Constitutional Brinksmanship

CONSTITUTIONAL BRINKSMANSHIP

Amending the Constitution by National Convention

Russell L. Caplan

Oxford University Press
New York   Oxford
1988

KF
4555
C35
1988

Oxford University Press

Oxford   New York   Toronto
Delhi   Bombay   Calcutta   Madras   Karachi
Petaling Jaya   Singapore   Hong Kong   Tokyo
Nairobi   Dar es Salaam   Cape Town
Melbourne   Auckland

and associated companies in
Berlin   Ibadan

Library of Congress Cataloging-in-Publication Data
Caplan, Russell L.
Constitutional brinksmanship.
Bibliography: p.
Includes index.
1. Constitutional conventions—United States
—History.
2. United States—Constitutional
history. 3. United States. Constitutional
Convention (1787)
I. Title. KF4555.C35   1988   347.73'0292   88-1529   347.302292
ISBN 0-19-505573-X

Printing (last digit): 9 8 7 6 5 4 3 2 1
Printed in the United States of America
on acid-free paper

To the memory of my father and mother
Alfred and June Caplan

Preface

Thirty-two states in the past decade have filed applications with Congress for a convention to propose a constitutional amendment requiring a balanced federal budget. At this writing petitions are being considered in several other states and only two more are needed to force Congress to issue the call, an event that might initiate a procedure never used in the Constitution's two-hundred-year history. Under article V of the Constitution, amendments can be proposed either by Congress, the method so far used for the twenty-six amendments that have been adopted, or by national convention, when the legislatures of two thirds of the states so request. The convention procedure, because it is untried, has been surrounded by uncertainties, but the principal fear is that a convention, if held, will propose amendments on subjects other than those for which it was called. The convention route has been used throughout the nation's history, and even now other campaigns for amendments regarding abortion, prayer in public schools, and English as the official national language ensure that article V will remain a fixture in the political life of the United States.

Former Associate Justice Arthur Goldberg has written: "Article V of the Constitution does not limit the agenda of such a convention to specific amendments proposed by the states in their petitions to Congress. There is nothing in article V that prevents a convention from making wholesale changes to our Constitution and Bill of Rights."

Retired Chief Justice Warren Burger has said of the balanced-budget convention campaign that "it would be a grand waste of time to have a constitutional convention and start over. . . . We can deal with these things one at a time." Associate Justice William Brennan is more direct: "I honestly doubt there's any prospect we want to go through the trauma of redoing the Constitution," a convention being "the most awful thing in the world."[1]

A "runaway" convention spewing a welter of unauthorized amendments might be expected to claim as precedent the Philadelphia Convention, which framed the Constitution in 1787. That "Grand Convention," as it was known at the time, exceeded its mandate to amend the nation's first federal constitution, the Articles of Confederation, and produced a new charter. It is likewise possible, according to Richard Rovere, for another convention to

reinstate segregation, and even slavery; throw out much or all of the Bill of Rights (free speech, free press, separation of church and state, the prohibition against unreasonable searches and seizures); eliminate the Fourteenth Amendment's due-process clause and reverse any Supreme Court decision the members didn't like, including the one-man-one-vote rule; and perhaps, for good measure, eliminate the Supreme Court itself.

Others, even supporters of a balanced-budget amendment, consider other dimensions. "Fettered or unfettered," Governor Thomas H. Kean of New Jersey has said, "the convention would intimidate all branches of government, confuse the financial markets, and chill international relations."[2] Could this happen under article V?

I

The Constitution sets out the central features of the convention route. Article V states:

The Congress, on the Application of the Legislatures of two thirds of the several States, shall call a Convention for proposing Amendments, which . . . shall be valid to all Intents and Purposes, as Part of this Constitution, when ratified by the Legislatures of three fourths of the several States, or by Conventions in three fourths thereof, as the one or the other Mode of Ratification may be proposed by the Congress.

The constitutional text describes in literal terms, and implies of necessity, a series of steps:

1. Two thirds of the state legislatures (currently thirty-four) must send applications to Congress.
2. Once Congress has received the correct number of applications, it must, if all other requirements are met, call the convention.
3. If a convention is called, delegates would be selected, meet at the convention, and decide whether to propose amendments.
4. Congress must determine whether the amendments proposed by the convention (if any) meet all constitutional requirements.
5. Whether a convention or Congress itself proposes the amendments, Congress must choose the method of ratification for the proposals— either by the state legislatures or by specially held state conventions.
6. Three fourths of the states (currently thirty-eight) must approve an amendment for it to become part of the Constitution.

If constitutional requirements are misunderstood or misapplied, a juggernaut resulting in a convention might be set in train unwittingly and even contrary to the wishes of convention proponents. If, on the other hand, Congress resists a mandate for change despite the fulfillment of all prerequisites, an amendment desired by an overwhelming part of the nation will have been unconstitutionally thwarted and confidence in the government lost.

Notwithstanding the despair of eminent students such as Laurence Tribe of Harvard Law School that the article V convention presents "many critical questions" that "are completely open" with no "authoritative answer," and Charles Black of Yale Law School that "neither text nor history give any real help," the convention clause, like every other in the Constitution, has a historical meaning that can be successfully retrieved. The clause is just as viable as the procedure for impeaching and removing the President, even though that mechanism also has never been employed to its completion. It was the mere threat of impeachment that drove Richard Nixon to resign from the presidency in 1974.[3]

The article V convention, Philip Kurland has said, "is not a weapon ready for use and its cumbersome method is both its virtue and its vice."[4] Now an exotic institution, the convention was a tradition already over a century old when it became part of the Constitution with article V. The convention clause was far from the Constitution's most obscure provision at the time of adoption. By 1787, in contrast, it had not been settled whether ex post facto laws, forbidden in article I, retroactively imposed liability in civil cases or related to criminal matters only. At Philadelphia John Dickinson had to consult Blackstone's *Commentaries on the Laws of England* to justify his position to the other delegates.

Once the underlying decisions were made the choice of words at Philadelphia was second nature, and one reason article V is so terse is because the salient features of conventions were generally well understood. In his *Manual of Parliamentary Practice*, composed for his own use as presiding officer of the Senate during his vice presidency, Thomas Jefferson remarked that for the most familiar rules of British practice "no written authority is or can be quoted, no writer having supposed it necessary to repeat what all were presumed to know." For the same reason, many aspects of the convention route have been hidden from view because conventions were a well-known part of the landscape when the Constitution was drafted, with the result that elaborate discussions of the subject that have survived are rare. Many original historical sources have been consulted, including a previously unnoticed early Supreme Court decision referring to the convention process, *Smith v. Union Bank of Georgetown*; this book is accordingly in the nature of a guide to the evidence.[5]

The question of a national convention's limitability is in reality two inquiries: (1) whether the states can apply for a convention on specific topics or, as some writers like Professor Black have held, must request a convention with full powers to revise the Constitution; (2) whether, if the states may apply for a convention on specific topics, amendments proposed by that convention on topics outside the applications become part of the Constitution if submitted to the states for ratification and the required three fourths do in fact approve. The evidence indicates that both plenary and limited-topic conventions may be applied for, and that a limited convention is bound by article V to propose only those amendments described in the triggering applications. Amendments proposed by a limited convention on topics not specified may be withheld by Congress from ratification and additionally can, for the most part, be challenged in the federal courts. If an irregularly adopted amendment is not contested over a period of years, probably decades, the amendment can attain a secure place in the Constitution by virtue of public acquiescence.

This book, the first systematic examination of the history and operation of the federal convention clause, is not a survey of the social and intellectual developments of the founding age. It is not, in other words, a rival or descendant of Gordon Wood's magisterial *Creation of the American Republic 1776–1787* (1969). Rather, its focus is first on a lost chapter of our constitutional history, namely, the role conventions and convention drives have played since colonial times; and second on the legal problems relating to the convention mechanism of article V, presenting the requisite case law and historical records to suggest specific answers.

II

Since 1787 no other national convention has met, but more than 230 state constitutional conventions have been held, a disparity explainable in part by the fact that each state is a much more compact and homogeneous region than the entire Union, and so an easier arena in which to effect political change; in part by the fact that the federal Constitution and Bill of Rights have come to be respected as the fundamental and indispensable bulwark on which the state charters depend.[6] State convention practice after 1787 is nonetheless of secondary importance in interpreting article V, because that practice was unknown to the founders, and is governed in the first instance by the provisions of state law, although subject at the periphery to the restraints of federal statutes and the Constitution through the supremacy clause of article VI, which proclaims that "This Constitution, and the Laws of the United States . . . shall be the supreme Law of the Land; and the Judges in every State shall be bound thereby."

It is sometimes assumed that there was a consensus to the effect that Revolution-era conventions possessed unlimited capacities; as this essay demonstrates, the reality was different. The misconception may have arisen because those early bodies were often both conventions and legislatures, acting as provisional governments in first framing a constitution and subsequently enacting legislation under it. In any event the idea that because a convention is in some sense "sovereign" it may override its commission flourished in the state conventions of the nineteenth century. After adoption of the federal Constitution, the states, both original and newly admitted, held conventions to draft and revise their constitutions. At the 1821 New York convention, delegate Peter

R. Livingston denied all limitations in an effort to show that the convention had the authority to disenfranchise blacks (a ploy to dilute their
voting strength in New York City):

the people are here themselves. They are present in their delegates. No restriction limits our proceedings. What are these *vested* rights? Sir, we are standing upon the foundations of society. The elements of government are scattered
around us. All rights are buried, and from the shoots that spring from their
grave, we are to weave a bower that shall overshadow and protect our liberties.
Our proceedings will pass in review before that power that elected us; and it will
be for the people to decide whether the blacks are elevated upon a ground which
we cannot reach.

At the Illinois convention of 1847, Onslow Peters added currency to
Livingston's doctrine:

We are here the sovereignty of the state. We are what the people of the state
would be if they were congregated here in one mass meeting. We are what
Louis XIV said he was—"We are the state." We can trample the constitution
under our feet as waste paper, and no one can call us to an account save the
people.

Other delegates shared Peters's perspective, although Thompson Camp-
bell "did not believe in the omnipotence of this body. . . . We must
abide by the law which has called us here for a particular purpose."
Arguments for the boundless powers of delegates were made at the
Kentucky convention of 1849 and the 1853 Massachusetts convention.[7]

The Illinois convention of 1862 was pivotal for convention scholarship. That body had been called to propose a new state constitution,
but in addition to submitting a charter for ratification—which was
rejected—the assembly engaged in numerous unauthorized acts that
were highly publicized and profoundly alienating to its constituents.
Among other measures, the convention ratified a proposed amendment
to the federal Constitution that Congress had stipulated was to be approved by the state legislatures, reapportioned the state's congressional
districts, approved a bond issue to aid wounded Illinois soldiers in the
Union army, and began investigating the conduct of the state governor's
office.[8]

A select committee of the convention was assigned to determine
whether the assembly was bound by the limitations of its enabling act.
The committee, influenced by the proceedings of the 1847 convention,
announced in its report (adopted by the full membership) that a convention represents "a peaceable revolution of the state government . . . a

virtual assemblage of the people of the state, sovereign within its own boundaries." Accordingly, "after due organization of the Convention, the law calling it is no longer binding" and "the Convention has supreme power in regard to all matters incident to the alteration and amendment of the constitution." The Illinois convention was rebuffed on all fronts: the ratification of the federal amendment was rejected by Congress as invalid, and state officials refused to issue the relief bonds ordered by the convention. [9]

These extravagant claims of sovereign power followed on the secession of the Confederacy the year before. The state conventions that proclaimed withdrawal from the Union, and the Montgomery Convention that framed the Confederacy's two constitutions, had renounced the authority of the federal government and promulgated statutes in the manner of regular legislatures. The actions of the secession and Illinois conventions inspired the first scholarly examination of the subject, A *Treatise on Constitutional Conventions: Their History, Powers, and Modes of Proceeding*, originally published in 1866, by an Illinois superior court judge and later a distinguished law professor at the University of Chicago, John Alexander Jameson.

Jameson, reacting to the trauma of the Civil War, cited a wealth of precedents from state cases and conventions for his thesis that conventions are limited in their powers by the acts calling them into existence and by the federal Constitution; in the case of state conventions, by the respective state constitution as well. Intent on domesticating the procedure, he traced the "dogma" of illimitable convention power to the "pro-slavery fanaticism" of Livingston at the 1821 New York convention, and concluded that the convention-as-sovereign theory had been formulated to justify slavery and disunion:

it is difficult to resist the conviction, that the assertion of that theory was connected with the great conspiracy which culminated in the late Secession war. Was it foreseen, that to carry out the design of disrupting the Union, with an appearance of constitutional right, new conceptions must become prevalent, as to the powers of the bodies by which alone the design could be accomplished? [10]

The *Treatise* was one of a spate of Reconstruction-era commentaries, including Timothy Farrar's *Manual of the Constitution of the United States* (1867) and Thomas Cooley's *Treatise on Constitutional Limitations* (1868), that stressed the limits to state powers and the subordination of the states to the federal Union. For Jameson and Cooley, one concern was to demonstrate the limitability of state conventions. They agreed that the Philadelphia Convention had exceeded its powers by proposing the Constitution, rendering that submission invalid as a controlling precedent. To the 1862 Illinois convention's claim of unrestrainable sovereignty based on parity with the Philadelphia Convention, Jameson countered that the Illinois assembly, as an instance of delegated power, could act only within the scope of its enabling act. Judge Cooley wrote: "The constitutional convention is the representative of sovereignty only in a very qualified sense, and for the specific purpose, and with the restricted authority, to put in proper form the questions of amendment upon which the people are to pass." The limits to state powers were enforceable, if necessary, but henceforward in court rather than in battle. In 1867, The United States Supreme Court for the first time decided that a clause in a state constitution violated the federal Constitution.[11]

The commentators who followed Jameson, notably Professor Walter Fairleigh Dodd of the Johns Hopkins University, and later Yale, and Roger Sherman Hoar, a state senator and lawyer who practiced with Louis Brandeis and served as legal adviser to the Massachusetts constitutional convention of 1917, were also concerned with the conventions held in the states to establish or revise their own constitutions, and touched incidentally on article V only insofar as it shed light on state practice. As the Civil War receded into history, fewer constraints were held to apply. Both Dodd, writing in 1910, and Hoar, writing in 1917, agreed with Jameson that the results of a state convention are invalid if repugnant to the federal Constitution—for example, to the prohibition against ex post facto legislation. Both agreed also, contrary to Jameson, that a state convention could disregard the legislative act calling it into existence. Hoar even argued that for extraconstitutional conventions, held despite the absence of an enabling provision in the constitution, the state charter imposes no limits because such an assemblage, like a regular convention or constitution, derives its authority from a higher source "inherent in the people."[12]

Though Jameson's book was well received and went through four editions by 1887, the convention-as-sovereign notion persisted. In 1869, when Congress considered submitting the fifteenth amendment for ratification by state conventions, Senator Orris Ferry of Connecticut, probably recalling the 1862 Illinois gathering, warned that a convention cannot be limited to "the simple amendment which you are proposing to it. It may go on to amend your State constitution and to subvert the whole machinery of your State government, and there is no power in your State to stop it." Congress has by and large kept with this theory, and has used it to repel subsequent national convention drives. The denouement of this tug-of-war may be a monumental confrontation should two thirds of the states ever file applications on the same subject, a balanced-budget amendment being currently the most likely candidate. "It is not inconceivable," Michael Kammen has written, "that the Constitution's Bicentennial will be observed amidst the largest governmental ruckus the nation has seen since 1860–61."[13]

III

The sources for the history of article V extend, in time, from seventeenth-century England right up to the present. The principal focus for interpreting the convention provision is necessarily on the framing of the Constitution at the Philadelphia Convention in 1787 and the deliberations in the ratifying conventions to which the Constitution was transmitted for the states' decisions on adoption. Before the final ratification, by Rhode Island in 1790, a campaign by opponents of the Constitution for another convention to revise the work done at Philadelphia generated a fair amount of commentary on the convention clause.

Original documents relating to the framing and adoption of the Constitution are located chiefly in the Library of Congress, the National Archives, the Library of the Supreme Court of the United States, and to a lesser extent the state libraries and historical associations. With four exceptions, only published documents have been used in this study. The actions of Congress during the Revolutionary War and under the Articles of Confederation are detailed in Worthington Chauncey Ford et al., eds., *Journals of the Continental Congress 1774–1789* (34 vols., 1904–1937), which are supplemented by Edmund C. Burnett, ed., *Letters of Members of the Continental Congress* (8 vols., 1921–1936), and a recent work in progress, Paul H. Smith et al., eds., *Letters of Delegates to Congress 1774–1789* (13 vols. to date, 1976–   ).

The indispensable record of the Philadelphia Convention remains the full set of notes taken by James Madison, delegate from Virginia. Though he disclaimed the title "Father of the Constitution," Madison was its chief architect, having drafted the Virginia Plan, which formed the nucleus of the instrument; left the fullest record of the Constitution's drafting, notes he later revised for publication from his own and other delegates' private papers; earned the reputation at Philadelphia, according to a fellow delegate, of being "the best informed Man of any point in debate," taking the lead in "the management of every great question" before the convention; advocated ratification as the coauthor with Alexander Hamilton and John Jay of *The Federalist*, the series of newspaper essays written to persuade New York to ratify, and eventually recognized as the preeminent commentary on the Constitution; served in the Virginia ratifying convention; and as a member of the First Federal Congress, which concluded the work of the Philadelphia Convention in establishing the new government, devised and shepherded the Bill of Rights to its successful proposal.

The proceedings of the Philadelphia Convention remained, on the whole, secret for many years. Only when Madison's notes were published in 1840, appearing posthumously by his wish, could an intelligible notion be had of the Constitution's gestation.[14] The Philadelphia delegates had conducted their proceedings behind closed doors, and entrusted the official journal to Congress. The journal was kept by William Jackson, the convention secretary, and is a bare-bones recital of motions made and carried or made and rejected, with none of the discussion behind them. Even this sparse account was not published until 1819, at the direction of Congress. The decision of Congress was taken by the surviving delegates as a signal lifting the ban on disclosure, and the private records of several members—Hamilton (who had died in 1804), Rufus King, John Lansing, Luther Martin, James McHenry, William Paterson, William Pierce, and Robert Yates—began to appear.

The notes, working papers, and correspondence of the delegates are the core of Max Farrand's *The Records of the Federal Convention of 1787*, first issued as three volumes in 1911, with an additional volume containing subsequently discovered material in 1937. In conjunction with the bicentennial observance of the Philadelphia Convention, Dr. James H. Hutson of the Library of Congress Manuscript Division published his *Supplement to Max Farrand's The Records of the Federal Convention of 1787* (1987), incorporating delegates' notes and correspondence brought to light during the intervening fifty years.

Our knowledge of the framers' understanding has been enriched by publication of comprehensive editions of the writings of the founders along with the essays and pamphlets written during ratification. These works include, in particular, Julian P. Boyd's edition of *The Papers of Thomas Jefferson* (22 vols to date, 1950–   ), which set the standard for projects of the type; Gaillard Hunt's collection of *The Writings of James Madison* (9 vols., 1900–1910), soon to be completely replaced by William T. Hutchinson, Robert Allen Rutland, et al., eds., *The Papers of James Madison* (15 vols. to date, 1962–   ); John C. Fitzpatrick's edition of *The Writings of George Washington* (39 vols., 1931–1944), prepared for the bicentennial of Washington's birth; and the exhaustive compilation of Hamilton's writings by Harold C. Syrett and Jacob E. Cooke, *The Papers of Alexander Hamilton* (26 vols., 1961–1979).

The publication of these reliable editions affords now a better picture of eighteenth-century constitutional ideas than was available in 1832 or 1861. "Not until Max Farrand's *The Records of the Federal Convention* appeared in 1911," one historian has written, "was it possible to see clearly just what had occurred in Philadelphia." Yet, in an eye-opening appraisal of the shortcomings of the records, Dr. Hutson found that reportorial inexperience and partisan bickering severely compromised many recollections. According to Dr. Hutson, even Madison, while a reliable reporter, can have set down no more than ten percent of the entire proceedings on the floor of the Philadelphia Convention.[15]

The proceedings in the states when the Constitution was transmitted for their decisions on adoption are preserved in the records of the state legislatures and ratifying conventions. At a minimum, outlines of the proceedings are documented for all thirteen states, but the fullest accounts exist for the legislatures of New York, Pennsylvania, Virginia, and South Carolina, and the conventions in New York, Virginia, Massachusetts, Pennsylvania, Virginia, and North Carolina. Very little, by contrast, is known of the ratifying assemblies in Connecticut and Georgia, outside of a few speeches.

For over a century the standard compilation of the ratification debates has been Jonathan Elliot's *Debates in the Several State Conventions on the Adoption of the Federal Constitution*, which appeared in 1830 and, as revised, in 1836. In the 1820s and 1830s Elliot, a political journalist rather than a scholar, collected the published accounts of the ratifying assemblies, originally committed to print by commercial publishers. Elliot admitted in his first edition that "the sentiments" contained in the published accounts "may, in some instances, have been inaccurately taken down, and, in others, probably, too faintly sketched," but scrupulous reporting of all sides in the debates was not the objective. The intended audience would be more interested in learning the opinion of Patrick Henry than of Zachariah Johnson. Consequently, the words of the less celebrated were slighted, omitted, or, as in the case of Massachusetts, doctored by the editors. Still, in the better renditions (Virginia, particularly, and New York) the flavor of individual speakers and their ideas often shines through. Many additional sources—delegates' notes, contemporary newspaper accounts—have since been uncovered and are included in what promises to be a thorough and reliable replacement for Elliot, *The Documentary History of the Ratification of the Constitution*, the first volume of which was published in 1976 under the late Merrill Jensen's editorship.[16]

The considerable body of writings produced by opponents of ratification, who were called antifederalists, has only recently been collected in Herbert J. Storing's definitive *The Complete Anti-Federalist* (7 vols., 1981). Abridged versions of the corpus are available in William B. Allen, Gordon Lloyd, and Margie Lloyd, eds., *The Essential Antifederalist* (1985); Morton Borden, ed., *The Antifederalist Papers* (1965); and Cecelia M. Kenyon, ed., *The Antifederalists* (1966). A recent study is Steven R. Boyd's *The Politics of Opposition: Antifederalists and the Acceptance of the Constitution* (1979).

The primary reference for the early years of the Federal Congress, as that body was called starting in 1789, is *The Debates and Proceedings in the Congress of the United States*, better known as the *Annals of Congress*, which began publication in 1834. This compilation is not a complete or systematic record, consisting mostly of speeches that private journalists had been reporting since the first session of Congress in 1789. Reporters, with the rest of the public, were not even permitted to attend sessions of the Senate until 1795, with the result that the record of the early Senate is much leaner than that of the House. The quality of reporting is uneven, and met at various times with praise and condemnation from the quoted members. One stenographer, according to Madison, was indolent and drank too much. It is, of course, impossible to assess the accuracy either of the reports or the reviews, for some of the protest may have come from politicians chagrined upon seeing their words in cold print. Granting the deficiencies, Madison's latest editors claim that the various contemporary sources reveal fundamental agree-

ment in the reporting of his speeches, perhaps because he spoke un-
usually slowly.[17]

Congress has never kept regular track of incoming convention applications, and there exists no official catalogue of the applications
adopted by the states since 1789. No federal official has ever been
designated to receive and keep track of applications separately, although
the rules adopted by the Senate and House of Representatives specify
that memorials to Congress (which state a grievance but do not ask for
any remedy) and petitions (which request specific action) are to be
delivered to the Secretary of the Senate and the Clerk of the House.
Convention applications are usually deemed to fall under one or the
other category of submission.[18]

This study has necessarily relied on several publications for application listings. The listings have been verified from original sources: usually the state statute reporter, but occasionally the official journals of the
Senate and the House of Representatives, kept pursuant to the command in article I of the Constitution that "Each House shall keep a
Journal of its Proceedings." The application totals for convention campaigns is more often than not inexact; even the question whether there
are thirty-two valid applications for a convention to propose a balanced-
budget amendment is disputed.[19]

Arriving at a consensus has been the watchword not only in Madison
studies but also in reconstructing what article V's convention procedure
meant to the founding generation—to the Philadelphia Convention
delegates, the members of the ratifying conventions, and those contemporaries who, like Noah Webster and Tench Coxe, propagandized for
the Constitution and left important writings. The central task of reconstruction was primarily one of recovering the meaning of words whose
definitions had quietly changed, or unearthing the history behind a
clause that illuminated its relationship to the amending process, rather
than one of construing a provision in accordance with the precepts of
one or another school of constitutional interpretation. The difference
between the competing schools of thought, now and in various incarna-
tions over the last two hundred years, has chiefly been the amount of
emphasis placed on the constitutional text and its history vis-à-vis judicial decisions and social values. Article V is a provision that, unlike
some others, can be sensibly and objectively interpreted in accordance
with its original meaning because of its unique features: the wealth of

data from the founding era, the existence of broad agreement among the founders, and the sparseness of judicial precedent.[20]

The framers themselves denied that the "intent" or discernible purpose of the Philadelphia Convention was necessary or even significant; complete records, after all, were hidden until 1840. Madison in particular demurred, emphasizing instead the debates in the ratifying conventions; he considered the Philadelphia proceedings as, at most, "presumptive evidence of the general understanding at the time of the language used," and reportedly "did not believe a single instance could be cited in which the sense of the Convention had been required or admitted as material in any Constitutional question." The framers shared the traditional assumption, bred by their training in the common law, that the document would be construed mostly by reference to the intrinsic meaning of its words—what Hamilton called in *The Federalist* "the natural and obvious sense of its provisions." Failing that, the standard judicial process of case-by-case interpretation would be employed. This procedure allowed for construction of a word or phrase when, as the framers knew was inevitable, unforeseen situations arose.[21]

The meaning and history of the text, however, should not be minimized. Some scholars have pointed to early applications requesting a "general" convention as proof that only wide-ranging assemblies are contemplated by article V.[22] Yet "general" at the time primarily referred not to deliberative scope but to breadth of attendance. In April 1783, a member of Congress reported to his colleagues that the New England states were planning a convention with the intent of developing a uniform tax code for that region. The proposed convention, which never met, was criticized by various members as a dangerous precedent under the Articles of Confederation. "Mr. Madison & Mr. Hamilton disapproved of these partial conventions, not as absolute violations of the Confederacy, but as ultimately leading to them," Madison wrote in his notes, "the latter observing that he wished instead of them to see a general Convention take place."[23] A "general" convention was simply one inviting representatives from all the states; a "partial" convention included delegations from fewer than the total number. In the preamble to the Constitution, the framers declared the national scope of the enterprise: to "provide for the common defence" and "promote the general Welfare." A wide-ranging convention was "plenary" or "plenipotentiary," signaling that the delegates had received full deliberative powers from their constituents. [24]

In this book, disagreements among the sources as well as agreements have been noted. The original spelling and punctuation have been retained; italicized words reflect the original unless otherwise indicated. There is still much about the Constitution's drafting and adoption that we do not know, and perhaps never will know. The convention portion of article V seems derived in important respects from the equivalent clause in Georgia's 1777 constitution, but as yet no evidence has turned up that explicitly links the two provisions. The journal of the 1777 convention is a two-page summary of the proceedings, with no material on the amending clause. [25]

The purpose of this essay is not to recommend or disparage any specific amendment proposal, but to heed Madison's admonition that in constitutional analysis "the danger of error must increase with the increasing oblivion of explanatory circumstances, and with the continual changes in the import of words and phrases." In 1974, the Special Constitutional Convention Study Committee of the American Bar Association, among its members Dean Albert Sacks of Harvard Law School, former Deputy Attorney General Warren Christopher, and federal judge Sarah T. Hughes, reported:

> We recognize that some believe that it is unfortunate to focus attention on this method of amendment and unwise to establish procedures which might facilitate the calling of a convention. The argument is that the establishment of procedures might make it easier for state legislatures to seek a national convention, and might even encourage them to do so. . . .
>
> If we fail to deal now with the uncertainties of the convention method, we could be courting a constitutional crisis of grave proportions. We would be running the enormous risk that procedures for a national constitutional convention would have to be forged in time of divisive controversy and confusion when there would be a high premium on obstructive and result-oriented tactics.

Of an expedient but dubious stratagem during a constitutional dispute in New York, Secretary of the Treasury Alexander Hamilton wrote to Senator Rufus King: "The precedent may suit us to day; but tomorrow we may rue its abuse." [26]

This study is the better for the encouragement and advice of those who assisted in providing the evidence and refining its conclusions—but share no responsibility for the result—especially Charles Chehebar, Gary Waxbar, Owen Fiss, Linda Grant DePauw, Jack P. Greene, Gerald A. Greenberger, Dr. James Hutson, John P. Kaminski, H. Jefferson Powell, Walter F. Pratt, Jr., Richard A. Ryerson, Celeste Walker, and G. Edward White. Critical documents were furnished by the staffs of the Library of Congress Rare Book Room, the American Antiquarian Society, the Connecticut State Library Archives, the Indiana State Library, the Office of the Secretary of State of the Commonwealth of Massachusetts, the Rare Books and Manuscripts Division, New York Public Library, and the United States Supreme Court Bar Library. My editors at Oxford University Press, Valerie Aubry and Marion Osmun, were unfailingly gracious and helpful.

Washington, D. C.   R. L. C.
November 1982

Contents

PART I

History

1

Prelude to the Grand Convention

English and Colonial Antecedents

In antiquity, Aristotle is known to have collected 158 "constitutions" of the Greek city-states, but these were nothing more than historical narratives joined to descriptions of the various political systems extant at the time of writing. Essentially the written constitution, like the convention as a means of framing or amending fundamental law, was conceived in England and first put into practice in this country. The convention was one of the three stages in the nation's constitutional development: first arose the distinction between constitutional and statutory law; second, the emergence of the constitutional convention as a body apart from the regular legislature; and third, the submission by conventions of constitutions for popular ratification.[1]

Before the Revolutionary War, the term "constitution" had the same meaning for the colonists as it did for the native English: not a fundamental charter of government specifying powers and rights unalterable by ordinary legislation, but rather, as defined by Henry St. John, Viscount Bolingbroke, "that Assemblage of Laws, Institutions and Customs . . .that compose the General System, according to which the Community hath agreed to be governed." The *Commentaries* of William Blackstone, much read in the colonies, did not distinguish between England's constitution and its system of laws as a whole.[2]

Among the first to distinguish the legislative from the constituent power was Sir Henry Vane, Governor of Massachusetts in the 1630s and a leading member of the Parliament that overthrew Charles I. To mend the breach between England's civil authorities and Oliver Cromwell's army, Vane in 1656 prescribed "a generall councill, or convention of faithfull, honest, and discerning men, chosen for that purpose. . . . Which convention is not properly to exercise the legislative power, but only to debate freely, and agree upon the particulars" which, in the form of "fundamentall constitutions, shall be laid and inviolably observed as the conditions upon which the whole body so represented doth consent to cast it self into a civil and politick incorporation."[3] Under the colonial charters no laws could be passed inconsistent with the laws of England; by 1678, "constitution" was in use among colonists to distinguish a written code of government from legislative enactments.[4]

When relations with Parliament deteriorated after the close of the Seven Years' War in 1763 as it attempted to spread the cost of defense with measures like the Stamp Act (1765) and enforce its taxation scheme with the Intolerable Acts (1774), the colonists reasserted entitlement to the laws of England, infringed by those measures, as their birthright. In time, the vindication of rights under the existing system ceased being the goal of the colonists. As Joseph Galloway of Pennsylvania admitted to the Continental Congress in 1774, his arguments that all acts of Parliament made since colonization violated the settlers' rights "tend to an Independency of the Colonies."[5]

Theory was shaped by the onrush of events, and the principles of natural justice held embedded in the English constitution, especially the writ of habeas corpus and trial by jury, became regarded as sacrosanct apart from their enaction into law, untouchable even by Parliament itself. In his famous speech against the wide-ranging search warrants called writs of assistance, Boston attorney James Otis in 1761 contended that acts contrary to the equitable principles of the British constitution were void. These principles of individual rights, distilled from English and colonial sources, were the foundation of the state constitutions and bills of rights, and so also of their federal counterparts.[6]

The final hallmark distinguishing constitutional from legislative acts was the use of a separate body, the convention, for the constitution's proposal. The first state constitutions of the Revolution were enacted by

state legislatures in the manner of statutes; the Articles of Confederation, the first constitution of the United States, was proposed by the
Continental Congress and approved by the state legislatures. Although
by 1787 the Articles had received recognition as "the law of the land"
unalterable by a state legislature, the Constitution's framers considered
the Articles of questionable supremacy. Madison wanted "to lay the
foundation of the new system"—the present Constitution—"in such a
ratification by the people themselves of the several States as will render
it clearly paramount to their Legislative authorities." This role was to be
played by the ratifying conventions.[7]

Prior to the start of the English Civil War in 1642, "convention"
seems to have meant simply "meeting," with no specifically political
overtones.[8] This old meaning survived alongside the new; General
George Washington in 1783 spoke of a "grand Convention of the
Officers." Although the gathering of barons at Runnymede who exacted
the Magna Carta from King John in 1215 has been considered a fore-
runner of the modern constitutional convention, applying the term
"convention" to a legislative body may have been suggested by the
Scottish Convention of Estates, which is known to have met in 1545.
The Convention of Estates, a quasi-legislative body that met without
the summons or concurrence of the Crown, was empowered to raise
armies and levy revenues, but could not enact legislation.[9]

It was commonplace by the eighteenth century that England's law-
making power was collectively vested in the three social orders, or
estates: the Crown, the peers, and the commons. Without a monarch
during Cromwell's Protectorate in the 1650s, Parliament—requiring a
royal writ to pass valid laws—was occasionally referred to as a convention because it was constitutionally deficient.[10] The Convention Parliament of 1660 effected the restoration of Charles II and declared itself a
true parliament "notwithstanding any want of the Kings Majesties writ
or writs of summons . . . or any other defect." After James II's abdica-
tion in the Glorious Revolution, another Convention Parliament met
on January 22, 1689, offered the throne to William and Mary, and as in
1660 proclaimed itself a true parliament.[11]

During this period government by convention underwent a sea
change in respectability. In the 1650s the term "convention" as applied
to Parliament had been pejorative, denoting an irregular assembly, but
by 1689 some saw the defects as virtues. John Milton, the poet and
radical tractarian, rejoiced that the Convention Parliament is "now

call'd, not as heretofore, by the summons of a king, but by the voice of libertie." Another author maintained that the 1689 Convention Parliament,

being the Representative of the whole Kingdom gathered together in an extraordinary case and manner . . . seemeth to be something greater, and of greater power, than a Parliament. . . . If this Convention can do anything, cannot it make laws truly Fundamental, and which shall have the same Firmitude and continuance as the Government it sets up?[12]

The uncertainties occasioned by the King's departure ignited smoldering grievances in the colonies into major disturbances that established the tradition in America. New governments in Massachusetts, New York, and Maryland during 1689 were installed after "conventions," as the meetings were called by members and contemporaries; the changes were held to reproduce, and be justified by, the events in England. While the social and economic grievances in each colony varied, a common thread was the unfounded rumor of a conspiracy against the largely Protestant colonists, involving the Catholic James II, the French, and their allies in North America, the Indians. To the English, Catholicism was the symbol of arbitrary, absolutist government because of associations with Bourbon rule. The colonists were completing the work of the English Convention Parliament of 1689, which had confirmed a Protestant monarchy and extirpated a Catholic succession.

After the imprisonment and expulsion of Governor Edmund Andros, the Massachusetts Council of Safety in May 1689 called two successive conventions. The latter assemblage expressly styled itself a "convention" after the 1689 Parliament; representing fifty-four towns, it followed the constituent instructions issued to forty of the towns and voted to resume government according to the forms of the old charter.[13]

News of Andros's overthrow soon reached New York, where merchants refused to pay customs on the theory that the government had no legal foundation. In May, a detachment of the militia seized the royal fort in New York City and with it, under Captain Jacob Leisler, control of the government. Seeking legitimacy for his regime, Leisler proclaimed loyalty to William and Mary and sent circular letters to the towns to choose delegates for a convention, in apparent imitation of the Boston meetings. The New York convention, whose representatives were mostly from the southern part of the colony, met in the fort from late June until mid-August "to advise," Leisler wrote, "and order all things necessary to resist the Ennemy, and to conserve this fort, City, land and Protestant Religion." The convention appointed a ten-member committee of safety, which in turn named Leisler commander in chief of the province, with full executive and military powers. Officials opposed to Leisler held their own convention in Albany, but Leisler's regime became the de facto government. Leisler was never recognized by the Crown, however, and in 1691, after a trial, was hanged.[14]

Maryland insurgents, unaware of these upheavals, saw a Catholic plot to hold the colony for James in the proprietary government's failure to proclaim immediately the new King and Queen. Led by John Coode, an expelled assemblyman, they formed an "association in arms" on behalf of William and Mary. The Associators marched on the State House in July 1689, seized the governor's manor, and called a convention of four delegates from each county, which met the last week in August. The convention proclaimed the new monarchy, and sought assurance from the Crown that the rights of Englishmen extended to the colonists of Maryland. Coode's government swiftly gained control, and a second convention perfected the interim administration. Royal confirmation of the new Maryland government came in the spring of 1690.[15]

The convention remained the instrument of transition in the next century. Thoroughly dissatisfied with the neglect and maladministration of the proprietors, by 1719 the colonists of South Carolina were looking for an expedient method of coming under royal protection. In July 1719 the proprietors once again repealed the election laws, dissolved the colonial assembly, and ordered the governor to call new elections. Articles of association, reciting grievances against the proprietary government, were drafted by the military and circulated by rebel leaders. When the province's Commons House of Assembly met, on December 10, it declared that the election laws had been repealed in a fashion "contrary to the Design and original Intent" of the proprietary charter and hence were still in force; since the subsequent election was void, the members of the house were not a regular legislature. The members accordingly resolved "That we cannot Act as an Assembly, but as a Convention, delegated by the People, to prevent the utter Ruin of this Government . . . until His Majesty's Pleasure be known." The convention elected a new governor and petitioned the Board of Trade in London to have South Carolina made a royal province. In August 1720, the Privy Council accepted responsibility for the colony.[16]

So far, American conventions were temporary substitutes for the royal legislatures, with no thought of operating alongside or supplanting them. That began to change with the advent of revolution as a lat-ticework of county conventions, provincial congresses and conventions, and finally the Continental Congress, sprouted to fill the vacuum being left by disintegrating royal authority. These extralegal bodies not only permitted the airing of colonial dissatisfaction; their very existence was a standing repudiation of the King, whose governors were prone to "arbi-trary and abrupt Dissolutions" (as James Wilson said) of the regular colonial assemblies. [17]

This next step was first taken by the Massachusetts convention of 1768, a meeting of township representatives to obtain redress against British measures. When the Massachusetts House of Representatives refused to rescind its letter opposing the Townshend Acts, the royal governor dissolved the House amid rumors that the Crown intended to station regiments of soldiers in Boston. Governor Francis Bernard would not convene the assembly for debate on the matter, but Samuel Adams and Thomas Cushing developed the idea of a convention of towns to protest the arrival of troops and dissolution of the House. The idea was familiar in Massachusetts from the conventions of Congrega-tional ministers, as well as from the meetings of town commissioners in county conventions. Despite administration arguments that it was crim-inal to assemble without the governor's approval, representatives from 100 of the province's 250 towns met for a week in September, elected Speaker of the House Cushing as chairman, and adopted a petition to the King along with an address to the governor. The convention was ignored by England but won the esteem of the colonists. Lieutenant Governor Thomas Hutchinson noted: "We have had a mock Assembly, called by the Town of Boston who have made a ridiculous figure but not so in the eyes of the body of the people." [18]

The Suffolk convention of September 1774 comprised delegates from the towns in that Massachusetts county, who met to condemn the Intolerable Acts and urge resistance to the "tyrannical and unconstitu-tional" administration of the royal governor. As a result of the declara-tions issued by the Suffolk and other county conventions, Governor Gage thought it "inexpedient" to call the legislature into session. Nev-ertheless, ninety representatives met at Salem in October, organized as a convention, and declared themselves a Provincial Congress. But like the other provincial congresses and conventions that were now meeting, it was deemed constitutionally defective because it lacked the third estate, namely, the Crown's representative in the person of the governor, and so collected taxes and raised militia by passing declarations and resolutions backed by public opinion only, not statutes with the force of law.[19]

State Constitutions and Constitutional Conventions

Pushed toward reformation of its political system and rupture with England after the events at Lexington and Concord, the Massachusetts Provincial Congress requested of the Continental Congress instructions regarding "the defence of this colony" against "a corrupt administration in Great Britain." John Adams, a delegate to Congress from the Bay Colony, felt that "We must reallize the Theories of the Wisest Writers and invite the People, to erect the whole Building with their own hands upon the broadest foundation. That this could be done only by Conventions of Representatives chosen by the People in the several Colonies, in the most exact proportions." Congress on June 9, 1775, recommended to Massachusetts an interim course of moderation: elect a new legislature that would "exercise the powers of Government, until a Governor, of his Majesty's appointment, will consent to govern the colony according to its charter."[20]

When similar requests came from New Hampshire and South Carolina, Congress followed Adams's advice. On November 3, 1775, Congress recommended that New Hampshire "call a full and free representation of the people, and that the representatives, if they think it necessary, establish . . . a form of government . . . during the continuance of the present dispute between G[reat] Britain and the colonies." The same resolution was passed the next day for South Carolina, and Congress made the identical recommendation to Virginia the following month when Governor Dunmore declared martial law.[21]

Finally, on May 10, 1776, Congress adopted a resolution encouraging all the colonies to form new governments. There was no longer talk of "the present dispute," for these governments were not predicated on eventual reconciliation with England:

> *Resolved*, That it be recommended to the respective assemblies and conventions of the United Colonies, . . . to adopt such government as shall, in the opinion of the representatives of the people, best conduce to the happiness and safety of their constituents in particular, and America in general.

The resolution, Adams observed at the time, was "considered by Men of Understanding as equivalent to a declaration of Independence."[22]

Although the resolution did not distinguish the functions of legislatures and conventions, one pamphleteer made the leap in analogizing the framing bodies recommended by Congress to the Parliament of the Glorious Revolution. "Conventions," he wrote, "are the only proper bodies to form a Constitution, and Assemblies are the proper bodies to make Laws agreeable to that constitution." When James II fled, "the situation of England was like what America is now; and in that state a Convention was chosen, to settle the new or reformed plan of government, before any Parliament could presume to sit; and this is what is distinguished in history by the name of the Revolution.—Here, my Countrymen, is our precedent." Wrote "Consideration" in defense of the Pennsylvania framing convention, "The people at large, by their Delegates, are the only proper makers and amenders of such compacts." Mimicking the history of conventions in England, the American version had evolved from a constitutionally defective body into one that, because of associations with heroic and profound governmental change, might appropriately frame fundamental law.[23]

Eleven of the original thirteen formed new governments, producing the first state constitutions, while Connecticut and Rhode Island retained their colonial charters, with minor alterations, until the nineteenth century.[24] Vermont, though not admitted as the fourteenth state until 1791, held conventions that drafted constitutions in 1777 and 1786. The state of Franklin or Frankland, carved out by land speculators from Tennessee and what is now southern Kentucky, held two conventions to establish statehood and adopt a constitution. The state never won the stamp of Congress, and folded in 1789. Other conventions held in the western reaches of the provinces as early as 1772 met to organize the territories or to erect independent states.[25]

In some states moderates, desiring a smooth transition from colony to independence, opposed calling a convention on the ground that the May resolution had permitted framing by the sitting legislatures, which in any case were the only legal standing bodies. The states originally observed no real distinction between fundamental and ordinary statutory enactments, using their conventions to execute regular legislative business in addition to framing constitutions, as was the case in Delaware, Pennsylvania, Maryland, North Carolina, and Georgia. Pennsylvania's convention, which began deliberating on July 15, 1776, was the first in history to be elected for the purpose of framing a constitution. South Carolina, Virginia, and New Jersey used their regular legislatures to draft constitutions. In 1778 President (later framer) John Rutledge of South Carolina refused to sign the new constitution, which had been passed by the legislature as if it were a statute. One reason he gave was that the legislature did not have the power to alter "the constitution from which it is derived."[26]

When John Adams referred to "the Wisest Writers," he meant such figures as James Harrington, Algernon Sidney, the Anglican bishop Benjamin Hoadly, Robert Molesworth, John Trenchard, and Thomas Gordon.[27] These English writers of the late seventeenth and early eighteenth centuries, known as True Whigs, Real Whigs, Radical Whigs, or Commonwealthmen, were critics of political corruption.[28] Among the reforms they urged were equitable representation, rotation in office, and annual elections. Of these men Bernard Bailyn has said, "more than any other single group of writers they shaped the mind of the American Revolutionary generation." The collection of *Cato's Letters* by Trenchard and Gordon, published in book form in the 1720s, was as influential in the colonies as Locke's *Second Treatise of Government* (1690).[29]

The Whigs had been concerned with British politics, in particular the contest between the Stuart monarchy and Parliament. Their themes, however, were adapted to American circumstances: the principle of equitable representation, a condemnation of unrepresented "rotten boroughs" in Parliament, was enlisted to deny Parliament's power to tax the colonies, since they were not literally represented in Westminster. The Old Whigs trusted the Parliament over the Crown for the protection of civil liberty, but the true guardian was a vigilant populace employing constitutional restraints on those who wielded power. "Only the Checks put upon Magistrates make Nations free," said Trenchard and Gordon. "They are free, where their Magistrates are confined within certain Bounds set them by the People, and act by Rules prescribed them by the People."[30]

The Whig emphasis on the legislative power as the buffer between citizens and monarch, and the notion of distinct, fundamental law, meshed with American constitutional thought during the Revolution. The legislature, especially the lower house, had represented the colonists against the Crown. Whig ideas on fundamental law kept their force after independence, but the political picture changed: the governor was no longer the enemy, and legislatures, coming under scrutiny, lost prestige by their passage of arbitrary and conflicting acts. Between 1784 and 1792, Edward Corwin found, New Hampshire's legislature freely vacated judicial proceedings, annulled or modified judgments, authorized appeals, and granted exemptions to the standing laws. To be sure, legislative and judicial functions were not yet perfectly distinct, but the abuses rankled. This is why to Jefferson "173 despots would surely be as oppressive as one" and to Madison, shortly after the Philadelphia Convention adjourned, "the evils issuing from" the "mutability of the laws of the States" had "contributed more to that uneasiness which produced the Convention . . . than those which accrued . . . from the inadequacy of the Confederation."[31]

The stage was set for the emergence of a separate body, the convention, to frame constitutional measures. Numberless ad hoc associations, committees, and conventions of various types had flourished in the colonies, often assuming governmental powers when the regular legislature was dissolved or prevented from meeting. These shadow governments, the immediate ancestors of the earliest constitutional conventions, were by 1787 deemed essential for framing constitutions. The Massachusetts town of Concord explained in October 1776: "the Same Body that forms a Constitution have of Consequence a power to alter it," and "a Constitution alterable by the Supreme Legislative is no Security at all to the Subject against any Encroachment of the Governing part on any, or on all of their Rights and priviliges."[32]

Jefferson, from the perspective of the mid-1780s, held Virginia's 1776 constitution defective because it was framed by a legislative body not authorized by the electorate to draft unalterable law: "the electors of April 1776, . . . not thinking of independance and a permanent republic, could not mean to vest in these delegates . . . any authorities other than those of the ordinary legislature." The delegates "could not therefore pass an act transcendant to the powers of other legislatures." The other states "have been of opinion, that to render a form of government unalterable by ordinary acts of assembly, the people must delegate persons with special powers. They have accordingly chosen special conventions to form and fix their governments."[33]

"A convention," wrote Noah Webster in 1788, "is no more than a Legislature chosen for *one particular purpose* of supremacy; whereas an ordinary Legislature is competent to *all* purposes of supremacy." He traced its evolution: "The *nominal* distinction of *Convention* and *Legis-*

lature was probably copied from the English; but the American distinction goes farther, it implies, in common acceptation, a difference of *power*." The difference of power, legislative and constituent, comes to the fore when "a change of circumstances . . . may render alterations necessary to the safety or freedom of the State; yet there is no power existing, but in the people at large, to make the necessary alterations. A convention then must be called."[34]

A full-fledged constitutional convention—a representative assembly officially summoned explicitly and exclusively to frame or revise a political community's fundamental law, whose proposals are thereafter submitted for popular ratification—did not emerge until the end of the first round of constitution-building.[35] The Massachusetts convention of 1779–1780 was the first assembly in world history to qualify as a genuine constitutional convention. An offer by the General Court (as the legislature was called) to draft a constitution had been rejected in 1776 by the Massachusetts towns, on the theory that the General Court was not representative and had no authority to frame fundamental law. In 1777, the Massachusetts House of Representatives was authorized by the towns to draft a constitution, but it too was rejected, in part because it had not been drafted by a separate body. In June 1779, the legislature announced elections for a constitutional convention, which met in Cambridge on September 1. The draft constitution, written by John Adams and assembly president James Bowdoin, was submitted by the convention to the towns on March 2, 1780, with the recommendation that they return their decisions by June 7. The constitution was adopted and went into effect on October 25, 1780.[36]

Signaling the final stage of constitutional development, Massachusetts and New Hampshire submitted their instruments for popular ratification; the other constitutions were passed and went into effect like statutes. The Massachusetts practice was followed by New Hampshire's conventions, which submitted draft constitutions for popular approval in 1779, 1781, 1782, and 1783. The first three drafts were rejected, the fourth adopted. Popular ratification in these states evidently grew out of their strong tradition of the town meeting, where members of the local communities gathered to decide directly on questions affecting their governance. Massachusetts and New Hampshire were the only states, as well, to submit the Articles of Confederation for the consideration of the towns before their legislatures ratified. In fairness, popular ratification in the 1770s was often impracticable due to wartime conditions.[37]

Though charters were in practice revocable by the Crown, the earliest American constitutions were based on the theory that governments once created were immutable, a legacy of the divine right of kings. John Locke's 1669 constitution for the Carolinas declared that it "shall be and remain the sacred and unalterable form and rule of government of Carolina forever."[38] Yet the 1639 Fundamental Orders of Connecticut were amended in 1660 to allow the governor to succeed himself, and the first amending provision in a constitution was drafted by William Penn for his colony in 1682. With the introduction of amending procedures, Gordon Wood has written, "Americans had in fact institutionalized and legitimized revolution." At the Philadelphia Convention, George Mason argued that amendments "will be necessary, and it will be better to provide for them, in an easy, regular and Constitutional way than to trust to chance and violence."[39]

Eight of the twelve state constitutions written in the first months of independence specified procedures for their own alteration, the others omitting a clause either through the framers' oversight or failure to appreciate how useful the feature would be. Five constitutions permitted amendment by convention, three—those of Delaware, Maryland, and South Carolina—by legislature. Amendment by legislature in those states, however, was accomplished either by an extraordinary legislative majority or by additional procedures, thereby retaining popular control but insulating fundamental law from the transient majorities sufficient to enact ordinary legislation.[40]

The Pennsylvania Constitution of 1776 provided for a convention to be called by the Council of Censors, an institution taken from the ancient Roman republic, to be elected every seven years for inquiry into the conduct of the government and whether "there appear to them an absolute necessity of amending any article of the constitution which may be defective." The proposed amendments "shall be promulgated at least six months before the day appointed for the election of such convention, for the previous consideration of the people, that they may have an opportunity of instructing their delegates on the subject." The Pennsylvania Council of Censors met in 1783 and 1784, both times failing to achieve the majority needed, two thirds of the twenty-four members, to call a convention. A dispute as to whether a convention would be limited to the items agreed to by the Council of Censors (as the wording suggested) or could reconsider the entire document went unresolved, as the Council adjourned on September 25, 1784, never to reconvene. Vermont copied the clause along with the rest of Pennsylvania's constitution, although Vermont's Councils met every seven years from 1785 to 1869.[41]

The Georgia Constitution of 1777, attributed to Button Gwinnett, provided in article 63:

> No alteration shall be made in this constitution without petitions from a majority of the counties, and the petitions from each county to be signed by a majority of voters in each county within this State; at which time the assembly shall order a convention to be called for that purpose, specifying the alterations to be made, according to the petitions preferred to the assembly by the majority of the counties as aforesaid.

Article 63 was never used, as the Georgia legislature on its own called a convention to draft a new constitution in 1788, with the end result, after two more conventions, the 1789 Georgia constitution.

The Massachusetts Constitution of 1780 specified that in 1795 the General Court was to call meetings of the towns throughout the state "for the purpose of collecting their sentiments on the necessity or expediency of revising the constitution, in order to amendments." On a two-thirds affirmative vote a convention would be held, comprising delegates elected from the towns "in the same manner and proportion as their representatives in the second branch of the legislature [the state house of representatives] are by this constitution to be chosen."[42] Through Adams's reputation the Massachusetts provision was the model for the equivalent clause in New Hampshire's 1784 constitution. In the Massachusetts constitution, the decision whether to hold a convention was left to the voters, but in New Hampshire the convention, to be held in 1791 rather than 1795, was mandatory. In 1795 the Massachusetts towns decided against revision, while New Hampshire's 1791 election resulted in a convention and a new constitution.[43]

In 1783 Jefferson, anticipating a convention call by the Virginia legislature to replace the state's 1776 charter, drew up a constitution that provided for an amending convention upon a two-thirds vote of any two of the three governmental branches. Each county was to elect the number of delegates it was authorized to send to the House of Delegates (the Virginia legislature's lower house), and the convention delegates "shall be acknowleged to have equal powers with this present Convention." No convention was held, and Virginia did not receive a new constitution until 1830. Under the Ordinance of 1784, written principally by Jefferson and adopted by Congress but never put into effect, when the inhabitants of a potential state in the western territories reached twenty thousand, "they shall receive from [Congress] authority with appointments of time and place, to call a Convention of representatives to establish a permanent constitution and government."[44]

A century after the English Convention Parliaments, the convention was the accepted mode for constitutional change in the United States. Yet the English predecessors were not regarded, in their time, as establishing new governments. The convention parliament had been a pragmatic solution to a break in the royal line, a makeshift to repair the political fabric rather than a convocation of founding fathers to promulgate new constitutional doctrine. This transformation of the convention from a conservative into a revolutionary device reflected the new nation's pride in constructing entire governments by deliberation. "Happy for us that . . . we are yet able to send our wise and good men together to talk over our form of government," wrote Jefferson. "The example we have given to the world is single, that of changing the form of our government under the authority of reason only, without bloodshed." Hamilton exulted at the Philadelphia Convention: "our Situation is peculiar. It leaves us Room to dream as we think proper."[45]

The Confederation Experience

Richard Henry Lee's resolution, introduced in Congress on June 7, 1776, proclaimed that "these United Colonies are, and of right ought to be, free and independent States," and recommended that "a plan of confederation be prepared." On June 12, Congress appointed a committee to draw up the plan. The Articles of Confederation, largely the work of committee chairman John Dickinson, were approved by Congress on November 15, 1777, and went into effect with Maryland's ratification on March 1, 1781. Article XIII required that any amendment to the Confederation "be agreed to in a Congress of the United States, and be afterwards confirmed by the legislatures of every State." Benjamin Franklin's "Sketch," presented to Congress in 1775 but not formally considered, had allowed for ratification by "a Majority of the Colony Assemblies" instead of all thirteen.[46]

Among the Revolution's economic dislocations were shortages of critical supplies and of hard currency, leading to inflationary emissions of cheap paper money by individual states to underwrite military and other expenses. The spiral of ever-higher prices was exacerbated by profiteering, and the scarcity of goods by hoarding. In December 1776, delegates from Connecticut, Massachusetts, New Hampshire, and Rhode Island met in Providence to discuss the conduct of the war and the regulation of prices in that region in order to halt inflation. The convention, sitting from December 25, 1776, through January 2, 1777, approved a wage-price schedule that was enacted into law by the states represented.[47]

The Providence convention sparked debate in Congress as to "whether it did not stand in need of the Approbation of Congress to make it valid." Samuel Adams affirmed that "a right to assemble upon all occasions to consult measures for promoting liberty & happiness was the priviledge of *freemen*—that it was contested by govr Hutchinson & . . . dreaded only by tyrants." Richard Henry Lee concurred: "we were not yet confederated—therefore no law of the union infringed." On the contrary, argued James Wilson, "the business the Committee transacted was wholly *continental* and of course required the approbation of Congress." Deferring to the fait accompli, Congress decided that "the Meeting was right considering the Circumstances," a narrowly grounded determination that left the question open in other cases. As to the status of that particular convention, William Ellery (Rhode Island) reported that "after a long metaphysical Debate which took up Part of three Days Congress were equally divided."[48]

Not wanting to be upstaged by the states, yet not wanting to offend them by claiming power to disapprove the convention proceedings, Congress on February 15, 1777, referred the Providence plan "to the consideration of the other united States," resolving

That, for this purpose, it be recommended to the legislatures, or, in their recess, to the executive powers of the States of New York, New Jersey, Pensylvania, Delaware, Maryland, and Virginia, to appoint commissioners to meet at York town, in Pensylvania, on the 3d Monday in March next, to consider of, and form a system of regulation adapted to those States, to be laid before the respective legislatures of each State, for their approbation:

That, for the like purpose, it be recommended to the legislatures, or executive powers in the recess of the legislatures of the States of North Carolina, South Carolina, and Georgia, to appoint commissioners to meet at Charlestown, in South Carolina, on the first Monday in May next.

The York convention was attended by representatives from all six invited states, but did not agree on a code; the Charleston convention never materialized. At the instance of Massachusetts, committees from the

New England states and New York met in Springfield, Massachusetts, from July 30 through August 6, 1777, to confer on methods to prevent depreciation and counterfeiting of their issues, and to curb wartime profiteering.[49]

Upon considering the Springfield convention's report, Congress issued another call on November 22, 1777, for three interstate trade conventions: one for the northern states in New Haven, Connecticut, the following January 15; one for the mid-Atlantic states in Fredericksburg, Virginia, on the same date; the last for South Carolina and Georgia in Charleston on February 15. The conventions were to "regulate and ascertain the price of labour, manufactures, internal produce, and commodities imported from foreign parts," and "on the report of the commissioners, each of the respective legislatures [was to] enact suitable laws . . . for enforcing the observance of such of the regulations as they shall ratify." Of the three proposed conventions, only that recommended for New Haven was held. The New Haven convention met from January 15 through February 1, 1778, and adopted a wage-price schedule that was enacted into law by four of the eight states attending,[50]

The schedule was repealed by the enacting legislatures after Congress, sensible of widespread noncompliance, advised in June 1778 the removal of all controls. The program, however, was revived on the local level. Wage and price codes were adopted at myriad town meetings, or "committees," and county conventions in Massachusetts, New Hampshire, Rhode Island, New York, New Jersey, Pennsylvania, and Delaware. To some in Philadelphia the handbills, mass meetings, and parades in search of monopolizers portended mob rule. "I am apprehensive we shall shortly be overun by committees," wrote a correspondent to Jefferson, for "they are taking large strides towards the entire subversion of this government." Even Samuel Adams was mortified: "now we have regular & constitutional Governments, popular Committees and County Conventions are not only useless but dangerous." While they "servd an excellent Purpose" in advancing the Revolutionary cause, "Bodies of Men, under any Denomination whatever, who convene themselves for the Purpose of deliberating upon & adopting Measures which are cognizable by Legislatures only will, if continued, bring Legislatures to Contempt & Dissolution."[51]

In one more regional try at stabilizing prices, a convention of the New England states and New York met at Hartford, Connecticut, in October 1779. The delegates endorsed a "Limitation of the Prices of the principal articles of merchandize and produce" and recommended a convention for all states "as far westward as Virginia inclusive" to gather at Philadelphia in January to consider price limits that would be put into effect in those states.[52]

This convention of New England and mid-Atlantic representatives met at the Pennsylvania State House in Philadelphia (now Independence Hall), beginning on January 29, 1780. Virginia and New York did not attend, and although New York gave assurances that it would implement a schedule to regulate prices, the commissioners (including future framers Elbridge Gerry, Roger Sherman, and Oliver Ellsworth) felt it was impossible to proceed without those two states. A committee was appointed "to form a general plan for the Limitation of Prices, in the several States," but no resolutions were adopted by the convention. On February 8 the delegates adjourned to meet again in two months, expecting commissioners from Virginia and New York, but apparently never reconvened.[53]

The evident futility of regulation irked opponents in Congress like John Witherspoon, president of the College of New Jersey and delegate from that state, who derided the New Haven efforts as "impracticable & absurd." The candid instructions to the Massachusetts delegates attending the 1780 Philadelphia convention asked the appointees "to Consider, whether it has not been found that a Limitation of Prices, instead of appreciating or giving stability to our money has not rendered it in a manner Useless? . . . in short whether it has not created such a stagnation of Business . . . as has oblidged the People to give up the measure or submit to starving?" The Philadelphia meeting was the last regional convention dedicated to price-fixing. Attempts to establish wage-price controls subsided after March 1780, when Congress virtually disowned its Continental bills then in circulation.[54]

To advocates of a strong central government—which as of 1780 included Washington, Madison, Hamilton, and Robert and Gouverneur Morris—it was apparent even before ratification of the Articles of Confederation was completed that the Confederation government would not be adequate to the tasks ahead. Dickinson himself expected "a revision and alteration . . . at a more convenient season." Each state under article II retained "its sovereignty, freedom and independence," which meant that Congress had no power to tax, but could only request funds from the states to meet its obligations, one of them support of the Continental Army. These requests were routinely spurned by the states, which had financial troubles of their own. The states could lay tariffs on imports, preventing Congress from adhering to commercial agreements with other nations; each state in effect conducted its own foreign policy and could indulge in trade wars against its neighbors. Finally, there was no executive power or developed judicial system by which the laws of the Confederation government could be enforced. These considerations eventually led to the drafting and adoption of the 1787 Constitution. [55]

The Confederation, wrote Max Farrand, "had been devised for an entirely different condition of affairs. . . . It provided for a 'league of friendship,' with the primary purpose of considering preparation for action rather than of taking the initiative." The Articles codified the arrangements forged among the colonies during the War, and probably represented the best that could be done at the time in the way of a central government; anything stronger would have been judged by the states a threat and rejected. Yet as early as January 1776, Thomas Paine's *Common Sense* had proposed that "a Continental Conference be held . . . to frame a Continental Charter, or Charter of the United Colonies." [56]

Hamilton was an especially forceful proponent of a convention to overhaul the Articles. In September 1780, he recommended "calling immediately a convention of all the states . . . vested with plenipotentiary authority" to amend the Articles and bring about "a solid coercive union." In the Confederation so revised, "Congress should have complete sovereignty in all that relates to war, peace, trade, finance, and to the management of foreign affairs," with state legislatures entrusted with the regulation of "the rights of property and life among individuals and to raising money by internal taxes." Three years later he drafted a resolution for Congress to use in calling a convention "with full powers to revise the confederation" by proposing alterations "to be finally approved or rejected by the states," but "abandoned" it, as he recorded, "for want of support." [57]

In August 1780, a convention of delegates appointed by Massachusetts, New Hampshire, and Connecticut, meeting in Boston, called for revisions of the Articles "that the Union of these States be fixed in a more solid and permanent Manner." The convention suggested that "the Powers of Congress be more clearly ascertained and defined, and that the important national Concerns of the United States be under the Superintendency and Direction of one supreme Head."

Another "Meeting of Commissioners" was recommended for Hartford in November.[58]

Commissioners from New Hampshire, Massachusetts, Rhode Island, Connecticut, and New York attended. This second Hartford convention made suggestions in the same vein as those of the Boston meeting, resolving that the states should "enable Congress to levy and collect such taxes, duties or imposts, within them respectively" to pay the interest on the public debt, and proposing mandatory state compliance with military requisitions from Congress. With the same objects in mind, the New York legislature adopted a resolution on July 21, 1782, proposing "a general Convention of the States, specially authorised to revise and amend the Confederation."[59]

Sentiment grew in Congress as well for a broad-gauged convention. According to Richard Henry Lee, many members were now, in the early 1780s, suggesting "as a very necessary Step for Congress to take— The calling upon the States to form a Convention for the Sole purpose of revising the Confederation . . . to enable Congress to execute with more energy, effect, & vigor, the powers assigned it." Congressional proposal of alterations, the "friends to Convention" argued, "has been already done in some instances, but in vain." Washington protested the "want of energy in the Federal Constitution . . . which I wish to see given to it by a Convention of the People."[60]

To invest Congress with powers to execute a national commercial policy, Governor Bowdoin on May 31, 1785, recommended to the Massachusetts legislature that the state's congressional delegation be instructed to propose a convention for that purpose. The General Court agreed and issued the orders, but the delegates—Samuel Holten, Elbridge Gerry, and Rufus King—refused to submit the proposal. Imbued with the spirit of '76, they feared that revamping the Confederation would produce a dangerously powerful central government hardly better than the British despotism recently cast off, changing "our republican Governments, into baleful Aristocracies." Moreover, they doubted that amendments could be "proposed in a Way, not *expressly* pointed out by the Confederation." Even granting, they said, that "no provision is made, for or against a Convention," so that a convention was not inconsistent with the Confederation, friction would nonetheless arise between the states and Congress should Congress reject any amendments proposed by the convention. In separate addresses before the Massachusetts legislature, King and Nathan Dane (a new delegate) made the same arguments against a convention, and held to the view that Congress alone could propose amendments.[61] The legislature cooled to the convention idea, and withdrew it in November.[62]

A more successful approach to amendment was meanwhile nearing fruition. From March 25 through 28, 1785, commissioners from Maryland and Virginia met at Washington's Mount Vernon home and settled a dispute pertaining to shipping and navigation rights on the Chesapeake and Potomac. Having originally assembled at Alexandria, as George Mason related, the commissioners, "upon the particular Invitation of the General, adjourn'd to Mount-Vernon, and finished the Business there." Washington, soon to be president of the Potomac Navigation Company, acted as host but did not join the negotiations. Under the compact, equal use of the waters was guaranteed to the two states: the "River Potomack shall be considered as a common High Way, for the purpose of Navigation and Commerce to the Citizens of Virginia and Maryland and of the United States." Mason and Alexander Henderson, the two commissioners who signed for Virginia (despite the enabling act's requirement that three participate), suggested to their legislature that representatives from those states meet annually to review commercial questions.[63]

When ratification of the compact was taken up in Maryland, its legislature recommended that Delaware and Pennsylvania be included in the annual conference. In the prospect that Delaware and Pennsylvania "will naturally pay the same compliment to their neighbours &c. &c.," Madison, who steered the compact through Virginia's General Assembly while downplaying the commissioners' exceeding of their powers, recognized the opportunity for "a Meeting of Politico-Commercial Commiss[ione]rs from all the States for the purpose of digesting and reporting the requisite augmentation of the power of Congress over trade." On January 21, 1786, the Virginia legislature adopted a resolution by John Tyler, father of the tenth president, for a convention to survey trade issues affecting the country as a whole, with a view to alterations in the Articles that would enhance Congress's power to regulate commerce.[64]

Virginia's resolution appointed five commissioners to meet with counterparts from the other states

to take into consideration the trade of the United States; . . . to consider how far a uniform system in [the states'] commercial regulations may be necessary to their common interest . . . ; and to report to the several States such an act relative to this great object, as, when unanimously ratified by them, will enable the United States in Congress effectually to provide for the same.

The choice having been left to them, the Virginia deputies transmitted to the states along with the resolution a circular letter proposing "the first Monday in September next as the time, and the city of Annapolis as the place for the meeting." Any reforms introduced at the Annapolis Convention would be instituted according to the procedure set out in the Articles, but suspicions of a more drastic hidden agenda were bruited. As Madison informed Jefferson, "Many Gentlemen both within & without Congs. wish to make this Meeting subservient to a Plenipotentiary Convention for amending the Confederation."[65]

To the suggestion of Fredericksburg attorney James Monroe (who succeeded Madison as President) that the Annapolis Convention might be too narrow in scope to be effective, Madison replied:

The efforts for bringing about a correction thro' the medium of Congress have miscarried. Let a Convention then be tried. If it succeeds in the first instance, it can be repeated as other defects force themselves on the public attention, and as the public mind becomes prepared for further remedies. The Assembly here [Virginia] would refer nothing to Congress. They would have revolted equally against a plenipotentiary commission to their deputies for the Convention. The option therefore lay between doing what was done and doing nothing.

Virginia, Madison perceived, would reject amendments emanating from Congress as well as a convention with plenary powers: in both cases alterations might issue that were too strong for its taste. As one scholar has observed, this concern "would not threaten a convention appointed for limited and carefully defined purposes and meeting under the auspices of the states rather than Congress." Of the forthcoming convention, Monroe guessed that "recommendations will meet with more attention from a body assembled under the particular direction of the States for a temporary purpose in whom the lust for power cannot be supposed to exist."[66]

Madison and Hamilton were among the commissioners from five states—Virginia, Delaware, Pennsylvania, New Jersey, and New York—who convened for four days beginning September 11, 1786, probably at Mann's Inn, a short walk from the Annapolis State House. Connecuticut and host state Maryland declined to send delegates, apprehensive that the meeting would cast doubt on the ability of Congress to handle matters of national moment. Massachusetts and Rhode Island appointed deputies, but so tardily that those delegations met on the way with news that the convention had ended.[67]

The convention's report, written by Hamilton and presented to Congress on September 20, concluded that "the power of regulating trade is of such comprehensive extent" that "to give it efficacy" may "require a correspondent adjustment of other parts of the Foederal System," as well as consultation with more than the five states attending. With one exception, said the report, the powers granted to the commissioners extended to deliberation on "the Trade and commerce of the United States." Only New Jersey had empowered its delegates to consider non-trade matters: "commercial regulations and *other important matters,*" as the report itself emphasized. Abraham Clark of that state therefore had been prevailed upon, said Madison later, to move for another convention "with more enlarged powers." The address recommended that each state appoint "Commissioners, to meet at Philadelphia on the second Monday in May next, to take into consideration the situation of the United States, to devise such further provisions as shall appear to them necessary to render the constitution of the Foederal Government adequate to the exigencies of the Union." No amendments were proposed by the commissioners; indeed, none were ever added to the Confederation.[68]

New Jersey's lower house in the meantime passed a resolution declaring its refusal to comply with a revenue requisition of Congress. To obtain a rescission, Congress sent a delegation to the state, including Charles Pinckney of South Carolina. On March 13, 1786, Pinckney exhorted New Jersey in a speech before the lower house "immediately to instruct her delegates in congress, to urge the calling of a general convention of the states, for the purpose of revising and amending the federal system," to which measure he pledged his support. A few days later the resolution was repealed, but the incident fueled talk in Congress of a constitutional convention.[69]

Agreeing to Pinckney's motion of May 3, 1786, to sit as a committee of the whole to consider "the state of public affairs," Congress nevertheless rebuffed his suggestion to appoint a convention for increased powers. Unwilling to cede the task of constitutional reform to another body, Congress on July 3 appointed a "grand Committee" to draft amendments that "will render the federal government adequate to the ends for which it was instituted." The committee's seven proposals among other things gave Congress exclusive control of interstate and foreign commerce together with the ability to enforce revenue requisitions levied on the states, but they were never approved by Congress after presentation on August 7, nor submitted to the states for ratification. The refusal was a repeat performance of the previous year, when Congress declined to approve an amendment (drafted by Monroe) granting it power to regulate foreign and domestic trade.[70]

The constant deadlocks on amendments arose from sectional jealousies and a reluctance by Congress to alienate the states by forcing them to surrender powers. The interest of northern states in untrammeled commercial activity squarely conflicted with southern claims to free use of the Mississippi, a right disputed by Spain; the North was willing to sacrifice navigation rights in exchange for trade advantages in the ports of Spanish Florida. The small states, meanwhile, opposed any plan that would diminish their weight in national councils.[71]

Last, as Monroe saw, many members believed that "all attacks upon the confideration were dangerous & calculated even if they did not succeed to weaken it." A respectable body of members and nonmembers alike did not think the situation was so desperate as to warrant remodeling the constitution; Monroe himself was "thoroughly persuaded the govt. is practicable & with a few alterations the best that can be devised." By the autumn of 1786, a distinguished historian concluded, "the men most anxious to create a strong central government had pinned all their hopes on a constitutional convention entirely apart from Congress."[72]

The Revolution had left the nation in debt, and the economic depression was acutely felt by heavily taxed farmers in the Northeast who were no longer allowed to repay creditors in crops. Requiring scarce hard money, they were forced to sell their land and livestock to merchants and speculators on the coast. In the summer of 1786 county conventions all over New England stated the agrarian community's grievances and demands for paper currency, but passing resolutions soon turned into mob action to intimidate the courts, which executed actions against debtors. The most notorious outbreak was led in western Massachusetts by Daniel Shays, for this insurrection came to symbolize the need for a stronger central government, and hastened the appointment of delegates to Philadelphia. Wrote Stephen Higginson, a federalist banker who had a major part in quelling Shays's Rebellion, "I never saw so great [a] change in the public mind . . . as has lately appeared in this State as to the expediency of increasing the powers of Congress, not merely as to commercial Objects, but generally."[73]

Even more ominous in early 1787 was the specter of the Union's partition into three or four separate regional confederacies, an idea that, Madison wrote, "after long confinement to individual speculations & private circles, is beginning to shew itself in the Newspapers." By the time Congress decided to act on the Annapolis report, seven states had already voted to send delegates, with more likely to follow. Congress, jealous of its prestige but confronted with the inevitable, acceded to the states by issuing, on February 21, 1787, its call for the Philadelphia Convention:

> Whereas there is provision in the Articles of Confederation and perpetual Union for making alterations therein by the Assent of a Congress of the United States and of the Legislatures of the several States. . . .
>
> Resolved that in the opinion of Congress it is expedient that on the second Monday in May next a Convention of delegates who shall have been appointed by the several States be held at Philadelphia for the sole and express purpose of revising the Articles of Confederation and reporting to Congress and the several legislatures such alterations and provisions therein as shall when agreed to in Congress and confirmed by the States render the federal Constitution adequate to the exigencies of Government and the preservation of the Union.

That day Madison wrote to Washington: "Congs. have been much divided and embarrassed on the question whether their taking an interest in the measure would impede or promote it."[74]

The Annapolis and Philadelphia gatherings were a rebuke to the inactivity and "imbecillity" of Congress. At Philadelphia, George Mason said: "I consider the federal government as in some measure dissolved by the meeting of this Convention." Washington, doubting the "legallity of this Convention," was persuaded to attend in part because of his conviction that Congress was not the "most efficatious channel for . . . alterations" and the other mode, as the "shortest course," was to be preferred. "Otherwise, like a house on fire, whilst the most regular mode of extinguishing it is contended for, the building is reduced to ashes."[75]

2

Philadelphia and After

Drafting Article V

The adjustment of shared power between central and state governments continued at the Philadelphia Convention, which met from May 14 until September 17, 1787, in the East Room of Pennsylvania's State House. When article V was shaped the delegates were occupied by three major concerns: (1) who could propose amendments; (2) whether ratification by the states should be required and, if so, by what fraction; and (3) what limits to place on the scope of the amending power.[1]

The Power to Propose

Article V began as the thirteenth of fifteen proposals together known as the Randolph or Virginia Plan, the work of Madison but presented to the convention on May 29 by the Governor of Virginia, Edmund Randolph:

> Resd. that provision ought to be made for the amendment of the Articles of Union whensoever it shall seem necessary, and that the assent of the National Legislature ought not to be required thereto.

The exclusion of Congress was the result of its failure to propose amendments in the immediately preceding years. When several delegates questioned the wisdom of an amending clause (five states still lacked one), Mason, the principal drafter of Virginia's 1776 constitution and declaration of rights, "urged the necessity of such a provision. . . . It would be improper to require the consent of the Natl. Legislature, because they may abuse their power, and refuse their consent on that very account."[2]

The convention referred the clause to the Committee of Detail, whose task it was to collect the various proposals, as revised by the delegates, and produce a working draft. Article XIX of the Committee's draft, reported to the convention on August 6, provided:

On the application of the Legislatures of two thirds of the States in the Union, for an amendment of this Constitution, the Legislature of the United States shall call a Convention for that purpose.

The figure of two thirds, or nine states, was derived from articles IX–XI of the Confederation, where that number was required for certain important actions relating to war and coinage.[3]

Including a convention mechanism was no empty gesture, for the conclave at Philadelphia was not thought to be the last of its kind. "Accommodation is absolutely necessary," Elbridge Gerry warned the delegates on July 2, "and defects may be amended by a future convention." Gunning Bedford, Jr., of Delaware also urged conciliation: "It will be better that a defective plan should be adopted, than that none should be recommended." There was "no reason why defects might not be [remedied] by meetings 10, 15 or 20 years hence."[4]

On September 10 Gerry began the first of the two major discussions of the amendment process by moving to reconsider article XIX. Since the Constitution would be "paramount to the State Constitutions," he wondered if the states would be protected, since under the article "two thirds of the States may obtain a Convention, a majority of which can bind the Union to innovations that may subvert the State-Constitutions altogether." Hamilton agreed to reconsider but would not confer proposal power on the states: "The State Legislatures will not apply for alterations but with a view to increase their own powers— The National Legislature will be the first to perceive and will be most sensible to the necessity of amendments," which militated in favor of granting Congress sole power to call a convention, especially since "the people would finally decide" whether or not to ratify any of the amendments proposed.[5]

Roger Sherman offered to return Congress as an alternative proposing agent: "or the Legislature may propose amendments . . . , but no amendments shall be binding until consented to by the several States." Madison followed up with a substitute that jettisoned the convention method altogether:

The Legislature of the U—— S—— whenever two thirds of both Houses shall deem necessary, or on the application of two thirds of the Legislatures of the several States, shall propose amendments to this Constitution . . . .

This method of proposal, by Congress upon petition by the states, copied the ratification method of the Confederation, in which the states were to "authorize their delegates to ratify the same in the Congress." Madison's substitute was kept in the second major draft, by the Committee of Style and Arrangement, reported to the convention on September 12.[6]

The amending clause was discussed at length for the second and last time on September 15. Mason, protesting the elimination of the convention and the resulting pivotal role given to Congress,

thought the plan of amending the Constitution exceptionable & dangerous. As the proposing of amendments is in both the modes to depend, in the first immediately, and in the second, ultimately, on Congress, no amendments of the proper kind would ever be obtained by the people, if the Government should become oppressive, as he verily believed would be the case.

Consequently, Gouverneur Morris and Gerry jointly "moved to amend the article so as to require a Convention on application of ⅔ of the St[ate]s."[7]

Madison responded that a Congress refusing to propose amendments demanded by the states was no likelier to call a convention for the same purpose, but verbally shrugging his shoulders professed to see no harm in the provision. In his words, "Mr. Madison did not see why Congress would not be as much bound to propose amendments applied for by two thirds of the States as to call a Convention on the like application. He saw no objection however against providing for a Convention for the purpose of amendments." With that, the Morris-Gerry motion was approved.[8]

The division of the amendment power was the essential compromise of article V, for determining who could propose amendments went far to determining what kind of amendments would be adopted. A source independent of Congress was necessary for what Mason called "amendments of the proper kind"; this translated, Hamilton knew, into applications by the states for alterations "with a view to increase their own powers" at the expense of the central government. On the subject of amendments, Hamilton wrote in *The Federalist*: "We may safely rely on the disposition of the state legislatures to erect barriers against the encroachments of the national authority."[9]

Ratification Requirements

It was at the outset unclear whether amendments to the Constitution, regardless of how proposed, would have to be ratified by the states. On September 10 Madison agreed to further discussion of the amending procedure: "the vagueness of the terms, 'call a Convention for the purpose' [w]as sufficient reason for reconsidering the article. How was a Convention to be formed? by what rule decide? what the force of its acts?" Madison's comment apparently reflects uncertainty as to whether amendments proposed by a convention would be immediately effective (as was true in the early state conventions), for as yet there was no ratification requirement. Gerry assumed no such requirement when he said a convention "can bind the Union to innovations." John Jay, who did not attend, was unsure whether the Philadelphia Convention itself would "ordain," that is, promulgate as binding, or "only recommend."[10]

Hamilton's recommendation assumed some form of ratification. Sherman's addition stipulated the assent of every state, but James Wilson's emendation to a three-fourths requirement for ratification was accepted, and kept in the final version. The three-fourths requirement was a triumph for the nationalists, since a unanimity requirement that repeated the Confederation's provision would have allowed one state to veto an amendment. Measures proposed in 1781 and 1783, giving Congress the power to tax imports, were in fact killed by, respectively, Rhode Island and New York.[11]

Limitations on the Power

Certain delegates, Hamilton among them, wanted to do away with state governments entirely, leaving Congress with "indefinite authority" and the states as bare administrative shells. Rufus King, sympathetic, said that the Philadelphia Convention could offer that alteration because it had the same vast discretion to propose amendments as did the Confederation Congress. That Congress, in which each state had one vote, might propose any change in the Articles, said King, including "that relating to the equality of suffrage."[12]

This onslaught led to restrictions on the amending power under the new Constitution. On September 10 John Rutledge of South Carolina objected to the amendment provision as then framed, since "he could never agree to give a power by which the articles relating to slaves might be altered by the States not interested in that property and prejudiced against it." To meet his objection a clause was added stating "that no amendments which may be made prior to the year 1808 shall in any manner affect" the slave trade.[13]

Roger Sherman, vigilant of Connecticut's land holdings in the Old Northwest, "expressed his fears" on September 15 that some states might be absorbed by their neighbors or at least deprived of their equal representation in the Senate. These injuries, he said, could be sanctioned by properly ratified amendments. "He thought it reasonable" in consequence "that the proviso in favor of the States importing slaves should be extended so as to provide that no State should be affected in its internal police, or deprived of its equality in the Senate." After a short, desultory consideration of subsidiary issues the convention approved Sherman's proviso minus the prohibition of interference with the states' internal "police," or regulation of public health and morals. The proviso now declared that "no State, without its consent shall be deprived of its equal suffrage in the Senate."[14]

In *The Federalist* Madison referred to the power "[t]o provide for amendments to be ratified by three-fourths of the States, under two exceptions *only*," a description indicating that the slave trade exception (obsolete by its own terms in 1808) and the equal suffrage exception were absolutes, placed beyond the scope of the amending power. Noah Webster wrote: "three fourths of their number may alter and amend . . . except in two or three particulars, expressly reserved in the compact."[15]

The final version of article V, with the rest of the Constitution, was officially approved by the members at the close of proceedings on September 15:

> The Congress, whenever two thirds of both Houses shall deem it necessary, shall propose Amendments to this Constitution, or, on the Application of the

Legislatures of two thirds of the several States, shall call a Convention for proposing Amendments, which, in either Case, shall be valid to all Intents and Purposes, as Part of this Constitution, when ratified by the Legislatures of three fourths of the several States, or by Conventions in three fourths thereof, as the one or the other Mode of Ratification may be proposed by the Congress; Provided that no Amendment which may be made prior to the Year One thousand eight hundred and eight shall in any Manner affect the first and fourth Clauses in the Ninth Section of the first Article; and that no State, without its Consent, shall be deprived of it's equal Suffrage in the Senate.

Two days later, after the engrossed Constitution was signed by the approving delegates (Randolph, Mason, and Gerry abstained), the convention rose.

Article V, no less than the other provisions of the Constitution, displays the compromises reached in the allocation of power. "Look through that instrument from beginning to end," said Jonathan Dayton of New Jersey, "and you will not find an article which is not founded on the presumption of a clashing of interests." As the article V proceedings show, the contest for economic and political power between the central and state governments did not stop at Philadelphia, nor was it expected to abate in the near future. Indeed, wresting power from the strengthened national government was the motive force behind the ensuing campaign for another constitutional convention.[16]

The Antifederalist Drive for a Second Convention

Rumblings of another constitutional convention surfaced before the Philadelphia Convention was out. On August 31, George Mason pronounced himself so upset with the direction the Constitution was taking that "he would sooner chop off his right hand than put it to the Constitution as it now stands." If changes were not made, "his wish would then be to bring the whole subject before another general Convention." Gouverneur Morris from the opposite corner welcomed "another Convention, that will have the firmness to provide a vigorous Government, which we are afraid to do."[17]

Edmund Randolph then suggested that the state ratifying conventions be allowed "to propose amendments to be submitted to another General Convention which may reject or incorporate them." Randolph introduced a motion on September 10 for another convention which Franklin good-naturedly seconded but which, at Mason's request, was tabled. Randolph reintroduced his motion five days later, seconded by Mason, who said: "A second Convention will know more of the sense of the people, and be able to provide a system more consonant to it. As the Constitution now stands," Mason could not sign it nor support it back in Virginia without "the expedient of another Convention." Charles Pinckney was apprehensive about "the consequences of calling forth the deliberations & amendments of the different States on the subject of Government at large" in a second convention. "Nothing but confusion & contrariety could spring from the experiment," he prophesied. "Conventions are serious things, and ought not to be repeated."[18]

Gerry then registered his objections to the Constitution, foremost among them the bold power given to Congress under the necessary and proper clause and the absence of a guarantee of jury trials in civil cases. These objections were grounded in the fear of an uncontrollable central government uprooting personal freedoms along with state prerogatives. "Under such a view of the Constitution," Gerry concluded, "the best that could be done . . . was to provide for a second general Convention." Yet when Randolph's proposal was put to a vote the delegates, feeling it would be a self-proclaimed lack of confidence in their own work, rejected it.[19]

In the convention's waning days, the delegates had brushed aside Mason's suggestion that the Constitution be prefaced with a bill of rights. After the Constitution was submitted to the state conventions held to decide on ratification pursuant to article VII, it became clear that the omission was a critical misjudgment that would make adoption an extremely close question. Though Hamilton in *The Federalist* argued against the necessity of a bill of rights and warned of "the utter improbability of assembling a new convention, under circumstances. . . so favourable . . . as those in which the late convention met," antifederalists demanded a second convention to supply amendments, with variations in content depending on the advocate.[20]

The antis, united only in their opposition to the Constitution as submitted, had no uniform position on other issues. Some were against the Constitution on the ground that the Articles of Confederation, with modifications, would suffice; others, that the Constitution was acceptable but required amendments before adoption; still others preferred dissolution of the Union into regional confederacies. A second convention, either to prepare a bill of rights for the 1787 Constitution or to draft a new charter, was the sole item of antifederalist consensus. The federalists, to be distinguished from the later political party, were, as Gerry said, "for ratifying the constitution as it stood."[21]

Randolph's report to the Virginia House of Delegates, explaining his refusal to sign the Constitution, recommended that the upcoming Virginia ratifying convention decide on amendments for submission to "another federal convention" in which "the amendments proposed by this or any other state be discussed; and if incorporated in the Constitution, or rejected." If the states did not want a convention, the Constitution would again be submitted to the ratification conventions for adoption or rejection as it was. Richard Henry Lee, who had failed in Congress to get a bill of rights added, concurred in the tactic: "the plan for us to pursue will be to propose the necessary amendments" and "to suggest the calling [of] a new convention for the purpose of considering them."[22]

Jefferson, the Minister to France, anticipated rejection of the Constitution by Virginia and an outcome like that envisaged in the Randolph-Lee plan. "Should it fall thro'," he wrote, "it is probable that Congress will propose that the objections which the people shall make to it being once known, another Convention shall be assembled to adopt the improvements generally acceptable." John Adams, the Minister to Britain, would take the Constitution "as it is, and promote a convention after some time to amend it"—a position he held as late as 1790, while Vice President.[23]

The federalists hoped that a convention would not soon be called. "The very attempt at a second Convention strikes at the confidence in the first," Madison thought, "and the existence of a second by opposing influence to influence, would in a manner destroy an effectual confidence in either." It is worth bearing in mind that a convention to amend the Constitution would not have tacked on clauses at the end: this was the method chosen by the First Federal Congress only after extended debate. Rather, the amendments would have been interwoven with the main text and the new charter would have been sent out again, in its entirety, for ratification.[24] While technically the 1787 Constitution would be in effect until superseded, it was realistic to assume that resubmission would jeopardize the fledgling government by effectively suspending it during the second round of ratification. Madison foresaw an "infinitely precarious" set of events were "the Constitution re-edited with amendments" at another convention.[25]

Expecting that the Virginia ratification convention would recommend amendments for consideration by another national convention, Mason and Patrick Henry were behind resolutions introduced in the legislature on November 30, 1787, defraying the expenses of "the deputies to a Federal Convention in case such a Convention should be judged necessary," which were grafted onto a bill providing for compensation of delegates to the ratifying assembly. The resulting act, passed on December 12, provided for the expenses of delegates to the ratifying convention, and in muted tones under pressure from the federalists, provided for reimbursing delegates at another federal convention in the name of reserving funds for the ratification convention to hold "communications with any of the sister states" and for "collecting the sentiments of the union respecting the proposed foederal constitution."[26]

The December act was circulated to the governors of the other states, but Governor George Clinton of New York, a leading proponent of a second convention, did not receive his copy until March 7, 1788. The (highly suspicious) delay prevented New York's legislature from acting in concert with Virginia. Randolph, whose support for another convention was growing lukewarm, strategically withheld Clinton's response, which promised cooperation "with any sister State," from the Virginia convention. The delegates learned of the response the day after they had voted to ratify, when it was read to the legislature. Without those crucial delays, according to one early study, a second convention "would have been inevitable."[27]

The federalists hit upon a compromise in the Massachusetts ratifying convention, held in January and February of 1788. A series of recommended amendments, drafted by Theophilus Parsons but presented to the convention by president John Hancock as his own, placated the opponents of the Constitution. The amendments, it was understood, would be proposed by Congress once the new government was adopted. The stratagem let ratification proceed unhindered, and was imitated in other conventions. Jefferson was converted from skeptic to supporter, favoring adoption provided a bill of rights was attached.[28]

The Constitution went into effect on June 21, 1788, when New Hampshire, the ninth state, ratified; Virginia (June 25) and New York (July 26) soon followed. At the Virginia ratification convention, only Madison's last-minute promise to obtain a bill of rights in the new Congress won the votes necessary for approval by his state. Patrick Henry, who had refused his appointment to Philadelphia, could not believe that a strong central government could administer the entire territory of the United States without detriment to Virginia's interests, especially her claims to western lands and navigation rights on the Mississippi. "I am persuaded," he told the assembly in Richmond's New Academy building on Shockoe Hill, "that one government cannot reign over so extensive a country as this is, without absolute despotism."[29]

Henry drafted a series of amendments for consideration by a second constitutional convention, which as slightly revised by the Virginia convention, was submitted to Congress with the state's ratification notice. With Virginia's approval a fact, Henry pledged to "remove the defects of that system in a constitutional way," but his amendments were radical surgery: in addition to reiterating the guarantees of personal freedom in Virginia's bill of rights, they hemmed in Congress's power to conclude treaties on territorial and navigation entitlements, and drastically reduced the power of Congress to levy taxes and regulate federal elections. "It is clearly seen by the enemies of the Constitution," wrote Madison, "that an abolition of that [taxation] power will re-establish the supremacy of the State Legislatures, the real object of all their zeal in opposing the system." Even the sympathetic nineteenth-century historian who was Henry's first major biographer conceded that an anti-federalist-led second convention "would have reconstructed, from top to bottom, the work done by the convention of 1787."[30]

The Virginia legislature, preparing to embark under the Constitution, was totally under the sway of Patrick Henry. "He has only to say let this be Law," Washington grumbled, "and it is Law." On October 29, 1788, Henry introduced in the House of Delegates his measure for a new convention, which was approved by the House the next day. Virginia's ratifying convention, stated Henry's preamble, had assented to the Constitution "and did also declare that sundry amendments to exceptionable parts of the same ought to be adopted" because "the subject matter of the amendments agreed to by the said [ratifying] Convention involves all the great essential and unalienable rights, liberties and privileges of freemen" that are "rendered insecure under the said constitution until the same shall be altered."[31]

A motion by federalist and ratifier Francis Corbin to amend the measure so as to ask Congress to propose its own amendments was voted down, 85 to 39. The committee appointed to draw up the convention application, which included Henry and Monroe, presented its draft with revisions by Theodorick Bland, another committee member, to the House on November 14. After the draft was read on the floor, Corbin made another counter-motion to substitute a "form of an application" permitting Congress itself to decide whether to propose amendments or call a convention; Corbin's substitute was rejected, 71 to 50. The committee draft was approved by the House of Delegates, and sent to the Senate. On November 19 the Senate, after making minor changes, concurred. The following day the Senate was notified that the House had agreed to the changes. "The weight of business that would devolve on the government," Monroe reported, "was suppos'd a sufficient reason why this trust should be repos'd in another body. It could in no event be productive of harm."[32]

Virginia's application, presented to Congress by Representative Bland on May 5, 1789, was steeped in the rhetoric of the Revolution. It proclaimed the "anxiety with which our countrymen press" for amendments, and rejected the "slow forms of Congressional discussion" in favor of "a convention of the States." The convention was to have "full power" to consider the "defects of this constitution that have been suggested by the State Conventions," and report amendments that would "secure to ourselves and our latest posterity the great and unalienable rights of mankind." In New York City's Federal Hall, where Congress was headquartered, the application was filed with the Clerk of the House of Representatives pending the receipt of applications from the remaining necessary states.[33]

In New York the price of ratification was a circular letter drafted by John Jay but sent to the governors of each state over the signature of Governor Clinton, president of the New York convention at Poughkeepsie, calling on Congress for a second convention to add amendments. Several articles of the Constitution, said the letter, were "so exceptionable" that "nothing but the fullest confidence of obtaining a revision of them by a general convention, and an invincible reluctance to separating from our sister states, could have prevailed upon a sufficient number to ratify it." Accordingly, "we ardently wish and desire that the other states may concur in adopting and promoting the measure."[34]

The proposal was well received by antifederalist contingents in North Carolina and Rhode Island, but was never seriously considered in any other legislature. Washington, resolutely opposed to another convention, knew that the Clinton circular was designed to "set every thing afloat again." New York indeed stood to lose revenues from a strong federal taxing power, since it had reaped the benefit of collecting duties on goods passing through its port to neighboring states. Called into early session by Governor Clinton, the legislature passed a resolution for a second convention on February 7, 1789. On May 6, Congress was presented with an application that hewed closely to its Virginia model.[35]

Rhode Island, the only state refusing to send delegates to Philadelphia, at first did not comply with article VII's requirement that ratification be accomplished by convention. The antifederalists disliked the amplitude of congressional power, the absence of a bill of rights, and the ban on state issuance of paper money. The antis, who dominated the legislature, tried to avoid a ratifying convention on the likely assumption that it would have voted for the Constitution. Although a referendum was attacked by federalists as inconsistent with the specified ratification mode, the Rhode Island legislature ordered the Constitution submitted directly to the towns for a vote, where in March 1788 it was rejected.[36] In October the legislature submitted the Clinton letter's proposal for another federal convention, but the response from the towns was too late and too scattered to be effective. On May 29, 1790, as Congress threatened a trade embargo, Rhode Island by state convention ratified the Constitution.[37]

North Carolina's convention, meeting at Hillsborough, adjourned in August 1788 without deciding the question of ratification, but having "taken for granted" that "Congress wou'd soon call a fresh general Convention," approved a number of amendments "to be laid before Congress, and the convention of the states that shall or may be called for the purpose of amending the said Constitution." On November 20, the state legislature passed resolutions calling another ratification convention and one for the appointment of "five Persons to represent this State in a Convention of the United States." All five delegates appointed by the legislature to this second federal convention were antifederalists, including the outspoken critic Timothy Bloodworth. The second ratification convention, which met at Fayetteville and voted to adopt on November 21, 1789, recommended amendments that were to be obtained through another federal convention.[38]

The conference held during September 1788 in Harrisburg, Pennsylvania, consisting of antifederalists disgruntled by the state's ratification the year before, issued a recommendation for amendments. The report was prefaced by a resolution asking the Pennsylvania legislature to obtain alterations to the Constitution "by a general convention of the representatives from the several states in the Union." The recommendation, ignored by the legislature, was written by Albert Gallatin, the Swiss immigrant who would serve in the House of Representatives and as Jefferson's Secretary of the Treasury.[39]

At the outset of the ratification contest, antifederalists outnumbered federalists in the voting (white male) population by approximately 52 to 48 percent. As was usual for the time, voting for the delegates to the ratifying conventions was sparse, involving perhaps only 5 percent of the entire population of nearly four million.[40] The low participation gave the towns and commercial regions, the areas with the highest percentages of voter turnout as well as the most likely to be federalist, a representational advantage in the conventions. This advantage proved critical: Virginia ratified by a ten-vote margin, Massachusetts by nineteen, New York by three. Since there could be no Union without the most important states, a shift of six, ten, and two votes in those assemblages—eighteen out of the more than fifteen hundred cast in the ratifying conventions of 1787 and 1788—would have meant a different outcome.[41]

In the end, only the two applications from Virginia and New York were sent to Congress, but a second convention, which would have mortally threatened the Constitution, was averted only because the antifederalists in each state were splintered and poorly organized. Some antis, like Patrick Henry, pushed for a second convention out of opposition to the Constitution itself, hoping the convention would produce a renovated charter with an enfeebled central government. Others, like George Mason, approved of the Constitution on the whole but held out for a convention as a bargaining chip to obtain a bill of rights.[42]

Madison kept watch over the election of the incoming representatives and appointment of senators "to ascertain precisely the complexion of the new Congress," for the second convention still hung like a sword of Damocles over the government. "The new Constitution is not yet out of the reach of its enemies," warned "Plain Truth" at the end of 1788. "I have no doubt," wrote a New York antifederalist, that "our Represent's in Congress, can be of service in calling another convention." Delay in submitting amendments after the pledge to obtain them from Congress, Madison knew, would encourage antifederalists "to blow the trumpet for a second Convention" and "complain of being deceived."[43]

Under Jefferson's tutelage, Madison urged an indifferent First Federal Congress to propose amendments, amendments that confirmed personal rights without touching the essential powers of the central government. Pursuing a strategy of divide and conquer, Madison's aim was "to give satisfaction to the doubting part of our fellow-citizens" and isolate into harmlessness the minority of diehard opponents. If the states were to see that amendments "cannot be secured in the mode they had wished," said Representative Thomas Tudor Tucker of South Carolina, "they will naturally recur to the alternative, and endeavor to obtain a federal convention," perhaps engendering such "discord, as to sever the Union asunder." Representative Gerry went along with amendments "to prevent the necessity which the States may think themselves under of calling a new convention." Gerry, who had made his peace with the Constitution and would be Vice President under Madison, was not "one of those blind admirers of this system," but "if it is referred to a new convention, we run the risk of losing some of its best properties; this is a case I never wish to see."[44]

By September 25, 1789, when Congress submitted to the states for ratification the amendments now known as the Bill of Rights, the pressure for another constitutional convention had evaporated, and Congress was launched as the method of choice for initiating amendments. "The first Congress will probably mend the principal" faults of the Constitution, Benjamin Franklin predicted, "& future Congresses the rest."[45]

3

The Nineteenth Century

Commentary on Article V

After the Constitution's adoption a confident Madison intimated, perhaps as a conciliatory gesture, that he might not be averse to a convention that met after the government was firmly in place. To Jefferson he wrote: "an early Convention . . . will certainly be industriously opposed" by those preferring no alterations or else proposal by Congress, "and who would moreover approve of a Convention for amending the frame of the Government itself, as soon as time shall have somewhat corrected the feverish state of the public mind." For newspaper publisher and Harvard naturalist Samuel Williams in 1794, the article V convention exemplified the dynamic nature of the federal Constitution: "it is one of the constituent and essential parts of American government, that conventions shall be called at certain periods of time, to alter, amend, and improve the present form and constitution of government; as the state, circumstances, and improvements of society, shall then require." But in the decades following ratification, a convention remained more a theoretical than a live prospect.[1]

That the founding age considered the convention a genuine part of the Constitution was demonstrated when the Adams administration secured passage of the Alien and Sedition Acts in 1798. At the time, armed conflict with France was on the horizon after skirmishes at sea and Talleyrand's attempt to extort a bribe in the XYZ Affair. The Alien and Sedition Acts allowed the President in wartime to imprison and deport aliens without trial, and forbade conspiracy to oppose measures of the government or publication of criticism that would bring either Congress or the President "into contempt or disrepute."[2] The legislatures of Virginia and Kentucky passed resolutions (drafted by Madison and Jefferson respectively) proclaiming these harsh laws unconstitutional.

In his *Report on the Virginia Resolutions*, written in December 1799, Madison held that any state could issue a declaration that certain "proceedings of the Federal Government are not warranted by the Constitution." Each state has the right of "communicating the declaration to other States, and inviting their concurrence in a like declaration." This right of communication, said Madison, extends to the amending power: "The Legislatures of the States have a right also to originate amendments to the Constitution, by a concurrence of two-thirds of the whole number, in applications to Congress for the purpose." Accordingly, the state legislatures might obtain repeal of the Alien and Sedition Acts by requesting Congress to "propose an explanatory amendment to the Constitution" declaring the rights such acts violated; "or two-thirds of themselves, if such had been their option, might, by an application to Congress, have obtained a Convention for the same object." The *Report* was adopted by the Virginia legislature on January 11, 1800, but no state ever applied, the acts expiring shortly thereafter.[3]

In the election of 1800, Jefferson and his running mate on the Republican-Democratic party ticket, Aaron Burr, received an equal number of electoral votes for President, throwing the decision into the House of Representatives. The Federalists had been eliminated from the top offices by the election, but some talked of preventing a decision in the House altogether and hanging on by granting in a statute the chief magistracy to the president pro tem of the Senate or some other designated official, such as the Chief Justice of the United States (Federalist John Marshall). In Virginia and Pennsylvania, Republican contingents were prepared to resist "usurpation" by the Federalists, by force if necessary. Amid impending anarchy and rumors of civil war, the unconstitutional plan to legislate the presidency dissipated as the Federalist leadership in Congress rallied to install Burr.[4]

From February 11 to 17, 1801, until the thirty-sixth ballot, the House was deadlocked; Jefferson, sitting as Vice President, was convinced that a constitutional convention was a real possibility. Should the government "expire on the 3d of March by the loss of it's head," he confided during the voting, "there is no regular provision for reorganizing it, nor any authority but in the people themselves. They may authorize a convention to reorganize & even to amend the machine." To the Governor of Virginia, his close friend Monroe, Jefferson wrote that if the Federalists enacted a law "putting the government into the hands of an officer," the Republicans would defy the measure, and "the middle States would arm." This news "shook them," he reported,

and they were completely alarmed at the resource for which we declared, to wit, a convention to re-organize the government, & to amend it. The very word convention gives them the horrors, as in the present democratical spirit of America, they fear they should lose some of the favorite morsels of the constitution.[5]

Looking back after his inauguration, Jefferson hypothesized that "in the event of a non-election of a President" by March 4, the original date for beginning a new term,

the federal government would have been in the situation of a clock or watch run down. . . . A convention, invited by the Republican members of Congress, with the virtual President & Vice President, would have been on the ground in 8 weeks, would have repaired the Constitution where it was defective, & wound it up again.

To Jefferson's way of thinking, the convention, which "would have commanded immediate and universal obedience," was part threat and part legitimizing device to replace the flawed method of electing the nation's highest officers.[6]

Albert Gallatin, who was Jefferson's lieutenant in the House during the impasse, years later denied that the Republicans had considered anything of the kind, and Dumas Malone was inclined to believe that Jefferson read too much into a proposal by Gallatin for a meeting of the Republican party to devise a "uniform plan of acting" in case a new election had been required. The contest of 1800 led to the proposal by Congress in 1803 of the twelfth amendment, adopted the following year, which provides for the separately designated elections of the President and Vice President.[7]

Senator William Plumer of New Hampshire digressed on a convention during consideration of the proposed twelfth amendment. Plumer's remarks as reported in the *Annals of Congress* for December 2, 1803, are an abbreviated version of the extended discourse he gave on that date. Plumer recorded a fuller commentary in his notes:

If this [convention] mode is adopted, Congress have nothing to do but to ascertain the fact whether the necessary number of States require a Convention. If the necessary number require it, Congress shall call it—The language of the Constitution is imperative—it does not give Congress any discretion upon the subject—it only gives them the authority, & makes it their duty, to summon a Convention. That Convention when assembled will then have the sole authority of proposing amendments, if any should by them be thought necessary. . . . Neither Congress [n]or the State Legislatures, can instruct that Convention what amendments are requisite.

Plumer regarded each unit of federal and state government as a separate and independent check on the other units, with no overlap or sharing of functions. For Plumer, a state legislature could not ratify a convention-originated amendment; only a state convention could do so. Similarly, Plumer held, only amendments that originate in Congress may be ratified by the state legislatures. "Congress, & the State Legislatures, are. . . distinct tribunals, and each have a check & controul upon the acts of the other."[8]

Plumer's national convention is independent in its agenda not only of Congress but also of the state legislatures, in keeping with his eccentric vision of the Constitution's system of checks and balances. His notion that there is a proper ratifying body (as between state legislatures or conventions), depending on whether Congress or a convention has proposed the amendment, is refuted by the text of article V, which gives to Congress exclusive discretion to select the mode of ratification.[9]

Unlike Plumer, Senator James Jackson of Georgia favored the twelfth amendment; Jackson, however, agreed with Plumer on the proposing scope of an article V assembly. Answering the implied question "why we do not resort to a convention, if we wish to amend the Constitution," Jackson said he was "averse to calling conventions, [except] when no other remedy was provided; bodies of that description are invested with boundless power; the physical and political powers of the State are in their hands; and they are therefore more exposed to the zeal and the intrigues of the ardent and ambitious."[10]

Of the treatises written in the early years of the Republic that consider the amending procedure, only St. George Tucker's annotated edition of Blackstone's *Commentaries*, first published in 1803, takes up the convention route in any detail. Wrote Tucker, himself an Annapolis Convention delegate:

the fifth article provides the mode by which future amendments to the constitution may be proposed, discussed, and carried into effect, without hazarding a dissolution of the confederacy, or suspending the operations of the existing government. And this may be effected in two different modes: the first on recommendation from congress. . . . The second, which secures to the states an influence in case congress should neglect to recommend such amendments, provides, that congress shall, on application from the legislatures of two thirds of the states, call a convention for proposing amendments. . . . Both of these provisions appear excellent. Of the utility and practicability of the former, we have already had most satisfactory experience. The latter will probably never be resorted to, unless the federal government should betray symptoms of corruption, which may render it expedient for the states to exert themselves in order to the application of some radical and effectual remedy.

Tucker was persuaded that the convention would be used only when Congress refused to propose specific amendments desired by the states, in which event "the concurrent sense of two thirds of the state legislatures may enforce congress to call a convention."[11] Though article V itself speaks of equal alternatives with no preferred order, this Congress-convention sequence was an inherent expectation if not a requirement, common sense dictating that the easier method of proposal be tried first. The difficulties in calling a convention, Madison had written, are "much greater than will attend the origination of amendments in Congress."[12]

The United States Supreme Court referred to the convention procedure in *Smith v. Union Bank of Georgetown*, an 1831 decision involving the estate of a naval officer who had died without leaving a will. Speaking for the Court, whose personnel that Term included John Marshall and Joseph Story, Justice William Johnson announced the rule: distribution of an intestate's property is governed by the law of the place where the estate is administered, not that of the state where the deceased had been domiciled. "Each government," said Justice Johnson, as part of its sovereign character "thus assert[s] the power of its own laws over the subject matter, when within its control."[13]

The argument was made to the Court that the law of the domicile governed, but the victorious opposing counsel, led by Francis Scott Key, contended that "[t]he municipal law is against this claim" because that position would "overthrow our own laws, and destroy rights derived under them." Key's charge was tantamount to saying that a constitutional amendment was required to support the opposing position, and Justice Johnson replied:

> Whether it would or would not be politic to establish a different rule by a convention of the states, under constitutional sanction, is not a question for our consideration. But such an arrangement . . . would most materially interfere with the exercise of sovereign right, as at present generally asserted and exercised.[14]

To court and counsel, a convention on a single subject—here, the power of a state to determine the disposition of property within its borders—seems to reflect common and unremarkable knowledge.

The Nullification Crisis

In one way or another, the national convention drives and interstate conventions of the early nineteenth century all dealt with the rights of states in a federal Union, the residue of controversies dating from colonial times. The infamous Hartford Convention of December 1814 was a response to the grim progress of "Mr. Madison's War," the War of 1812. The twenty-six New England delegates had contemplated secession, and recommended constitutional amendments that among other things would have given the states a free hand in conducting their own defense. The tension between state and federal interests, increasingly a contest between South and North, reached its acute phase in the nullification crisis of the late 1820s and early 1830s.[15]

Nullification doctrine, long in brewing, was employed to counteract programs such as the national bank, the protective tariff (above all the 1828 "tariff of abominations"), and the building of roads and canals—developments viewed, especially in South Carolina, as a systematic federal invasion of the states' internal governance. The tariff imposed high duties on manufactured goods and was viewed by detractors as a subsidy of the industrial North by the agrarian South. Constitutionally, it was argued that the protection of manufactures was an abuse by Congress of its power to regulate commerce, or else that the tariff, since it transferred wealth from one region to another, violated the fifth amendment's prohibition against taking private property for public use without just compensation. The nullification doctrine reached its classic formulation in the South Carolina *Exposition and Protest*, written in 1828 by John C. Calhoun, Vice President of the United States, at the behest of the South Carolina legislature, though not officially adopted by it. Calhoun in the *Exposition* contended that each state had the right to "nullify" any federal law—to deem it of no effect within its borders until the nullifying state's action was reversed by an amendment to the Constitution.

Calhoun had been inspired by, and invoked, the arguments of Madison and especially Jefferson made thirty years before on the right of states to protest infringement of their prerogatives by the federal government. [16] Jefferson had contended in the Kentucky Resolutions that the federal government "was not made the exclusive or final judge of the extent of the powers delegated to itself, . . . but that, as in all other cases of compact among parties having no common judge, each party has an equal right to judge for itself, as well as of infractions as of the mode and measure of redress." Later, Jefferson would cast the article V convention as a route of appeal by the states from actions taken by the federal government. "It is a fatal heresy to suppose that either our State governments are superior to the federal, or the federal to the States," he wrote in 1821 to Judge Spencer Roane; "in differences of opinion between these different sets of servants, the appeal is to neither, but to their employers peaceably assembled by their representatives in convention." To Justice Johnson he commented: "The ultimate arbiter is the people of the Union, assembled by their deputies in convention, at the call of Congress, or of two-thirds of the States. Let them decide to which they mean to give an authority claimed by two of their organs." By "arbiter" Jefferson did not necessarily mean a body that could resolve questions in the manner of a court, as Calhoun seems to have understood, but probably one that could settle disputes by proposing amendments that, if adopted, would determine the issue. [17]

The Roane letter was quoted in the *Exposition* to justify nullification, or as Calhoun preferred to call it, "interposition." By mixing Jefferson's claim for the states as judges of constitutional infractions with the idea of a national convention as arbiter of jurisdictional disputes, Calhoun arrived at a nullifying power that could be exercised by a state convention. For Calhoun, a single contested federal power might be resolved by a constitutional amendment "in the ordinary form," that is, proposal by Congress; but "should the derangement of the system be great, embracing many points difficult to adjust, the States ought to be convened in a general Convention; the most august of all assemblies, . . . and having power & authority to correct every error." Madison, while admitting to some inexact language, denied that the Kentucky Resolutions or his own *Report* sanctioned nullification. Madison's *Report* had, in fact, explained that the state declarations were "expressions of opinion, unaccompanied with any other effect than what they may produce on opinion."[18]

Since both sides to the nullification dispute claimed his support, Madison was compelled to answer publicly—especially after the great Senate debate in January 1830 between Daniel Webster, arguing for the constitutionality of protective tariffs, and Robert Y. Hayne, defending nullification. Both sent copies of their speeches to Madison, who responded to Hayne with an elaborate rebuttal. When the Hayne letter came to the attention of Edward Everett, a Massachusetts congressman and editor of the influential *North American Review*, Everett requested and received Madison's permission to publish it. The 3,500-word letter, which Madison refined and readdressed to Everett, appeared in the *Review* for October 1830. The performance, enthusiastically received by, among others, John Marshall, was praised by one Madison biographer as his "final, most carefully considered interpretation of . . . the federal constitution."[19]

In the letter, Madison repudiated Calhoun's doctrine on the constitutional ground that a national convention, rather than nullification, is the states' legal refuge when Congress exercises a questionable power and will not propose an amendment circumscribing the power:

> Should the provisions of the Constitution . . . be found not to secure the Government and rights of the States, against usurpations and abuses on the part of the United States, the final resort within the purview of the Constitution, lies in an amendment of the Constitution, according to a process applicable by the States.

The right of resistance or revolution, said Madison, is a natural right exercisable only upon dissolution of the constitutional compact.

> If the doctrine were to be understood as requiring the three fourths of the States to sustain, instead of that proportion to reverse the decision of the appealing State, the decision to be without effect during the appeal, it would be sufficient to remark, that this extra-constitutional course might well give way to that marked out by the Constitution, which authorizes two thirds of the States to institute and three fourths to effectuate an amendment of the Constitution,

establishing a permanent rule of the highest authority, in place of an irregular precedent of construction only. [20]

Madison denied that each state has the power to disregard the Constitution at its pleasure: such "diversity of independent decisions" would "speedily put an end to the Union itself." The nullification prerogative was in any case contrary to the supremacy clause as well as to article III, which vests the power to decide constitutional cases in the federal judiciary. Yet Madison was hardly endorsing a convention. "To refer every point of disagreement to the people in Conventions," he had written some years earlier, "would be a process too tardy, too troublesome, & too expensive; besides its tendency to lessen a salutary veneration for an instrument so often calling for such explanatory interpositions." Madison placed himself among those who, recollecting "the happy result of the original Convention," should "deprecate the experiment of another with general power to revise its work."[21]

On October 26, 1832, the South Carolina legislature provided for a state convention to consider the tariff passed by Congress the previous July. The convention, the embodiment of Calhoun's doctrine, met from November 19 to 24, 1832. On its last day the convention passed an ordinance pronouncing the tariff acts of 1828 and 1832 "null, void, and no law," forbidding the collection of duties under those tariffs, and barring appeals to the United States Supreme Court on the question. The ordinance also warned that use of force by the federal government would be "inconsistent with the longer continuance of South Carolina in the Union." As a remedy, the convention proposed either lowering the tariff or "the call of a General Convention of all the States."[22]

South Carolina's actions incurred a proclamation on December 10 from President Andrew Jackson, affirming that the United States Constitution established a distinct federal government, not a league of independent states. The proclamation was written by Secretary of State Edward Livingston, who had been corresponding with Madison on strategies to counter nullification. To Governor James Hamilton, who advocated a convention, Jackson issued a virtual invitation:

the Governor of the State speaks of the submission of their grievances to a convention of all the States . . . . Yet this obvious and constitutional mode of obtaining the sense of the other States on the construction of the federal compact, and amending it, if necessary, has never been attempted by those who have urged [nullification]. . . . If the Legislature of South Carolina "anxiously desire" a general convention to consider their complaints, why have they not made application for it in the way the constitution points out?[23]

South Carolina's convention application, the first submitted to Congress since 1789, was passed by its legislature on December 18:

> Whereas serious causes of discontent do exist among the States of this Union, from the exercise by Congress of powers not conferred or contemplated by the sovereign parties to the compact, therefore,
> *Resolved*, That it is expedient that a convention of the States be called as early as practicable, to consider and determine such questions of disputed power, as have arisen between the States of this confederacy and the General Government.

The legislatures of Ohio, Massachusetts, and Illinois replied that it was inexpedient to hold a convention. The Massachusetts legislature's report faulted the application because it "studiously avoided" the "uniform practice" observed in convention applications since 1789, that of specifying "the precise points wherein the existing provisions of the system were supposed to be doubtful or insufficient, and the . . . correction proposed"; the implied accusation was of surreptitiously threatening disunion by means of a wide-open convention. Delaware correctly explained that the Supreme Court is the only proper tribunal to decide constitutional disputes between the state and federal governments.[24]

South Carolina, as its application illustrates, saw the article V assembly as a more hospitable forum than the Supreme Court for resolving state-federal controversies. In an 1827 report the South Carolina legislature had concluded that "it would not only be unwise, but even unsafe to submit questions of disputed sovereignty to any judicial tribunal." The Supreme Court, it was hinted, was not "wholly impartial" in such matters. Mississippi's legislature disagreed with the convention tactic: a convention assembled at that time might well affirm "those very powers which are so obnoxious" to the South. The tariff's constitutionality was supported by eighteen of the twenty-four states, and "the power of the smaller States is greater in Congress than it would be in a Convention," since under any conceivable plan of representation "the co-ordinate power held by us in the Senate, would be merged in the mass of the popular representation of the larger states."[25]

Georgia proposed a convention of southern states to consider means of relief against the tariff, condemning nullification as "neither a peaceful, nor a constitutional remedy," but rather as "tending to civil commotion, and disunion." Georgia then submitted an article V application, approved by its legislature on December 20, 1832. After a preamble alluding to the "many controversies, growing out of the conflicting interest[s] which have arisen among the people since the adoption of the Federal Constitution," the heart of the application requested an amendment to determine whether tariffs may be imposed "for the direct protection of domestic industry" and an amendment to establish an equitable system of federal taxation, along with "such others, as the people of the other States, may deem needful." Georgia's application elicited the disapproval of Massachusetts, Mississippi, Connecticut, and New Hampshire.[26]

Alabama followed with resolutions adopted on January 12, 1833, recommending "the call of a Federal Convention, to propose such amendments to our Federal Constitution, as may seem necessary and proper, to restrain the Congress of the United States from exerting the taxing power, for the substantive protection of domestic manufactures." Alabama's application was accompanied by resolutions denouncing nullification as "unsoun[d] in theory and dangerous in practice," and advocating "as a last resort" the call of a "Federal Convention, to . . . recommend such plan, which will satisfy the discontents of the South" either by an express denial of congressional power to impose protective tariffs or by upholding and defining the power. When Governor Henry Edwards dispatched the three convention applications to the Connecticut General Assembly, he said in the accompanying message:

> The resolutions of the States of Georgia and Alabama, propose no less than the call of a Convention with nearly unlimited powers. The necessity of such a Convention at the present time is not perceived. When we recollect the extreme difficulties the framers of the present Constitution had to contend with . . . , the task of commencing this work anew, would indeed be appalling.

In March 1833, Jackson approved a compromise tariff together with a "force bill" enabling the President to call up the military for collection of the tariff proceeds. When the South Carolina convention met again that same month, it rescinded its ordinance of nullification and declared the now-mooted force bill null and void.[27]

Nullification was never as popular elsewhere in the region as it was in South Carolina, mostly because only that state endured a severe depression in the late 1820s. Some states had long experienced a depression and were not prone to blame tariffs entirely; others were enjoying a boom from their cotton crops. The anti-tariff sentiment that certainly existed regionwide produced, outside Calhoun's state, only the moderate response of seeking a convention under article V, not the radical response of nullification, which denied the Constitution's operation. Alabama's application was to be the last until the Civil War, and Jefferson Davis in his memoirs regretted that "in earlier and better times, when the prospect of serious difficulties first arose, a convention of the States was not assembled to consider the relations of the various States and the Government of the Union."[28]

The Civil War

Always just beneath the tariff controversy was the South's concern that a federal government interpreting the Constitution to permit high tariffs would also, eventually, construe it to ban slavery. Calhoun wrote: "I consider the Tariff act as the occasion, rather than the real cause of the present unhappy state of things. The truth can no longer be disguised, that the peculiar domestick institution of the Southern States . . . has placed them in regard to taxation and appropriations in opposite relation to the majority of the Union." This issue was addressed at the Nashville convention of 1850, where delegates from nine slave states recommended extension of the Missouri Compromise line of 36°30', dividing slave from free territories, to the Pacific.[29]

While the nation hurtled toward sectional conflict in late 1860, proposals from Delaware, Arkansas, and Tennessee for a national convention to resolve North-South differences came to nothing. On January 19, 1861, Virginia proposed a conference of the states on the slave question. Although the meeting, known as the Washington Peace Conference (or Peace Convention), was intended as a substitute for a national constitutional convention, Virginia's proposal did not represent an article V application: it did away with the two-thirds filing requirement, no congressional call was envisioned, and any amendments passed had to be approved by Congress before submission to the states.[30]

As a basis for settlement, Virginia recommended the Crittenden Compromise, a set of constitutional amendments introduced in Congress on December 18, 1860, by Senator John J. Crittenden of Kentucky. The Crittenden amendments would have revived the Missouri Compromise line, held unconstitutional by the Court in *Dred Scott*, with the difference that an entering state could decide for itself whether to allow slavery. The federal government was to reimburse owners for fugitive slaves not recovered, and no constitutional amendment "shall be made" giving Congress "power to abolish or interfere with slavery in any of the States by whose laws it is . . . permitted."[31]

Kentucky's response to Virginia's invitation was to appoint commissioners to the Peace Conference, as well as to submit a convention application that came within the ambit of article V. The application proposed, "as a basis for settling existing difficulties," adoption of the Crittenden plan. Kentucky's convention recommendation was a tactical alternative to Virginia's conference initiative, which contemplated secession if it failed: a separate resolve passed in Richmond declared that if reconciliation efforts proved "abortive," then "Virginia shall unite her destiny with the slaveholding states of the south." Kentucky's convention request, the first in nearly thirty years, was followed by article V applications from New Jersey, Indiana, Illinois, and Ohio. The Illinois and Indiana applications informed Congress that those states saw no need for amendments, concurring only for the sake of national unity. An Arkansas state convention held in March 1861 to decide on secession recommended a national convention, but the state left the Union before the legislature could act; the same proposal from a Missouri convention was rejected by the legislature.[32]

The Peace Conference was regarded as an estimable successor to the Philadelphia Convention by those intent on compromise, and as illegal by northern radicals unconditionally opposed to slavery. The Conference met in the national capital's Willard Hotel (then Willard's Hall) from February 4 through 27, 1861, and was chaired by ex-President John Tyler. Present were 133 commissioners from twenty-one of the thirty-four states (one died during the proceedings), including former cabinet officers, ambassadors, governors, senators, and representatives, with such luminaries as former Attorney General Reverdy Johnson and future Chief Justice Salmon P. Chase. The Maine and Iowa delegates were also members of Congress, and divided their time between the two bodies.

Meant to arrest the drift toward disintegration, the Conference did postpone secession by the border states. Yet none of the six states already in the Confederacy sent delegations, an absence all but precluding success. The Pacific states were too far away to be represented. Thomas Ewing of Kansas advised his fellow commissioners to be "firm as a rock in battle, but conciliatory in council." Nevertheless the deliberations, while courtly in tone, were in substance marked by intransigence. "Our opinions are formed," said George Davis of North Carolina almost immediately, and they "will not be changed by debate."[33]

Each side offered amendments calculated to outrage the other, the better to justify positions already taken. The North would not recognize a constitutional right to property in slaves or a right to secede, nor would the South accept mandatory compensation for citizens injured by mob action in the slave states. Proposals for an article V convention to iron out differences, a stall touted by Republicans, were defeated by the commissioners. The amendment the Conference approved, a Crittenden variation, was rejected by the Senate, and the House of Representatives refused even to consider it.[34] The Crittenden plan itself, rejected by President-elect Abraham Lincoln, died in Congress as well. Lincoln, resigned to protecting slavery where it existed but inflexibly opposed to any extension, refused to endorse the Peace Conference and had not even wanted Illinois to send delegates.[35]

In the weeks before the capture of Fort Sumter in April 1861, a flurry of proposals for a national convention were put forward in Congress. Doubting that two thirds in each house would approve his amendments, Crittenden with the backing of Stephen A. Douglas unsuccessfully proposed a national, nonbinding plebiscite on his resolutions, in the hope of demonstrating wide support and inducing congressional assent. Senator Joseph Lane of Oregon introduced resolutions requesting a convention that was avowedly extraconstitutional, for it was "apparent that the present system of government," including article V, "is not adequate to the exigencies of the times." In similar straits, said Lane's preamble, the framers discarded the Confederation "to devise another plan of government, and that course was adopted and crowned with success." Other convention resolutions were offered in the Senate by George Pugh of Ohio and William H. Seward of New York, and by various members in the House of Representatives. All attempts at compromise—Crittenden's plan and permutations thereof, a national convention or plebiscite—broke down in Congress for the same reason that they had failed at the Peace Conference.[36]

On the afternoon of November 9, 1860, President James Buchanan, hoping to avert disunion at least for the remainder of his term, floated the idea of a national convention at a cabinet meeting. If the North refused the overture, he said, the South would be justified to the world in leaving the Union. The cabinet split on the idea's advisability. Citing

Madison's *Report* in his last annual message to Congress, on December 3, Buchanan recommended adoption of a constitutional amendment along the lines of the Crittenden plan. Proposal might be through Congress or a convention: "This might originate with Congress or the State legislatures, as may be deemed most advisable to attain the object." Buchanan conveyed his design to Lincoln in late December.[37]

Challenged by Buchanan either to accept a convention or to appear disdainful of a constitutional solution, Lincoln nevertheless could not afford to alienate either the moderate flank of his party, which favored compromise, or the radical abolitionist wing, which did not. To Buchanan's emissary he wrote: "I do not desire any amendment of the Constitution. Recognizing, however, that questions of such amendment rightfully belong to the American People, I should not . . . withhold from them . . . a fair opportunity of expressing their will thereon, through either of the modes prescribed in the instrument." Lincoln, opposed to a convention himself, was to reiterate the crafted answer in his first inaugural address.[38]

On March 4, 1861, the new President would "make no recommendation of amendments" but "recognize[d] the rightful authority of the people" in amending the Constitution, "to be exercised in either of the modes prescribed in the instrument itself," and declared that

to me, the convention mode seems preferable, in that it allows amendments to originate with the people themselves, instead of only permitting them to take, or reject, propositions, originated by others, not especially chosen for the purpose, and which might not be precisely such, as they would wish to either accept or refuse.

Lincoln averred, perhaps to head off a convention, that he had "no objection" to a constitutional amendment that had been proposed by Congress two days before, prohibiting federal interference with slavery. This proposal, known as the Corwin amendment after a House sponsor, was ratified by only three states and rendered obsolete in 1865 by the adoption of the thirteenth amendment, which abolished slavery in all states and territories.[39]

Ordinances unilaterally declaring secession were void, said Lincoln, and acts taken toward that end were "insurrectionary or revolutionary." Yet a State Department memorandum of March 15, 1861, held that a state could leave the Union "with the consent and concert of the people of the United States, to be given through a National Convention, to be assembled in conformity with the provisions of the Constitution of the

United States." Seward, Lincoln's Secretary of State and a spokesman for compromise, had while in Congress declared that the Union could be dissolved not by secession, "but only by the voluntary consent of the people of the United States, collected in the manner prescribed by the Constitution." The Corwin committee's minority suggested an article V convention to effect a "dignified, peaceful, and fair separation," settling issues such as the partition of common property and navigation of the Mississippi.[40]

During the Civil War, members of Congress continued to offer plans for a constitutional convention to bring the conflict to a negotiated rather than a military conclusion. On December 2, 1862, Senator Garrett Davis of Kentucky proposed a national convention to meet in Louisville in April 1863 "to take into consideration the condition of the United States, and the proper means for the restoration of the Union." Other public figures, including Democratic national chairman August Belmont and former Iowa chief justice Charles Mason, promoted a convention, but the idea received little encouragement from the major parties. A convention seemed a confession of inadequacy on the part of the President and Congress, and was considered a method that had been discredited by the failure of the Peace Conference. The South in addition, had seceded by means of state conventions, and the device now carried the taint of treason.[41]

"So we had a Peace Convention," wrote Philadelphia attorney Sidney George Fisher, "but it could not prevent war." Fisher, deciding that the Constitution's amending provision was outmoded, saw a national convention held in wartime as divisive and uncontrollable: "Conventions are ever prone to exceed their commission." Invested with "the omnipotence of an English Parliament, but without any of its restraining influences, internal or external, the Convention, dressed in a brief authority, might play some fantastic tricks, which, if they did not make the angels weep, would more than ever divide sections and parties, inflame passion and very probably produce the anarchy it was intended to prevent." Despite Fisher's pessimism, applications were adopted by Delaware, Kentucky, and Oregon.[42]

Fisher's apprehension regarding uncontrolled delegates was influenced most immediately by the conventions held in ten of the eleven states that withdrew to form the Confederacy (Tennessee used its legislature). On December 20, 1860, South Carolina became the first to leave when its convention, meeting in Charleston, unanimously passed the ordinance of secession. Nominally reversing the process by which the states had joined the Union, the ordinance repealed South Carolina's ratification of the federal Constitution. The state was then declared an independent sovereignty, and the convention proceeded to enact bills and ordinances accordingly.[43]

The convention that met in the Senate chamber of the Alabama legislature in Montgomery on February 4, 1861, to frame a constitution for the Confederacy was supremely aware of its Philadelphia antecedent. The Confederacy's founders regarded themselves not only as the heirs of the 1776 revolutionaries, but also as the heirs of the 1787 delegates, vindicating a constitutional heritage corrupted by judicial and congressional interpretations that siphoned power from the states to the central government. On the evening of February 8 the Montgomery Convention, which was also the Confederate Congress, adopted a provisional constitution. Drafted in haste as a stopgap until a permanent constitution was framed, it was, said Vice President of the Confederacy and Georgia delegate Alexander Stephens, "the constitution of the United States with such changes and modifications as are necessary to meet the exigencies of the times," deviating from its 1787 model primarily to reflect the Confederacy's views on states' rights and slavery. This document's article V read in its entirety: "The Congress, by a vote of two-thirds, may, at any time, alter or amend this Constitution."[44]

The permanent constitution, adopted by the Montgomery Convention on March 11, 1861, brought the amending procedure more in line with states' rights doctrine. Article V of the permanent constitution eliminated the Confederate Congress as an amending agent, entrusting proposal exclusively to a convention:

Upon the demand of any three States, legally assembled in their several conventions, the Congress shall summon a convention of all the States, to take into consideration such amendments to the Constitution as the said States shall concur in suggesting at the time when the said demand is made; and should any of the proposed amendments to the Constitution be agreed on by the said convention—voting by States—and the same be ratified by the legislatures of two-thirds of the several States, or by conventions in two-thirds thereof—as the one or the other mode of ratification may be proposed by the general convention—they shall thenceforward form a part of this Constitution. But no State shall, without its consent, be deprived of its equal representation in the Senate.

The provisional document had been passed into law by the Montgomery Convention, but the permanent charter included a ratifying clause and was sent to the states. The proposal requirement, allowing three

states to initiate the amendment process, was a constitutionalized substitute for nullification: belatedly, the South took Madison's advice to
settle jurisdictional disputes by national convention.[45]

Since the 1787 Constitution was, as President Jefferson Davis later
wrote, "the model followed throughout," the Confederate amending
clause represents a considered judgment as to what the original article V
meant in 1861. Yet the journals of the Montgomery Convention reveal
only that Alexander De Clouet of Louisiana inserted the phrase "at the
time when the said demand is made" to ensure that the agenda of the
convention would be, in the words of Alabama delegate Robert H.
Smith, "confined to action on propositions put forth by three States."
The journals do not indicate whether De Clouet's addition was meant
to confirm an existing understanding of the original article V or to
establish a departure from it.[46]

Lowering the proposal requirement from two thirds to three states,
like reduction of the ratifying requirement from three fourths to two
thirds, was intended to prevent one or a few states from being locked
out. The South considered itself, as Calhoun said, "in opposite relation
to the majority of the Union," a victimized minority at the mercy of
expanding federal might propelled by a North-dominated Congress and
an antagonistic Supreme Court. De Clouet's addition, therefore, may
have been designed specifically to protect individual states against the
submergence of their interests by a majority acting through the convention. No Confederate article V convention was ever held; the only
amendment to either of the Confederate constitutions was added to the
provisional charter, and, like article III of the 1787 document, gave
Congress the power to determine the judicial districts in the states.[47]

Reconstruction and Beyond

Two years after Lee's surrender North Carolina passed an application
for a national convention "to compose the animosities growing out of
the late war" in hopes of reversing or reducing the effects of emancipa-
tion, but received no support elsewhere. The federal government, instead, entered on Reconstruction by conventions in the returning states.
The conventions of 1865 and 1866, held in fulfillment of proclama-
tions by President Andrew Johnson, and those held in 1867 and 1868
under the Reconstruction Acts, were required to draft new constitutions

abolishing slavery and correspondingly extending the right to vote. The Reconstruction conventions, not governed by article V, in addition to framing constitutions also acted as legislatures to establish the new state governments—heralding federal involvement in civil liberties. While early amendments to the Constitution refined the operation of the federal apparatus, the thirteenth, fourteenth, and fifteenth amendments were designed to eradicate slavery and its vestiges—in other words, to effect broad social reform.[48]

A constitutional crisis, forgotten now but at the time compared in gravity to the Civil War, was precipitated by the disputed Hayes-Tilden election of 1876. Whether the Republican Rutherford B. Hayes or the Democrat Samuel J. Tilden (who had won the popular vote) would be the next president hinged on conflicting sets of electoral vote returns from three southern states and Oregon. During the winter of 1876–1877, wrote a student of the events, "probably more people dreaded an armed conflict than had anticipated a like outcome to the secession movement of 1860–61." President Grant was ready to declare martial law if, as rumored, Tilden carried out a plan to be inaugurated in New York.[49]

To resolve the "delicate and critical" impasse, Senator John J. Ingalls of Kansas in December 1876 offered a resolution inviting the states to apply for an article V convention. The convention was to report "alterations and amendments in the nature of an entire instrument" to the President, who would submit the revised Constitution to ratification by state conventions. The national convention was to assemble at Columbus, Ohio, in May 1877, with the Chief Justice as the presiding officer. Each state was to be represented by as many delegates as it was entitled to senators and representatives in Congress; two delegates in each state were to be chosen by the state legislature, and one elected by voters in each congressional district. No action was taken on the Ingalls measure, but when a commission established by Congress determined that Hayes had won, Congress ratified the decision after the Democrats were promised withdrawal of federal troops from the South and nonenforcement of the fifteenth amendment's guarantee of voting rights to freed slaves. With this quid pro quo, Reconstruction came to an end.[50]

The convention proposals of the late 1800s bespeak a Constitution that had come of age, and perhaps one that had not kept pace with the states. In 1884 Representative Moses McCoid of Iowa introduced a resolution declaring that many worthy amendments developed in the past century "have been incorporated in the constitutions of the several States, more easily amended than that of the Federal Government," but "have not and are not likely to be adopted" by Congress. Accordingly, the resolution provided for appointing a commission to decide whether to recommend that the states apply for a convention to meet on July 4, 1887. The commission was never appointed. In 1886, a House select committee favorably reported a constitutional amendment creating the office of Second Vice-President. The minority concurred, but expressed the view that the country's phenomenal economic growth in the preceding hundred years, together with the accumulation of amendments left unexamined in Congress, mandated a thorough revision. It was therefore "not expedient to amend the Constitution in this fragmentary way," the minority decided; rather, "a general convention should be held at an early day to consider and determine all amendments which may be proposed."[51]

Modernization was likewise the theme of James Schouler's presidential address to the American Historical Association in December 1897. The lawyer and Johns Hopkins lecturer found that the states "have developed organic improvements of practical detail in government to suit our modern society, which well deserve to be nationalized." First on the agenda was the method of amendment, which presented the danger that "changes so crude, so numerous, and so incongruous might proceed from any plenary convention" that the nation risked "being launched, at length, into a worse rather than a better government." Praising from the drafting standpoint the Confederate example, Schouler advised applying states "in concert to frame concrete propositions of amendment carefully in advance" and wished that "our Constitution clearly authorized a limited general convention." Among Schouler's other amendments, taken from state models, were the direct election of the President and United States senators, as well as a two-thirds vote of Congress to borrow on the public credit beyond a certain limit in order to reduce federal spending—objectives that would inspire convention drives in the century ahead.[52]

4

The Twentieth Century

Direct Election of Senators

Until the twentieth century, convention applications were submitted by the states or encouraged by Congress out of actual demand for a convention. As the great conventions of the eighteenth century faded from national consciousness, the procedure evolved into a "protest clause" to goad or scare Congress itself to act on a desired amendment. The first modern convention campaign, organized almost precisely at the turn of this century, aimed to replace article I's method of choosing United States senators by the state legislatures with direct election by the voters—an aim realized with the adoption of the seventeenth amendment.

After establishment of the government in 1789, new states were admitted by Congress and drafted constitutions at their founding conventions. Connecticut and Rhode Island adopted their first post-Revolution charters, and other states held conventions to revise their original constitutions. Most organic reform was concerned with the intertwined goals of broadening suffrage, equalizing representation in the legislature, and extending the roster of officials elected by popular vote. This was the movement, as one study put it, from property to democracy— the expansion of citizen sovereignty begun during the Jefferson and Jackson "revolutions" as the population fanned out westward and demanded commensurate voting power. This trend was mirrored on the federal level by attempts to obtain the popular election of senators. A constitutional amendment to that effect, first proposed in Congress by Representative Henry Storrs of New York in 1826, was backed by Andrew Johnson during the 1850s and 1860s while he served in Congress, and in 1868 while in the White House.[1]

During the 1890s the popular movement for direct election of senators started in earnest, receiving the support of political organizations, particularly in the western states: farmers' associations, or granges, together with Democratic and Populist party platforms in state elections. The national Democratic party endorsed direct election in 1900, 1904, 1908, and 1912. The Republican national convention of 1908 rejected Robert La Follette's plank embracing the amendment, but the presidential nominee, William Howard Taft, said in his acceptance speech: "With respect to the election of Senators by the people, personally I am inclined to favor it." As of 1910 direct election was supported by the American Federation of Labor, the National Grange, and reputedly nine tenths of the public, although the *New York Times* was to oppose it.[2]

State legislatures at this time were often engaged in pitched battles over senatorial candidates, resulting in deadlocks that prevented action in other matters as well. Delaware had no representation in the Senate at all from 1898 to 1902. Pennsylvania, Utah, and California were periodically deprived of senators because their legislatures could not agree. Between 1891 and 1905, forty-five deadlocks occurred nationwide. These contests were marked by bitter acrimony among factions in the legislatures, numberless but meaningless votes in assembly chambers after candidacies were settled in caucus cloakrooms, and the pandemic buying of influence. A five-month deadlock in Illinois during 1909 resulted in the election of a senator later expelled by Congress for bribery. Even after proposal but before final ratification of the seventeenth amendment, stalemates bedeviled four legislatures.[3]

In 1904 Oregon pioneered the de facto popular election of senators without an amendment in a law that permitted candidates for the state legislature to sign, in their petitions of candidacy, either "Statement No. 1" or "Statement No. 2." In Statement No. 1, the signer promised to vote for the senatorial candidate receiving the highest popular vote at the following general election, without regard to the signer's own preference. In No. 2, the signer declared that he would deem the vote nothing more than a recommendation that could be disregarded. Few politicians would sign Statement No. 2, and by 1909 a healthy percentage of the legislature had subscribed to No. 1. The signers honored their pledge that year, for although the legislature was controlled by Republicans, the winner of the popular contest, a Democrat, was sent to Washington.[4]

The "Oregon System" received national attention and was copied in numerous states, with varying degrees of success. In December 1910, fourteen out of the thirty newly chosen senators had been selected by popular vote. Supporting the electoral reform were the progressive, "muckraker" journalists who popularized the image of the Senate as a millionaires' club beholden to the great corporations and indifferent to the average citizen. Lincoln Steffens in *The Shame of the Cities* (1904) detailed the corruption rampant in state and municipal governments, while David Graham Phillips's series of articles on "The Treason of the Senate" in *Cosmopolitan Magazine* during 1906 turned a harsh spotlight on a body depicted as a citadel of wealth recklessly abusing its public trust and dubbed by the magazine "The House of Dollars."[5]

As early as 1874 the states had transmitted to Congress requests for a constitutional amendment, with Nebraska in 1893 the first to submit a convention application on the subject.[6] Five times between 1893 and 1902 the House of Representatives approved an amendment, but the Senate never went further than a favorable report in 1896 by the committee on privileges and elections. No state followed Nebraska's lead until 1899, when the Pennsylvania legislature appointed a standing committee to coordinate efforts with other states for obtaining the amendment. The committee reported to the next session of the legislature its conviction that the Senate would not approve an amendment until faced with convention applications from two thirds of the states. The committee therefore recommended that the states apply to Congress for a convention, and that a copy of the model convention application appended to its report be sent to the secretary of state in each state. The recommendation was adopted, and the model was used by many states for their petitions. Georgia and Arkansas soon established equivalent committees, and where initially states filed memorials that "most respectfully request" Congress to propose the amendment, the applications filed after Pennsylvania's action relied on the command of article V that Congress "shall call a Convention."[7]

By 1903 thirteen more petitions had been filed, and by 1912 thirty-one states, according to most counts—one short of the number then required—had sent applications. Henry Litchfield West wrote that "very few persons realize how close the nation is to a constitutional convention. . . . It would take but a slight degree of missionary work among these legislatures to secure the two-thirds action." West, who desired neither the amendment nor a convention, predicted that a national convention "would open Pandora's box" because it could not be restricted to a single issue. The convention "would, in all probability, be in session for a year, during which time the business interests of the country would pass through a period of uncertainty that would be almost disastrous."[8]

Walter Clark, North Carolina's chief justice, doubted that "the great corporations which control a majority of the Senate will ever voluntarily transfer to the people their profitable and secure hold upon supreme power." He concluded in the *Yale Law Journal* for December 1906: "It is high time that we had a Constitutional Convention." George Haynes wrote that if the necessary applications accrued and the Senate still refused to concur in the call, the amendment would nevertheless issue because "such an arrogant assumption of power will speedily react upon the men who commit it, and the personnel of the Senate will soon be changed."[9]

In the Senate opponents of the measure, anxious over defeat at the hands of the citizenry, argued that an amendment was unnecessary: the existing method of election had produced some of the country's greatest statesmen, and any defects could be remedied by statute. Senator Elihu Root of New York introduced a bill providing that if a state legislature failed to choose a senator within twenty days of the first convening of the legislature's two houses, a plurality vote rather than a majority would govern. In February 1911, Weldon B. Heyburn of Idaho expressed his desire to avoid a convention at all costs, insisting that article V

does not contemplate that any constitutional convention shall assemble with a limitation on it to deal with a particular question. When the constitutional convention meets it is the people, and it is the same people who made the original Constitution, and no limitation in the original Constitution controls the people when they meet again to consider the Constitution.

The senator hoped, he said four months later, that "we would never again meet to make a constitution. With all the conflicting interests of this day and this age, with the great corporations, with the great labor question, with the hundred issues, you never could get 90,000,000 people to agree upon a constitution." Heyburn, bitterly opposed to the amendment as well as a convention, was not "to be dragooned into the support of a measure" until the constitutional number of states weighed in for a convention.[10]

On February 28, 1911, the Senate for the first time voted on the amendment. The measure lost by five votes, but the handwriting was on the wall. The proposal was submitted to the states for ratification in May 1912, and its adoption as the seventeenth amendment was proclaimed by Secretary of State William Jennings Bryan on May 31, 1913. Although the simultaneous accumulation of thirty-one applications for direct election and its proposal by Congress suggests that the drive played a key role, there remains no evidence that the convention threat by itself forced the Senate to approve the amendment. At least as influential was the growing quota of senators chosen by popular vote, among them the instrumental advocate William E. Borah of Idaho, who by personal inclination and sensitivity to constituent pressure were in favor of direct election. "I should not have been here if it had not been practiced," said Borah on the eve of proposal, "and I have great affection for the bridge which carried me over."[11]

Reform and Reaction

Direct election of senators was integral to the program espoused by the Progressives, a political movement at its zenith in the first two decades of the twentieth century. Believing that the federal government was not adapting quickly enough to meet the social and economic opportunities of the new era, the movement advocated among other reforms simplification of the amending process. In the Progressive-backed amendment to article V introduced by Representative Walter Chandler, future constitutional amendments might be proposed on a simple majority vote of both houses, by one fourth of the states, or by national conventions to be held every thirty years beginning in 1920.[12] Conservatives generally opposed new amendments to the Constitution, taking the view that more alterations would make it "as flexible as an ordinary statute" and impair its dignity. Yet they were divided on such issues as polygamy and Prohibition, some favoring amendments on those subjects, others holding that social reforms should be effected by statute instead of amendment. Others objected to legislated reform, no matter how laudable on the merits, as an infraction of individual liberty. James M. Beck, Representative from Philadelphia and the epitome of conservatism in the 1920s as Solicitor General of the United States under Harding and Coolidge, was aghast at Prohibition: "That the federal government should prescribe to the peoples of the States what they should drink would have been unthinkable to the framers of the Constitution."[13]

Despite the aversion in some parts to legislating personal conduct, anti-polygamy measures had been recommended by President Grant as early as 1871 to correct the "anomalous, not to say scandalous, condition of affairs existing in the Territory of Utah." Congress for years afterward debated but never proposed an amendment, although the days of that practice were numbered when the Supreme Court upheld a criminal conviction for polygamy against a first amendment claim of religious freedom. Utah's admission as a state in 1896 was conditioned on including a polygamy ban in its constitution, but Utah did not rigorously enforce the ban. Between 1906 and 1916, twenty-six states responded to Utah's laxity by submitting applications for an anti-polygamy convention.[14]

Less than four months after the eighteenth (Prohibition) amendment was declared adopted in 1919, the first of numerous proposed amendments repealing or gutting it was introduced in Congress. In the 1920s and early 1930s, before adoption of the twenty-first amendment, five states (Massachusetts, Nevada, New Jersey, New York, and Wisconsin) applied for a convention to propose an amendment repealing Prohibition. Louis A. Cuvillier, a New York state assemblyman, pressed Congress in February 1933 to call a convention for a repeal amendment, asserting that Congress had the power to limit the convention's deliberations and reject any action taken on other matters. In a letter to John Nance Garner, Speaker of the federal House of Representatives and Vice President–elect, Cuvillier described "a national constitutional convention of all the States to meet forthwith to repeal the Eighteenth Amendment . . . , and each State in the national convention ratifying or rejecting the proposed amendment." Cuvillier wrote that President-elect Franklin Roosevelt endorsed a convention on the ground that, as was true, Roosevelt while Governor of New York had signed the state's 1931 convention application for a repeal amendment.[15]

Cuvillier, as he had written in a magazine years earlier, supported the "calling of a convention,—which, by adopting an entirely new constitution, would rid us at a stroke of the Eighteenth Amendment and such other portions of our governmental machine as have proved themselves impractical." He was, however, under the mistaken impression that a national convention could be used both to frame an amendment and to permit the states to decide whether to ratify it.[16]

To Cuvillier's argument that Congress was bound to call one inasmuch as two thirds of the states had filed since 1900, Wayne B. Wheeler, General Counsel of the Anti-Saloon League of America, observed that the petitions, most of which dealt with polygamy and direct election of senators, were "no longer alive." Wheeler also touched on the costs of a convention, financial and otherwise:

The dislocation of our economic life, the uncertainty of business, the unsettling of every part of our national structure would mean losses difficult to imagine. Every wild-eyed champion of impractical reform would turn to such a gathering. The lunatic fringe would provide the most sensational news for the world's press. The enemies of constitutional government would see in such a gathering an invitation to propagandize, both during the interval before the convention met and during its sessions.[17]

As the Great Depression lingered on into the 1930s, various proposals for radical revision of the Constitution, including a national convention, appeared. Jessie Wilson Sayre, President Wilson's daughter, recommended a convention in a May 1932 address to the Massachusetts League of Women Voters, saying that the Constitution was 120 years out of date. But lecturing a month later at King's College, Cambridge University, James Beck feared that "we could not repeat the success of the convention of 1787" not only because "we have not public statesmen who are comparable with the statesmen of 1787, but also because we could no longer make any successful attempt to embody the needs of a highly complex age in a written form of government." As a result, "thoughtful Americans," while appreciating that "changes are needed," would nevertheless almost unanimously oppose another convention because "it might prove a 'witches' Sabbath' of socialistic demagoguery."[18]

On May 27, 1935, the Supreme Court in *Schechter Poultry Corp. v. United States* struck out part of the National Industrial Recovery Act, a linchpin of Roosevelt's New Deal economic program, ruling that it invaded powers over local transactions reserved to the states exclusively. Days later the President, at a White House press conference, hinted that he was mulling a constitutional amendment to neutralize the "horse-and-buggy" decision by broadening congressional power to regulate commerce and so permit the continued functioning of agencies like the National Recovery Administration and the Agricultural Adjustment Administration.[19]

Federal officials for a time considered what was termed the "quick" method of amendment, by which Congress would propose the amendment and specify ratification by state convention. The "quick" method was based on a (probably incorrect) interpretation of article V originated by former Attorney General A. Mitchell Palmer, that allowed Congress rather than the states to determine the time and place of the ratifying conventions; in the White House plan, the time for holding the conventions would have been fixed at sixty days after *Schechter* was handed down. Representative Maury Maverick, on behalf of a bloc of House liberals, appealed in a nationwide radio broadcast for a constitutional convention "called as quickly as is humanly possible" to propose an amendment enabling Congress "to pass legislation for the betterment of the people."[20]

Like many other liberal scholars, Harvard political scientist William Yandell Elliott perceived the existing Constitution as an obstruction of the majority will expressed by the New Deal. For Elliott in a 1935 book, the times demanded a state-managed economy led by a strong (Rooseveltian) executive assisted by an Economic Advisory Council, and "amplification of governmental machinery" in the form of federal administrative agencies. Rather than allowing the "difficulty of amending the Constitution to hold us in the grip of a fatal inertia," there must be "[a]greement on fundamental principles" preliminary to a "constitutional convention for 1937—to recreate the work of a century and a half ago and mold it to new uses." This re-creation would regroup the states into ten or eleven "commonwealths," large regions approximately equal in population and economic integration, in order to "reduce the terrific waste of multiplied state capitals, legislatures, and bureaucracies," in the process "redrawing the political map into areas more suited to the cultural and economic needs of modern America."[21]

The dramatic rise in federal taxes starting in 1933 provoked a movement for an anti-tax amendment among those who held that increased taxes would reduce the capital available for investment in industry and that tax proceeds would be spent by the federal government on services better left to the states. The amendment was a strike at the welfare state by striking at its source of revenue. In 1938, the American Taxpayers

Association promoted an amendment that would repeal the sixteenth amendment (authorizing federal income taxes) and limit Congress to a maximum 25 percent tax on income.[22]

Representative Emanuel Celler introduced the Association's amendment in Congress, where it was reported to the House Judiciary Committee and went no further. Seeing that the congressional path was hopeless, the Association with very little national publicity turned to the convention route. The aim was not to hold a convention, one anti-tax leader testified, but rather "to put the fear of God" into Congress to propose the amendment. By 1950, eighteen states had adopted applications, and in 1952 the amendment received the blessing of the American Bar Association's House of Delegates.[23]

The amendment was attacked by members of Congress and other high federal officials, notably Representative Wright Patman, who referred to the proposal as the "Millionaire's Amendment" and to a sponsoring organization, the Committee for Constitutional Government, as the "outstanding Fascist group in America." After consulting congressional staff attorneys on the legal question, Patman urged the adopting states to rescind their applications and stop the amendment's advocates from "sneaking this reactionary plot through unsuspecting State legislatures." At a congressional hearing on the amendment, Patman insisted that an article V convention could be used "for any purpose on earth" and "rewrite the whole Constitution."[24]

Perturbed by the momentum, Congress in 1952 assembled a report to demonstrate how the amendment would slow the government's ability to promote employment, seriously damage small business, benefit large corporations, and lead to higher taxes for low-income groups. The report, helped by opposition from national organizations such as labor unions, achieved its purpose by significantly discouraging the movement. In 1963, when Colorado filed, claims that thirty-four states had sent applications were ignored by Congress, and opponents questioned the effect of rescission by twelve states, the status of applications one or two decades old, and in two cases the impact of a gubernatorial veto.[25]

During and immediately after World War II, sentiment for United States participation in a limited world government produced resolutions from twenty-three states urging their delegations in Congress to support "an international sovereignty of reason, social justice and peace." Former Supreme Court Justice Owen J. Roberts headed a movement to draft a constitution organizing the democracies of the Atlantic alliance into an "interstate republic" or international federal union, complete with a popularly elected transnational Congress and executive. This constitution would be framed at an international constitutional convention to be called by a joint resolution of Congress, a plan informally approved by President Harry Truman and energetically backed by General George C. Marshall. In 1949 six of the twenty-three states filed petitions for an article V convention to frame amendments enabling United States participation. Cold War tensions, especially the Korean conflict, dampened enthusiasm, and by 1951 three had revoked their applications.[26]

The presidential election of 1940 resulted in an unprecedented third term for Roosevelt, producing a boomlet, in quarters opposed to the Democrat's policies, for an amendment limiting eligibility to two terms. In 1943 Illinois, Iowa, Michigan, and Wisconsin adopted applications for a convention to develop such an amendment. Montana joined on February 28, 1947, but the following month Congress proposed the two-term limitation in what became the twenty-second amendment, adopted in 1951.[27]

The close Kennedy-Nixon presidential race of 1960 focused national attention on changing the electoral college, the system created in article II and modified by the twelfth amendment for selecting the President and Vice President. Under the system, each state has a number of electors equal to the total of its senators and representatives; each state's entire electoral vote is awarded to the winner of a bare plurality of its popular vote. Congress had long debated various proposals, but no one version commanded two-thirds of each house since the votes were split among four plans: (1) direct election, (2) retaining the unit rule but eliminating the electors, (3) dividing each state's electoral votes among the candidates in the same proportion as the popular vote, and (4) assigning the individual electors to districts within each state.

The first two plans, in which the large, urban states would retain a lion's share of the power, were naturally favored by members of Congress from those areas; the last two were supported by the small, rural states, whose influence in elections probably would increase if either were adopted. In the winter of 1962–1963 a drive was launched for a convention that could consider only the last two plans, and amassed a total of eight applications—from Colorado, Kansas, Montana, Texas, Utah, Wisconsin, Arkansas, and South Dakota—all filed in 1963.[28]

The Supreme Court's landmark 1954 ruling in *Brown v. Board of*

Education that racial segregation in public schools was unconstitutional provoked hostile reactions from the South. Louisiana was the first to send Congress a protest resolution, declaring that "segregation of the races in the public schools, so long as equal rights are preserved, is a matter of legislative policy for the several States, with which the Federal courts are powerless to interfere." Similar protests followed from Georgia, Virginia, South Carolina, and Mississippi. Calhoun's interposition doctrine was revived by Louisiana when it passed statues to thwart a federal court order desegregating certain New Orleans public schools. The Supreme Court affirmed the lower court's invalidation of the statutes, and spurned the state's argument that Louisiana "has interposed itself in the field of public education over which it has exclusive control." In 1961 Arkansas requested an amendment, from Congress or a convention, permitting one fourth of the states to invalidate any Supreme Court decision that illicitly "transfers powers from the several States to the Federal Government" until subsequently approved by the legislatures of three fourths of the states.[29]

Applications for a convention to overturn *Brown* came from Georgia in 1955 and Arkansas four years later. Louisiana and Mississippi in 1970 filed applications for a convention to propose an amendment prohibiting compulsory attendance at a particular school on account of race, religion, color, or nationality. Busing to achieve racially integrated schools was approved by the Court the next year in *Swann v. Charlotte-Mecklenburg Board of Education*. United Concerned Citizens of America, a lobbying group, was formed in 1971 to obtain an amendment that would undo *Swann*; in 1972, the National Committee for a Constitutional Amendment to Prohibit Forced Busing was organized with the goal of securing convention applications from thirty-four states. Eight additional states—Michigan, Tennessee, Nevada, Oklahoma, Texas, Virginia, Kentucky, and Massachusetts—submitted applications between 1971 and 1976, but the convention effort, which highlighted a surprisingly widespread antipathy toward busing, has since been dormant.[30]

The Supreme Court's 1973 decision in *Roe v. Wade*, recognizing a constitutional right to abortion, was highly unpopular in the ranks of political conservatives and religious fundamentalists. Formal action to repeal *Roe* by amendment was begun in 1977, and in 1979 Justice Antonin Scalia, then a professor at the University of Chicago Law School, said that he "would favor a convention on abortion." In January 1980 presidential aspirant Ronald Reagan issued a message to demonstrators marching on the White House for an amendment to outlaw abortion. Reagan declared that he was "firmly committed to the right to life. . . . I hope Congress itself will propose an amendment and send it to the states for ratification. As a last resort, I support the right of the people of the United States to call a constitutional convention for the specific purpose of proposing such an amendment." By 1986 the anti-abortion convention campaign had garnered nineteen applications.[31]

In addition to the drives that accumulated a significant number of applications, individual states in this period sometimes requested Congress simply "to call a convention for proposing amendments," with no subject listed (Texas, 1899; Wisconsin, 1911), but most often petitioned for a specific purpose, among them: an amendment granting Congress the power to suppress monopolies (Illinois, 1911), requiring that all subsequent amendments be ratified by referendum (Louisiana, 1920), permitting Congress to tax income from federal and state securities (Idaho, 1927), establishing the Townsend Plan to give two hundred dollars a month to every person over sixty years of age (Oregon, 1939), forbidding "coercive" imposing of conditions on federal grants to the states (Pennsylvania, 1943; Oklahoma, 1976), "repudiating" a Supreme Court decision that oil reserves in waters adjacent to a state belong to the federal government (Texas, 1949), amending the treaty-making power (Georgia, 1952), apportioning federal gasoline tax proceeds among the states for the construction of highways exclusively (California, 1952), altering the method of selecting federal judges and fixing a definite term of office (Alabama, 1957), prohibiting state taxation of non-residents' income (Connecticut, 1958), allowing the reading of the Bible in public schools (Massachusetts, 1964), and giving the President authority to delete individual items in appropriations bills, generally called the "line-item" veto (Tennessee, 1977).[32]

Like those of the major drives, a good number of these applications reflect distaste for the burgeoning influence of the federal government, especially as articulated by the Supreme Court's expansive readings of congressional power to regulate commerce and race relations. "In view of the progressive inroads that Congress has made on what has been considered State functions and the action of a majority of the current Supreme Court in upholding Federal extension of power over local matters," wrote an Atlanta superior court judge in 1948, "the States should call a Constitutional Convention wherein the voices of the States and people might be heard."[33]

Everett Dirksen's Campaign Against Reapportionment

In 1962 the Supreme Court entered a formerly uncharted political thicket, holding in *Baker v. Carr* that issues relating to equitable apportionment of state legislatures—representation that accurately mirrors population distribution—can be decided by the courts, relief being available under the fourteenth amendment's due process clause. *Wesberry v. Sanders* in 1964 applied the "one-person, one-vote" principle to apportionment of congressional districts. The same year, *Reynolds v. Sims* extended the principle to both houses of each state legislature, fostering apprehension that the legislatures would be completely dominated by the heavily populated urban, liberal regions, with a corresponding decrease in the power of the rural and small-town, mostly conservative, areas. Coming on the heels of decisions handed down in the preceding decade ordering integration of and banning organized prayer from public schools, the apportionment cases were to conservatives a particularly unwelcome intrusion of federal power into what they considered the preserve of the states.[34]

Foes of these Court decisions sought to roll them back by constitutional amendment, and found an opening via the Council of State Governments, a research and advisory body made up of state legislators and other officials as well as government professionals. In December 1962 a coalition of members—generally rural legislators from the South long dominant in their state governments, who would be reapportioned out of their seats—obtained the Council's recommendation for three "states' rights" amendments. These amendments would (1) streamline the state initiation of amendments by requiring Congress to propose an amendment on the application of two thirds of the state legislatures (recalling early versions of article V), and eliminate the convention method of ratifying as well as of proposing amendments; (2) create a "Court of the Union," composed of the fifty chief justices of the state supreme courts, to hear appeals from Supreme Court decisions affecting "rights reserved to the states or to the people" under the Constitution; and (3) remove state legislature apportionment issues from federal jurisdiction. The Council's plan was for every state legislature to submit three uniform applications to Congress, each of the applications requesting a convention to propose one of the amendments.[35]

Addressing the American Law Institute in Washington on May 22, 1963, Chief Justice Earl Warren took issue with the convention campaign. Warren did not speak on the merits of the amendments, although on retirement he said that *Baker* was the most important case of his tenure; rather, he warned that the proposals, which "could radically change the character of our institutions," had received "very little public mention." He urged the bar to speak out to prevent the Constitution from being "changed unwittingly." The amending article, the Chief Justice added in terms that were strong for him, if "used unwisely by an uninformed public . . . could soon destroy the foundations of the Constitution."[36]

A few days later, the convention method was endorsed by former President Dwight Eisenhower in a commencement address. Eisenhower encouraged the graduating class of Defiance College in Ohio to help restore the rights and responsibilities lost to "a distant bureaucracy." Disclaiming reference to any pending measure but unavoidably hinting at his sympathies, he said: "Through their state legislatures and without regard to the Federal Government, the people can demand and participate in constitutional conventions in which they can, through their own action, adopt such amendments as can and will reverse any trends they see as fatal to true representative government."[37]

All three states' rights amendments were disapproved as "ill-advised" and too extreme by the American Bar Association's House of Delegates at its annual meeting in the summer of 1963. Assailed by the American Civil Liberties Union, the Conference of Mayors, and other groups, the amendments never produced applications from more than a scattered handful of states.

It was *Wesberry* and *Reynolds* that gained adherents to the amendment cause in Congress and lent the antireapportionment movement respectability. The Council of State Governments in late 1964 recommended an amendment permitting one house of a bicameral state legislature to be apportioned on factors other than population, and released a guide for states illustrating how to file an application for a constitutional convention with Congress. A San Francisco public relations firm, Whitaker & Baxter, was hired for a media campaign directed at Congress and state officials. In January 1965 the amendment was introduced in the Senate by Everett Dirksen, the Republican Minority Leader; after rejection by a Senate subcommittee, Dirksen reintroduced it as a rider to another resolution, which designated August 31 to September 6, 1965, as American Legion Baseball Week. The Dirksen amendment passed the Senate on August 4, 1965, by a simple majority but not the necessary two thirds. A week later Dirksen submitted a modified version and in April 1966, like its predecessor, it failed to muster a two-thirds vote. Just before the final tally, Dirksen warned his colleagues that the fight for an amendment would continue. "Just as old soldiers never die, but fade away," he said, "this issue will not die. Neither will it fade away, believe me."[38]

When the General Assembly of the Council of State Governments announced its endorsement of an apportionment amendment in 1964, sixteen convention applications had already been filed. At this early stage, however, the applications went unnoticed by Congress; they were not tabulated as they arrived, but simply printed in the *Congressional Record* and filed with the Judiciary Committees of both houses. Two states sent their petitions to the Library of Congress, which returned them.[39]

In some of the state legislatures approving applications, the members thought they were merely expressing disagreement with the Supreme Court decisions and did not appreciate the legal implications of their vote. The petition was passed in the New Hampshire lower house by voice vote and carried to the senate, where it was approved within minutes without a public hearing or reference to a committee. In Colorado, the resolution was not even printed. Dirksen, working closely with the state legislatures, planned to keep the campaign quiet until the final states had submitted applications, and then make a dramatic announcement that the requirements for an article V convention had been fulfilled.[40]

Congress and the public had been unaware that the convention drive was so near its goal when, in March 1967, the thirty-second state filed its petition. The campaign now attracted nationwide publicity, including a front-page story in the *New York Times*, and with it organized opposition in Congress and the state capitals. Senator Joseph Tydings, a liberal from Maryland averse to convention and amendment, held that Congress should turn away applications from legislatures that were malapportioned, which meant that most would be refused since twenty-six of the applying states were under a court order to reapportion. Senator Robert Kennedy declared that Congress "must possess power to rule upon the validity of the submitted resolutions" and felt that "Congress is justified in this case in setting a very short time period—certainly of no more than 2 or 3 years." Senators Proxmire and Javits expressed the preeminent fear: a convention could not be limited in theory or practice to the subject of apportionment—and Dirksen evidently agreed.[41]

A reporter for the *Wall Street Journal* speculated that an unlimited convention furthered rather than hindered Dirksen's strategy:

> Most Dirksen-watchers agree he doesn't really want a Constitutional convention. The idea rather is to terrorize liberal Senators with the thought of a runaway convention that would start tinkering with the Bill of Rights. To avoid such a calamity, the reasoning goes, Congress itself would propose to the states for ratification a Constitutional amendment.

Yet A. Willis Robertson, a conservative Democrat and former senator from Virginia, also dreaded a convention on the theory that it might be controlled by liberals who would rewrite the Constitution to their liking.[42]

In early 1969 Iowa's application brought the total to thirty-three, one short of the required number, but in November Wisconsin's legislature voted against becoming the thirty-fourth. Three states rescinded their applications, at least partially out of fear that a convention might be uncontrollable. A principal reason for North Carolina's retraction, according to one legislator, was the prospect of a nationally televised convention attracting unsavory characters and "some degree of violence," in a repeat of the 1968 Democratic presidential nominating convention in Chicago. Utah's petition was voided by a federal court because of its passage by an inequitably apportioned legislature.[43]

Republicans emerged as the major beneficiaries of reapportionment, as they picked up seats in newly redrawn suburban districts. Seeing that one-person/one-vote was not necessarily inimical to rural interests, a majority of the states began to comply with reapportionment, and support for the amendment waned. Reapportionment, unlike direct election of senators, mostly engaged the attention of local politicians rather than the electorate at large; this probably explains why Dirksen could operate for so long in privacy. The campaign effectively ended with Dirksen's unexpected death in September 1969.[44]

Senator Sam Ervin, who supported Dirksen's efforts and thought it desirable to allay fears of a "runaway" assembly, in August 1967 introduced the "Federal Constitutional Convention Act" (S. 2307), the first comprehensive legislative framework for a national convention. De-

signed to rein in any convention to prescribed limits and, not incidentally, maintain congressional hegemony in the amending process, the
bill addressed issues such as requirements for valid applications, the
period during which applications stay effective (six years), the capacity
of states to withdraw their applications (permitted), the convention's
proposing agenda (limited to amendments of the same "general nature"
as that stated in the call issued by Congress), the apportionment and
compensation of delegates (each state could send as many delegates as it
had members in the House of Representatives, to receive fifty dollars a
day plus travel expenses), the majority vote needed for the convention to
submit an amendment (a simple majority of the total number of delegates), and the length of its session (one year, unless extended by
Congress).

Reacting to the startling near-success of Dirksen's campaign, the
Senate Judiciary Committee's Subcommittee on the Separation of
Powers held hearings on the Ervin bill in October. The bill was revised
and reintroduced in the next legislative session, but the full Congress
took no action. The Ervin bill has been periodically reintroduced,
passing the Senate in 1971 and 1973 when a dozen states applied for a
convention on federal-state revenue sharing, only to receive no consideration in the House of Representatives.[45]

Picking up the mantle after Ervin's retirement and responding to the
drive for a constitutional balanced-budget amendment, Senator Orrin
Hatch (an amendment proponent) unveiled a similar "Constitutional
Convention Implementation Act" in 1979. The most recent version of
the Hatch bill, S. 40, cleared the Senate Judiciary Committee in September 1985 but failed to pass the Senate itself. Convention bills have
been introduced in the House as well, the latest by Representative
Charles Schumer in July 1987, but no congressional proposal has been
enacted into law.

This congressional activity coincided with increased application activity by the states. Of the 400 convention applications received by
Congress in the past two centuries (with every state represented at least
once), only a dozen or so applications were filed in the Constitution's
first hundred years; in the last two decades 150 have been submitted.
The activity is a symptom of deep conflict and pressure for major
structural change: the most serious convention threats, during 1787–
1789, the Civil War, the first two decades of this century, and finally
the 1960s, have also marked the periods during which the greatest

number of constitutional amendments have been introduced in Congress and ultimately adopted.[46]

The major convention campaigns of the late twentieth century (so far unsuccessful) reflect dissatisfaction, of a conservative and rural hue, with the social and economic policies associated with the federal government. Distressed by the growing federal bureaucracy and centralizing of power arising from President Lyndon Johnson's Great Society program, Dirksen told a business executives' conference in April 1965 that he was troubled by the "deeper and deeper intrusion of federal power into the affairs of the people," lamenting that "today we are indisputably in the welfare state."[47]

Meanwhile, three of the four constitutional amendments actually adopted between 1961 and 1971 curbed the power of the old southern political system and augmented the electoral strength of the eastern seaboard by granting the District of Columbia the right to vote in presidential elections, abolishing the poll tax, and lowering the voting age to eighteen. These amendments received their principal support in the populous eastern urban states, and their chief opposition in the states of the West and South.[48]

Controlling the Federal Budget

Reducing Washington's influence by imposing restraints on expenditures was the motive behind the drive for an amendment mandating a balanced federal budget, just as it had led to convention proposals for a tax-limitation amendment and a line-item veto. In 1784 Roger Sherman favored amending the Confederation to give Congress a tax power over imports as a way of retiring the national debt, "though I never wish to have the power in Congress to raise money extended beyond what may be necessary for the present debt." Jefferson in 1798 wrote, "I wish it were possible to obtain a single amendment to our constitution. . . . I mean an additional article, taking from the federal government the power of borrowing." Article I of the permanent Confederate constitution required all expenses of the Post Office Department to be paid out of its own revenues after March 1, 1863. Some kind of budget-balancing provision is now a part of forty-four state constitutions.[49]

The different versions of the proposed balanced-budget amendment all essentially require that, in the absence of a national emergency, congressional appropriations must not exceed expected federal revenues in any fiscal year. Starting in 1790 with obligations that totaled roughly $75 million, including debts inherited from the Confederation, federal budget deficits had been relatively mild and infrequent until 1900, when they increased dramatically. Escalating after the Depression, they were seen by a growing number of fiscal conservatives as a major cause of chronic inflation and decreased private investment. Many versions of a constitutional budget amendment have been offered in Congress since the first, the Knutson amendment of 1936, setting a per-capita limit on the federal public debt during peacetime; one introduced in 1956 by Senators Harry F. Byrd of Virginia and Styles Bridges of New Hampshire drew a convention application in support from Indiana.[50]

A renewed amendment drive two decades later coincided with and drew strength from the popular "revolt" against big government that was fashionable in the mid-1970s. In 1975, when the Senate Judiciary Committee held hearings on balancing the budget, the idea of combining an amendment to control federal spending and a convention campaign to obtain it occurred to a few legislators in assorted states. Two of these legislators, state representative David Halbrook of Mississippi and state senator James Clark of Maryland, got the measures through their own legislatures and then expanded their efforts. Halbrook lobbied across the South; Clark, failing to interest Common Cause, a public interest group, recruited the aid of the National Taxpayers Union, a conservative Washington-based lobbying organization, using its mailing lists and ties with other antispending groups. They hired a coordinator, drafted a model resolution, and began working with informal networks of other state legislators. As one chronicler of this stage relates, "the movement's sponsors nurtured their obscurity to keep opposition down. . . . They also encouraged impressions that their project was outlandish and their resolutions about as meaningful as endorsements of apple pie." A convention was never the sponsors' goal; the idea was to pressure Congress into submitting the amendment.[51]

North Dakota in March 1975 was the first state to apply for a convention as part of this concerted movement, and by the end of the year five more had signed on. The campaign was boosted by popular resistance to state taxation schemes, symbolized by California's adoption of Proposition 13, a state constitutional amendment drastically cutting local property taxes that was soon copied elsewhere. On June 7, 1978, the day after Proposition 13 was adopted, Senator Robert J. Dole sent a letter to all fifty governors asking their help for a convention: "I believe that Americans want to stop the onslaught of big government. The American taxpayer has reached his limit. . . . I hope that you will consider requesting and working with your state legislature to petition Congress to establish a Constitutional Convention calling for a Federal balanced budget." Although Proposition 13 coauthor Howard Jarvis later, under pressure, supported a convention, he was initially against opening up the Constitution to "weirdos" who could write their own "screwball" version of the document. [52]

In January 1979 a draft anti-spending amendment was presented to leaders in Washington by the National Tax Limitation Committee, set up four years earlier by Lewis K. Uhler, ex–John Bircher and member of Governor Ronald Reagan's California administration, and William Rickenbacker, son of Captain Eddie. The amendment was the creation of a panel that included Milton Friedman, the Nobel Prize-winning economist at the University of Chicago, and Robert H. Bork, the former Solicitor General of the United States, Yale law professor and unsuccessful nominee to the Supreme Court. To avert budget balancing by simply raising taxes, the NTLC amendment limited increased federal spending to a proportion of increases in the gross national product. Bork, who saw trouble in trying to enforce the amendment in the courts, found the merits "difficult to the point of being agonizing," although deserving of "serious consideration." A convention was out. "A constitutional convention ought to be the last resort of a foundering nation, not the casual practice of a successful one." [53]

Major impetus to the convention drive came from the support announced in the second inaugural address of California Governor Edmund G. (Jerry) Brown, as the application total approached thirty and many state officials predicted thirty-four applications by the summer of 1979. But Brown's entrance raised questions at the national level— from economists, members of Congress, and various lobbying groups— as to what safeguards existed against erosion of the Bill of Rights if a convention were held, whether the amendment would be a straitjacket on fiscal policy or else so vaguely worded as to be without meaning, and what kind of national emergency would justify suspending the balance requirement. The California Assembly's Ways and Means Committee held extensive hearings on the amendment and the convention process during February, the first state legislative body to do so. After testimony from fifteen witnesses, including Governor Brown, Senator Ervin, Professors Laurence Tribe, Charles Black, and Professor John T. Noonan of the University of California at Berkeley, as well as Dean Gerhard Casper of Chicago, the Democratic panel turned down the application.[54]

Convention applications no longer breezed through state legislative chambers but on the contrary faced tough, extended debate as lawmakers realized their votes mattered. "It was one thing when you could just pass the thing and send it off to Washington with nobody looking," said an Ohio state senator. "But now the newspapers are watching, you've got to have hearings. Everybody's more careful when this comes up in a legislature now." Commented Taxpayers Union treasurer William Bonner, "It would have been better to let a sleeping dog lie" and allow the number to rise to the required thirty-four. "There was no point in heating things up. When Brown announced, we had to go more public."[55]

Brown also enmeshed the convention drive in partisan politics, transforming it somewhat into a test of his strength as a presidential candidate. Though Brown was a Democrat, the balanced-budget issue appealed mostly to the Republican party (especially its conservative segment), which traditionally favors restraint in federal spending. Leading the counteroffensive from liberals and moderates in Congress, Edmund Muskie, chair of the Senate Budget Committee, warned in no uncertain terms that budget cuts under the amendment would come out of federal aid to the states. Opposition, however, was not confined to liberals. Senator Barry Goldwater, the Republicans' right-wing presidential candidate in 1964, backed the amendment but denounced the convention idea to the Senate as "very foolhardy" and "a tragic mistake," because "if we hold a constitutional convention, every group in this country—majority, minority, middle-of-the-road, left, right, up, down—is going to get its two bits in and we are going to wind up with a Constitution that will be so far different from the one we have lived under for 200 years that I doubt that the Republic could continue."[56]

President Jimmy Carter, seeking reelection, said at a news conference that a convention in line with Brown's proposal would be "extremely dangerous" because it "would be completely uncontrollable" and the Constitution "could be amended en masse with multitudes of amendments." In a letter to the speaker of the Ohio house of representatives, he called the amendment "flawed and harmful" and the convention a "radical and unprecedented action" that "might do serious, irrevocable damage to the Constitution." At the White House, a nine-member task force was organized to counter the drive in the state legislatures. Ohio declined to pass an application, but in April 1979 New Hampshire, where Brown had campaigned for the presidency and lobbied for a convention, became the thirtieth state to apply. The vote was seen as a pointed rebuke of Carter's economic record.[57]

To complement the White House task force, an anti-amendment lobbying organization called Citizens for the Constitution was established by Thomas P. O'Neill III, the lieutenant governor of Massachusetts and son of the Speaker of the House of Representatives, along with other national Democratic party leaders. Congressional staffs questioned the technical validity of the submitted applications, maintaining that some applications were out of date, others improperly required specific language for the proposed amendment, and two had not been signed by a state official. With such arguments liberal Democratic senators Alan Cranston and Birch Bayh, the latter chair of the Judiciary Subcommittee on the Constitution, found only fourteen or sixteen petitions, respectively, to be (said Cranston) "in good order."[58]

While the Taxpayers Union took the position that applications rejected by Congress would quickly be revised and resubmitted, Common Cause, which was opposed to a convention, was skeptical. Said Fred Wertheimer, a Common Cause vice president: "A lot of states that passed this back when nobody was looking very hard at it might think twice if they got another chance." Despite polls showing that more than three fourths of the American public favored a balanced-budget amendment, the *Washington Post* observed, "the amendment drive has been a victim of its own success. As it gained public attention, it spawned a counterattack from the Washington political establishment. Further, the balanced-budget campaign has become involved in all sorts of extraneous political battles."[59]

In July 1979 President Carter met at Camp David with his staff and national political leaders to chart national goals and recoup popular support for his administration. Carter's poll taker, Patrick H. Caddell, had suggested in a memorandum that one way of involving the public in shaping the nation's future was a constitutional convention that would, according to Caddell, allow the airing of ideas yet result in few if any permanent changes. At the Camp David session Vice President Walter Mondale was reportedly "apoplectic" regarding a convention, calling it the worst idea he had ever heard and reminding the group of the White House anti-amendment task force.[60]

Only one state filed an application in 1980, but the drive retained momentum with the election to the presidency of Ronald Reagan, an enthusiastic supporter of the amendment. His ardor was shared by many conservative elements in the Republican party brought to prominence by his election, and public support for the amendment remained strong, in some cases as high as 80 percent. Several states came close to petitioning in 1981, with Alaska becoming the thirty-first in 1982. Revealing a rift among proponents, NTLC president Lewis Uhler stated after the Alaska vote that the purpose of the campaign was not to have a convention summoned, but rather "to put pressure on the Congress to act on its own" by submitting the amendment, while Taxpayers Union founder and chair James D. Davidson maintained that a limited convention was possible, necessary, and the actual goal of his organization.[61]

In August 1982 a balanced-budget amendment was approved by the Republican Senate (the only time this measure has passed a chamber of Congress), but perished in the Democratic House. Missouri's convention application in March 1983, the thirty-second, was the reaction. "This thing," said Treasury Secretary Donald Regan a few weeks later, meaning a convention, "could suddenly jump on us." Griffin Bell, who had been Attorney General under Carter, believed the convention drive a legitimate strategy that had worked in the case of the seventeenth amendment. "Those who wring their hands over the prospects of a convention," he wrote, "run the risk of exposing their elitism, implying that the average citizen cannot be trusted." Bell doubted a convention would meet, but felt that one could be limited since "Congress would not be compelled, nor would it have any incentive" to submit for ratification any proposals that exceeded the call. The platform adopted in July 1984 at the Democratic presidential nominating convention opposed "the artificial and rigid Constitutional restraint of a balanced budget amendment" as well as "efforts to call a federal constitutional convention for this purpose." The Republicans at their convention a month later pledged to work for approval of the amendment. On the motion of a South Carolina legislator, the conservative-dominated platform committee added a rebuttal: "if Congress fails to act on this issue, a constitutional convention should be convened to address only this issue in order to bring deficit spending under control."[62]

After Missouri the drive endured a series of reverses. In September 1984, the Michigan senate had approved a petition and the membership of the lower house seemed ready to concur, but discharge from the house select committee for a tally was blocked, five to four. The swing vote, retiring Republican Ruth McNamee, favored a balanced budget but felt that the balancing was up to Congress, and despite pressure from the White House "realized I don't want the Constitution tampered with." California and Montana, whose legislatures had refused to pass applications, saw unsuccessful attempts to place on their ballots popular referenda directing the legislatures to submit applications. Justice Rehnquist let stand decisions by the respective state supreme courts that the referenda contravened state constitutional provisions as well as article V, which contemplated legislatures acting independently of external restrictions. [63]

President Reagan renewed his endorsement of a balanced-budget amendment in his second inaugural address, but in March 1985 Connecticut continued the refusals, an indication that the drive's strength was in the West and South. At a standing-room-only committee hearing in Hartford, a procession of witnesses debated the virtues of both amendment and convention. Republican Governor Pierre S. du Pont of Delaware testified that approving a convention resolution "is the only way to move the Congress of the United States to restrain spending." Professor James W. Tobin of Yale University, a Nobelist in economics, said that a budget amendment would create "a parliamentary morass" for Congress, while Thomas I. Emerson, professor emeritus at Yale Law School, stated that there was no assurance that a convention would confine itself to that amendment, possibly resulting in "a constitutional crisis that could tear the country apart." Despite telephone calls urging adoption from Senator Dole and in one case from Vice President George Bush aboard Air Force Two, and despite Republican control of the legislature, the senate upheld the committee's recommendation not to pass the resolution. [64]

The string of reversals extended through 1985 and 1986, a development attributable to the "runaway" scare, the loss of Republican seats in state houses and the likelihood of reduced federal grants (decisive in the Northeast, dependent on federal aid to its cities), and also the passage in late 1985 of the Balanced Budget and Emergency Deficit Control Act. The statute, popularly known after its senatorial sponsors as "Gramm-Rudman-Hollings," required the federal deficit to be reduced in stages to zero by 1991. Gramm-Rudman's centerpiece or "trigger provision" mandated automatic spending cuts if deficits exceeded specified levels.

In March 1986 the Republican Senate failed by one vote to approve a balanced-budget constitutional amendment; Gramm-Rudman, as a palatable excuse to oppose the convention or its object, was given credit for the defeat. An amendment advocate and a liberal, Senator Paul Simon, said after the vote: "Senators think Gramm-Rudman has passed and that will do the trick." On a television news program, Simon called the convention "a very dangerous path, and another reason why I favor" an amendment originating in Congress. "If we get those two additional states for a constitutional convention, number one, we don't know what kind of a budget amendment they might draft. Second, that constitutional convention can . . . modify the Bill of Rights, they can put an abortion amendment in the Constitution, they can raise all kinds of havoc." Denying he favored the amendment primarily to stave off a convention since it was "meritorious on its own," Simon considered the drive "an additional incentive" for proposal by Congress.[65]

Stung by the Senate's rejection, President Reagan indicated that he might become personally involved in obtaining convention applications from the last two states, apparently using the threat of a runaway convention to bludgeon Congress into proposing the amendment. On March 26, a White House deputy press secretary read the President's statement to reporters:

It remains the President's hope that Congress will act responsibly to pass a balanced budget amendment, avoiding the need for a constitutional convention. . . .

The President urges Congress to set aside its free-spending habits and to promptly act to propose a balanced budget amendment before the supporters of such an amendment have no other course than to pursue petitioning the remaining State legislatures.

The press secretary added: "It may be that the president feels [so] strongly about a balanced budget that he favors a constitutional convention, and take your chances." Soon after, the conservative *Washington Times* editorialized for the amendment but against a convention that could "put the Constitution up for grabs" and barter away guarantees against unreasonable search and seizure in exchange for school prayer.[66]

This was the first time the Reagan administration had officially taken a position on a balanced-budget convention, although in a 1982 interview Reagan had referred to the convention strategy for a budget amendment as "a last resort, because then once it's open, they could take up any number of things." At a news conference in Detroit during the 1984 reelection campaign, Vice President Bush was asked if a balanced-budget convention should be expanded to include abortion and school prayer. Bush responded: "I think the convention, if there is one, should address itself to the issue for which it was called. I don't think you should try to circumvent the constitutional process and ram some amendment in there whether it's from the left liberal side or from the right conservative side."[67]

Deciding in July 1986 a challenge brought against Gramm-Rudman by Representative Mike Synar, the Supreme Court held the trigger mechanism unconstitutional as a violation of the separation of powers because it assigned the executive function of determining automatic spending cuts to the Comptroller General, who was removable solely by Congress. Left intact was the statute's "fallback" mechanism, requiring Congress to pass a joint resolution mandating any spending cuts. Congress, forced again to make its own budget choices when the smoke cleared, began to consider ways of repairing the trigger as the deficit for fiscal year 1986 climbed to $220.7 billion, the highest in history. At the end of 1986 the balanced-budget convention drive stood at thirty-two states, at least nine other states having passed an application in one legislative chamber, with no rescissions or invalidations.[68]

Arguing to save Gramm-Rudman, the Comptroller General had reminded the Supreme Court of the thirty-two applications. If the trigger were struck down, "the result may be to add momentum to a convention and to unwise constitutional amendments." Yet in 1987 there was as much stalemate as momentum. Although efforts to rescind applications failed in Maryland, Nevada, Texas, and Georgia, the magic two petitions likewise eluded pro-amendment forces, despite increased public awareness of the convention drive due to the bicentennial observances of the Constitution's framing and President Reagan's intensified involvement in the campaign.[69]

While rejecting a draft for his State of the Union address that committed him to push for a convention, Reagan began sending letters to the legislatures considering applications. To a state senator leading the fight in Montana, he wrote:

It has now become obvious that without further State initiatives Congress will not act to impose a limit on its own spending. I therefore believe that further action by the States, and particularly by the Montana Legislature, in petitioning Congress to call for a constitutional convention for the sole purpose of writing a balanced budget amendment will go far towards convincing Congress to pass and submit to the States an amendment for this purpose. If your effort is successful, Montana would be the 33rd State to pass such a resolution, just one short of the 34 required to call a constitutional convention. I believe this may finally convince Congress to act on an amendment of its own, which has always been my goal.

Switching tactics, Reagan now saw an article V convention as limitable to stated issues, not the runaway hinted at in the wake of the Senate's 1986 rejection. Montana's house of representatives passed a resolution 51 to 49, but in March the senate voted it down, 46 to 4. Playing a role in the defeat, and active as well in the movement to repeal submitted applications, was an unlikely alliance of organizations ranging across the political spectrum from liberal to conservative, from the Americans for Democratic Action, the American Civil Liberties Union, Common Cause, and the American Jewish Congress to the John Birch Society, the Gun Owners Clubs of America, and the Eagle Forum, an organization headed by activist Phyllis Schlafly that helped derail ratification of the equal rights amendment. These groups shared the view that a convention would inevitably take up non-budget matters, a premise that administration officials called the "wild beasts theory."[70]

Reagan, undaunted, referred to the convention process with apparent approval on May 23, in his weekly radio address delivered from the Camp David presidential retreat. Even with the enactment of Gramm-Rudman, the now-Democratic Congress

has been returning to its old ways and forgetting the solemn promises it made under this law. That's why I'm one of those Americans who has always believed a constitutional amendment, mandating that Congress balance the budget, is the answer to what ails us. And we've tried to get such an amendment through the Congress so that the state legislatures could vote on it.

This reluctance by the Congress has inspired a number of Americans to try another method provided for in the Constitution, a constitutional convention, one with delegates from each state, who could propose a balanced budget amendment, and then send it on to the state legislatures for approval. Only two more states are needed to call such a convention. And believe me, if the Congress continues to balk at passing the balanced budget amendment, I think the drive for a constitutional convention will pick up steam.

"Two states more," said Senator Daniel Moynihan in a commencement address at Columbia Law School, "and either we have a new convention, with the crisis that will bring, or we do not, with a resulting crisis of a differing order."[71]

From the public at large during 1987, signals were mixed. Eighty-five percent of the respondents in a New York Times/CBS News poll favored an amendment requiring Washington to balance the budget, and a survey conducted by the Hearst Corporation to mark the bicentennial found 61 percent interested in a constitutional convention to consider amendments on school prayer, abortion, and freedom of the press. In a *Newsweek* poll, however, 72 percent said that a convention held to make basic changes would make things worse.[72]

Nor did constitutional lawyers and scholars follow a rigid party line. Conservative historian Forrest McDonald of the University of Alabama found a budget amendment "indispensable," yet in a television interview abhorred a convention: "There's so much incompetence in this country today—they'd make a horrible botch of it." According to Bruce Ackerman of Yale Law School, an admirer of the New Deal, "There is a fear among liberals that if we open up the Constitution to change we would do a bad job of it. . . . But there is also a chance that we will not fail in structuring and re-ordering a government capable of discharging the functions of a regulatory state and elaborating notions of freedom that we can understand."[73]

Kicking off Independence Day weekend in a July 3 speech on the steps of the Jefferson Memorial, Reagan promised, "I will again ask Congress to submit a balanced budget amendment to the States. And if the Congress will not act, I'll have no choice but to take my case directly to the States." One provision of the amendment, said Reagan, would require an unspecified supermajority of Congress (a vote greater than 51 percent) to raise taxes. He also mentioned the possibility in an address to the nation televised from the Oval Office on the evening of August 12. In his first public remarks after congressional hearings on the Iran-contra affair, Reagan outlined the remaining goals of his administration:

The Congressional budget process is neither reliable nor credible—in short, it needs to be fixed.

We desperately need the power of a constitutional amendment to help us balance the budget. Over 70 percent of the American people want such an amendment. They want the Federal Government to have what 44 state governments already have—discipline. . . .

If the Congress continues to oppose the wishes of the people by avoiding a vote on our balanced-budget amendment, the call for a constitutional convention will grow louder. The prospect for a constitutional convention is only two states away from approval, and, one way or another, the will of the people always prevails.

The first sitting Chief Executive since Lincoln to endorse the convention mechanism and the first ever actively to promote its use, Reagan stopped short of recommending a convention call while encouraging pressure on Congress. Reagan is "playing with matches when he uses the convention threat to push his pet amendment," offered the generally liberal *New York Times*, adding that Congress could well "take some of the anxiety out of the process by enacting procedures for dealing with state applications."[74]

Following Reagan's directive, White House personnel started evaluating prospects for the last two applying states. On the legislative front, Congress passed a revised Gramm-Rudman statute to eliminate the deficit by 1993, with a trigger intended to pass constitutional muster by lodging the authority to order automatic spending cuts in the President's Office of Management and Budget. Negotiations between Congress and the Executive in October to meet the first annual deficit-reduction goal under Gramm-Rudman II were infused with special urgency by the worst stock market slide since the Crash of 1929. The plunge, ascribed to the deficit at least in part, brought the problem home to many Americans, and fiscal issues looked to remain paramount in the 1988 national elections.[75]

PART II

Operating Principles

5

Judging Applications

Should the balanced-budget amendment drive, or any other convention campaign, proceed to the constitutional number of applications, Congress—and the states—would be forced to embark on a route never before taken. Of course, Congress does not have to do anything until thirty-four applications arrive. "Congs. have no authority to propose a Convention," said Hamilton at the New York ratifying convention, "but must wait for nine states to make the proposition to them."[1] If that point is reached, Congress will have to decide whether all the applications are viable. Any full-fledged analysis of a complement of thirty-four applications would be two-tiered, with one focus on validity or formal compliance with article V—whether a subject matter must be stated, for instance, or whether the governor must approve—and the other on the timeliness or contemporaneity of the submissions. A Congress that has rejected an amendment will naturally be prone to find technical fault with the applications, but will probably feel compelled to respect constitutionally adequate submissions, if for no other reason than because its findings would likely be challenged in the courts.[2]

"If the number of states calling for a constitutional convention fails to reach 34," a Hoover Institution study predicts of the budget amendment, "Congress will probably continue to hold hearings and talk of the need for a balanced budget or spending limitation, but is unlikely to do more than deliberate. But as the 34th state prepares to pass a resolution,

Congress will move with alacrity to offer its own amendment." Since modern convention drives have aimed not to hold a convention but to extract an amendment from Congress, in the Institution's scenario article V will have worked just as Madison envisioned in his proposed substitute. That is, the process will remain in the hands of the central government, for Congress will submit amendments either on its own initiative or upon application by the states. For its part Congress in the last two decades has considered, but never passed, constitutional convention implementation acts whose main purpose is to limit conventions to the subject matter contained in the applications. As if locked in a constitutional arms race, both sides are preparing for a confrontation neither really wants. Small wonder Gerald Gunther of Stanford refers to this state of affairs as "constitutional brinksmanship."[3]

In providing that "on the Application of the Legislatures" Congress "shall call a Convention," article V implies that Congress is the agent entrusted to receive, inspect, and decide on the validity of applications, and that applications must be submitted to Congress to be counted toward a convention call. The applications submitted to the House of Representatives by Virginia and New York in 1789 were each "entered on the Journal, and carefully preserved by the Clerk of this House, among the files in his office." These petitions, then, were considered valid by the First Congress. Of Virginia's application, Representative Madison declared: "The most respectful and constitutional mode of performing our duty will be, to let it be entered on the minutes, and remain upon the files of the House until similar applications come to hand from two-thirds of the States."[4]

As a threshold matter a convention application, obviously, must indeed ask Congress to call a convention; yet confusion has arisen, especially during the campaign for the seventeenth amendment, because submissions occasionally ask only that Congress propose the amendment. Other anomalies abound. Maryland's application for a federal income tax convention was invalid because it was passed by only one house. Both houses of the Texas legislature approved identically worded resolutions for a convention on the same subject, but neither house concurred in the resolution passed by the other, and no application was filed with Congress. Applications for a balanced-budget convention from Arkansas and Indiana, though passed by only one house, were inadvertently sent to Congress. The two states later submitted applications approved by each house of their legislatures.[5]

The Subject Matter Requirement

Article V does not expressly say that an application must specify a particular subject area or proposed text for an amendment, and Charles Black has argued that article V authorizes only a plenary assembly, hence that petitions for a limited convention are invalid. That rule would disqualify nearly all the balanced-budget applications, which purport to limit the convention to that topic or even the exact text of the amendment set out in the application. To judge, however, from evidence of the founding era, Black's position is erroneous.[6]

The Georgia Constitution of 1777 had language parallel to that of an early article V draft. Georgia's clause stated that "the assembly shall order a convention to be called for that purpose," and the Committee of Detail's August 6 draft, approved by the Philadelphia Convention on August 30, provided that "the Legislature of the United States shall call a Convention for that purpose." There is no concrete evidence showing reliance by the framers, but the Georgia legislature was to issue its call "specifying the alterations to be made, according to the petitions preferred to the assembly."

Georgia's procedure may well have been drawn from the practice of the interstate conventions of the colonial and Revolutionary periods. Delegates to regional conventions had always derived their powers from their home governments, a practice in use at the Albany Congress of 1754; that assembly was charged with strengthening intercolonial defenses against the French and, as the Lords of Trade in Whitehall put it, "burying the hatchet" with the Iroquois. The Massachusetts commissioners to the Albany Congress were "authorized and impowered" by the General Court "in Concert with Commiss[ione]rs from [the other provinces] to enter into Articles of Agreement and Confederation. . . for their general Safety & Interest, and for confirming & establishing the . . . Attachm[en]t of the Indians of the Six Nations to his Majesty our most Gracious Sovereign."[7]

The usage seems to have been adapted from the practice in international law by which sovereign nations invested emissaries with stated powers for negotiating agreements with other sovereigns. In *The Law of Nations*, a treatise well known and highly regarded during the founding era, the Swiss theorist Emmerich de Vattel had written: "Sovereigns treat with one another through the medium of agents or commissioners, delegated with requisite authority . . . . The rights of the agent are

defined by the commission given to him. He must not exceed it." The
agent can negotiate only within the commission, and "princes reserve
to themselves the right of ratifying agreements drawn up in their name
by their agents."[8]

Delegates to regional conventions in the 1770s and 1780s were appointed to meet with counterparts on particular urgent matters. Rhode
Island's delegates were authorized to attend the Providence convention
of 1776 "to confer with the Committees of the States of Massachusetts
Bay, Connecticut, and New Hampshire . . . upon the expediency of
raising and appointing an Army for the . . . Defence of the New England States." New York's enabling concurrent resolution for the 1780
Hartford convention appointed three commissioners "with powers . . .
to propose and agree to in the said Convention all such measures as
shall . . . give a vigor to the governing powers equal to the present
crisis." A modern single-issue application would follow the precedent of
the Annapolis Convention, for which Virginia empowered representatives "to take into consideration the trade of the United States," specifically "a uniform system" in the "commercial regulations" of the states.[9]

Stretching this pattern to the utmost were the commissions and call
for the 1787 Philadelphia Convention. Under the Annapolis report's
formula, repeated with differing nuances by the states and Congress, the
delegates were to "devise such further provisions as shall appear to them
necessary to render the constitution of the Foederal Government adequate to the exigencies of the Union." These "further provisions," it
was commonly supposed, would deal with trade regulation and related
matters such as the power of Congress to levy import taxes and enforce
its judgments, matters recently the subject of amendments debated in
Congress or recommended by conventions.[10]

The vague Annapolis wording allowed more far-reaching changes
than the limited-issue call of Congress suggested, which was apparently
what nationalists had had in mind for months. In April 1787, Madison
confessed that

it will be well to retain as much as possible of the old Confederation, tho' I
doubt whether it may not be best to work the valuable articles into the new
System, instead of engrafting the latter on the former. . . . In truth my ideas of
a reform strike so deeply at the old Confederation, and lead to such a systematic
change, that they scarcely admit of the expedient.

Washington, for one, was glad of the call's elasticity: "Had Congress
proceeded to a delineation of the Powers, it might have sounded an

alarm—but as the case is, I do not conceive that it will have that effect."[11]

In *Federalist* 40 Madison stated that the "powers of the Convention" at Philadelphia "ought in strictness to be determined, by an inspection of the commissions given to the members by their respective constituents," and John Jay wrote of those delegates, "they who hold commissions can by virtue of them neither retrench nor extend the powers conveyed to them." The pre-1787 interstate conventions had been governed by commissions—the credentials issued to the delegates by their home state legislatures—and the 1789 applications of Virginia and New York, reflecting that origin, speak of deputizing the convention delegates with the powers necessary to consider appropriate amendments. The applications submitted under article V, therefore, are the descendants of the pre-1787 convention commissions.[12]

"It is natural to conclude," said federalist Wilson Cary Nicholas at the Virginia ratifying convention, "that those states who will apply for calling the convention will concur in the ratification of the proposed amendments." It followed for Nicholas, later a governor, senator, and representative, that "the amendments, which shall be agreed to by those states" applying for a convention "will be sooner ratified by the rest than any other that can be proposed." The "amendments . . . agreed to" by the applying states can have been agreed to only in the applications. In late 1787 and early 1788, Pennsylvania antifederalists campaigned to repeal the state's ratification of the Constitution. The campaign resulted in petitions supporting the antis from at least eight counties. The sole recorded opposing petition, from Wayne Township in Cumberland County, was presented to the state legislature on March 1, 1788, and affirmed "That the proposed Federal Constitution cannot be very dangerous while the legislature[s] of the different states possess the power of calling a convention, appointing the delegates and instructing them in the articles they wish altered or abolished."[13]

Despite Professor Black's assertion that applications limiting a convention to a specified amendment are void, the Wayne Township petition, expressly construing article V, evinces the understanding that delegates may be empowered with regard to particular amendments. Illustrating that commissions may be either plenary or specific, Madison wrote that the Constitution's opponents are "zealous for a second Convention, and for a revisal which may either not be restrained at all, or extend at least as far as alterations have been proposed by any State."

The Massachusetts delegation refusing to submit Governor Bowdoin's convention proposal to Congress in 1785 explained: "if a Convention of the States, is necessary . . . , the Members thereof should be United in their Authority and confined to the revision of such parts of the Confederation as are supposed defective, and not entrusted with a General Revision of the Articles."[14]

Since specification was assumed in article V, often the states rather than Congress were regarded as the true initiators of the convention process. Before the Morris-Gerry convention provision was inserted, Congress itself was to propose amendments upon the application of the state legislatures. At this point, Mason recalled in 1792, "amendments might be proposed either by Congr. or the legislatures." The applications in this early article V would have specified particular amendments, for Congress could hardly submit amendments instigated by petitions that were blank or demanded a variety of different alterations. In any event, Congress elsewhere in the clause was empowered to submit its own amendments.[15]

"Cassius," the federalist Boston merchant James Sullivan, wrote: "The 5th article also provides, that the states may propose any alterations which they see fit, and that Congress shall take measures for having them carried into effect." Should the new Constitution be ratified, said Hamilton in *Federalist* 85, "alterations in it may at any time be effected by nine states," nine states being then two thirds. "And consequently whenever nine or rather ten states, were united in the desire of a particular amendment, that amendment must infallibly take place," Hamilton adding that "though two-thirds may set on foot the measure, three-fourths must ratify." It seems impossible for two thirds of the states to initiate or effect "a particular amendment" unless a particular subject is specified in each application, and unless the applications agree on the subject.[16]

This is why Madison at Philadelphia insisted that "Congress would . . . be as much bound to propose amendments applied for by two thirds of the States as to call a Convention on the like application." Madison and his colleagues understood, first, that the applications were to specify amendments ("bound to propose amendments applied for . . ."), second, that the applications were to agree on the nature of the amendments (each amendment is "applied for by two thirds of the States"), and third, that the same requirements are contemplated by the final article V ("the like application").

Despite the nebulous quality of article V's phrase "a Convention for proposing Amendments," applications must evidently specify particular amendments, and a convention need be called only if the requisite number of applications agree in text or subject matter with regard to at least one amendment.[17] The phrase "for proposing Amendments" refers to the purpose or type of convention intended, in this case, as Madison referred to it at Philadelphia, "a Convention for the purpose of amendments"—in contrast to, for example, the trade conventions of the 1770s held to propose state statutes. The phrase does not, as Charles Black and others have held, preclude limitation to a single subject.[18]

Contrary to what John Calhoun and Professor Black supposed, therefore, a convention is not to be used only for thoroughgoing revision of the Constitution. Each amendment under article V, said Hamilton in *The Federalist*, whether from Congress or a convention "would be a single proposition, and might be brought forward singly." One of Madison's points in his *Report on the Virginia Resolutions* was that a convention could be called for one well-defined purpose, a position unchanged in his 1830 *North American Review* essay ("two thirds of the States to institute and three fourths to effectuate an amendment") and echoed the following year by the Supreme Court in *Smith v. Union Bank of Georgetown*. There is, according to these examples, no restriction on the number or kind of amendments a convention may submit, as there is none on those submitted by Congress. St. George Tucker said that a convention would propose the amendments "congress should neglect to recommend."[19]

The procedures of article V developed organically from existing practices, such as the Confederation ratification procedure used by Madison in his substitute amending clause. Another familiar device was the circular letter, as used by Virginia and New York in proselytizing for a second convention. The winning of state applications was but an adaptation of the method used by the colonies in organizing for constitutional reform while under British rule, indeed for disseminating news of all kinds over large areas. Innumerable circular letters were sent by the committees of correspondence to share intelligence and coordinate strategies of resistance.[20]

A report received by Madison makes explicit the connection with the days of the correspondence committees: "Mr. Henry has declared his intention . . . of bringing in a bill for the purpose of promoting a second Convention at Philadelphia to consider amendments—& that the Speakers of the two houses shou'd form a Committee of Correspondence to communicate with our sister States on that Subject." The connection was further evoked by a transmittal letter from the Virginia General Assembly sent with the copies of its convention application to the state legislatures:

As we conceive that all the good people of the United States, are equally interested in obtaining those amendments, that have been proposed, we trust that there will be an harmony in their sentiments and measures, upon this very interesting subject. We herewith transmit to you a copy of this application, and take the liberty to subjoin our earnest wishes that it may have your concurrence. [21]

The founders apparently assumed that a single amendment or set of amendments would be circulated among the states and garner its support in that manner, as suggested by Virginia's invitation to the states for the Annapolis Convention and the echoes of Virginia's 1789 convention application in its New York counterpart.

Although there is no constitutional requirement that article V applications indicate a particular stance on the subject matter to be considered, there is evidence that delegates may be given instructions of that nature. Instructions to elected representatives, in Parliament, had been known in England since medieval times, and took root in the American colonies in the 1600s. [22] The practice flourished especially in the Northeast, where the towns had become particularly well established as units exercising many prerogatives of sovereignty. Members of the Confederation Congress could be recalled for disobeying instructions. [23]

Regarding the Philadelphia Convention, Washington was concerned that "if the delegates come to it under fetters, the salutary ends proposed will in my opinion be greatly embarrassed & retarded, if not altogether defeated." At Philadelphia, the credentials of the Delaware members not only formally contemplated revision kept within the Articles, but also substantively prohibited assent to any proposal unless equal state suffrage in Congress was preserved. Said New Jersey delegate William Paterson: "the Commissions under which we acted were not only the measure of our power[,] they denoted also the sentiments of the States on the subject of our deliberation."[24]

Not all states gave voting instructions to their delegates when the ratifying conventions were held, but the instructions as to whether to approve the Constitution were generally followed. Some delegates to the Massachusetts convention, originally instructed to vote against the Constitution, returned to their constituents and informed them that after discussion they could not honestly oppose ratification; they were sent back to Boston and directed to vote "as they thought best." Randolph, entertaining the idea of another national convention, informed Madison: "My object will be, (if possible) to prevent instructions from being conclusive, if any should be offered, and to leave the conventioners perfectly free."[25]

While delegates in the founding era were given instructions on the "up or down" question whether to vote for ratification, attempts to program delegates to a modern national convention too tightly may be struck down as invasive of the convention's deliberative powers. Consequently, although delegates may refuse their commissions (as Patrick Henry did), resign (as when George Wythe left Philadelphia because of his wife's illness), or be expelled (as at North Carolina's ratifying convention), the states probably cannot recall and replace delegates except perhaps if the delegates abuse or transcend their proposing powers. To Gerry, Rufus King wrote in January 1787: "if Massachusetts should send deputies for God's sake be careful who are the men."[26]

When the twenty-first (repeal) amendment was submitted for ratification by state conventions, the high courts of four states ruled that delegates to a ratifying convention cannot be bound to the outcome of a state referendum.[27] The Supreme Court of Ohio pointed out that a convention already has a built-in referendum: "The views of the candidates, for election as delegates to the convention, will be known in advance, so that the final action of the convention should be truly representative of the will of the people upon the one special question involved." As one repealer admitted to a fellow "wet" regarding the contest in Maine, "I am sorry but I don't think that we can do anything except try to get a decent body of men elected to the convention."[28]

The Method of Application

Convention proponents have sometimes attempted to bypass the state legislatures by obtaining an initiative vote directing the legislature to submit the application. In 1938 the electorate of Oregon approved by a substantial margin a measure requiring the legislature to file an application for a convention on the Townsend recovery plan. The legislature, citing the election results but acting on its own vote, submitted the application to Congress. Initiatives for a balanced-budget convention were stricken from the California and Montana ballots in 1984. Had they been allowed to stand, and been approved, they would have produced the last two states needed to activate the convention clause. The Supreme Court has said consistently that ratifying an amendment by referendum is unconstitutional, since the framers contemplated "action by deliberative assemblages representative of the people . . . . Ratification might have been left to a vote of the people," but article V "is plain."[29]

As the first of those decisions came down, William Howard Taft, while professor of law at Yale, wrote that the specification of two modes of ratification in article V "exclude necessarily any idea of further submission to the people directly of the proposed amendment." Taft could have added that the framers had before them a model for a plebiscite in the Massachusetts 1780 constitution, which provided for a convention to be called by popular vote. The Massachusetts application mechanism was not used, although its qualified executive veto did become the model for the federal procedure. Doctrine concerning ratification is probably transferable to the application stage: proposal and ratification are successive steps in the same undertaking, and Madison borrowed from the ratification procedure of the Confederation for the application stage of his substitute amending clause.[30]

The founders evidently assumed that any convention application would be submitted after a simple majority vote in each of the state's two legislative chambers. Indeed, the vote in the Virginia legislature on its 1789 application is recorded simply as having been "resolved in the affirmative" in the House of Delegates and "agreed to" in the Senate, with no indication that the measure was so extraordinary as to require a supermajority. New York's application was likewise "agreed to" in the Assembly; in the Senate "it was carried in the affirmative, by all the Members present, excepting Mr. Douw and Mr. Lawrance."[31]

Since the Constitution specifies no vote for the legislatures, it is a sound assumption that the decision is not with Congress but with the individual states. This reasoning was applied to article V by Associate Justice John Paul Stevens, then a federal appellate judge sitting with a district court panel, in *Dyer v. Blair. Dyer* upheld an Illionis legislative rule mandating a three-fifths vote to ratify an amendment to the federal Constitution. Finding no straightforward directions in the Constitution or its history illuminating the manner in which ratification was to occur, Stevens concluded that a bare majority is permitted but not required; the framers did not mean to impose a specific figure on the state legislatures "but, instead, intended to leave that choice to the ratifying assemblies." Exactly how much greater than a simple majority is permissible for application or ratification must be judicially decided on a case-by-case basis, but *Dyer* properly noted that the supremacy clause prohibits a state legislature from abolishing completely the ratification function.[32]

The Governor's Veto

Despite a long history and clear signals in the constitutional text, the role of the state governors has been controversial in modern convention drives. The campaign for direct election of senators was considered to have fallen one application short, but one other state passed an application in both houses and refrained from submission only because of the governor's veto. More recently, Governor Mike O'Callaghan of Nevada vetoed an application for a balanced-budget convention (a later submission reached Congress), yet the only court to consider the issue held that the governor's approval is not necessary for sending an application.[33]

In the eighteenth century only 20 percent of the colonial governors were American; as a result, the royal or proprietary governor symbolized foreign domination.[34] From the 1600s onward, struggles ensued between the governors and the assemblies over the power to appoint local officials, regulate the judiciary, and determine policy with respect to land and trade. Robert Treat Paine, a signer of the Declaration and member of the 1768 Massachusetts township convention, wrote at the time that the convention was held "in Consequence of Gov. Barnards dissolving the Genl Court." The Boston Tea Party of December 16, 1773, was as much as anything else a remonstrance against the executive, for it was widely known that Governor Hutchinson's sons were among the consignees who would sell the tea and collect the import tax. The Declaration of Independence condemned King George III for having "refused his Assent to Laws, the most wholesome and necessary for the public good" and having "forbidden his Governors to pass Laws of immediate and pressing importance."[35]

The role of conventions during the Revolution as a means of circumventing royal authority, in the person of the governor, is lucidly explained by Judge St. George Tucker:

The dissolution of the constitutional assemblies by the governors appointed by the crown, obliged the people to resort to other methods of deliberating for the common good. Hence the first introduction of conventions, bodies neither authorized by or known to the then constitutional government; bodies, on the contrary, which the constitutional officers of the then existing governments considered as illegal and treated as such. . . .

. . . The power of convening the legal assemblies, or the ordinary constitutional Legislature, resided solely in the executive. They could neither be chosen without writs issued by its authority, nor assemble, when chosen, but under the same authority. The Conventions, on the contrary, were chosen and assembled either in pursuance of recommendations from Congress, or from their own bodies, or by the discretion and common consent of the people. They were held, even whilst a legal assembly existed. [36]

The bitter experience of the colonies under the English was manifest in the state constitutions framed after independence, for the governor's powers were now sharply curtailed. Where the colonial governors had used their veto power freely and were unrestrainable by the assemblies, by 1787 only Massachusetts kept a veto in the governor exclusively, which in any event could be overridden by two thirds of the legislature. [37] Wrote Fisher Ames, a member of the Massachusetts ratifying convention and the First Federal Congress, "we looked for danger on the same side where we had been used to look." The executive's title in New Hampshire was changed to "president" because "governor" was reminiscent of imperial rule. Every state constitution delineated the legislative branch first, before the executive—a pattern kept by the Philadelphia delegates, half of whom had aided in drafting their states' constitutions or legal codes. [38]

This history is engrained in article V, which requires a convention to be called "on the Application of the Legislatures of two thirds of the several States." The framers kept the legislative and executive powers distinct, as shown by the guarantee clause, section 4 of article IV:

The United States shall guarantee to every State in this Union a Republican Form of Government, and shall protect each of them against Invasion; and on Application of the Legislature, or of the Executive (when the Legislature cannot be convened) against domestic Violence.

If the governor was to be included, that inclusion was explicitly set forth. A draft constitution used by James Wilson as a member of the Philadelphia Committee of Detail shows the contrast dramatically:

on the Application of the Legislatures of two thirds of the States [to amend the Constitution], the Legislature of the United States shall call a Convention for that Purpose.
   The Members of the Legislature, and the executive and judicial Officers of the United States . . . shall be bound by Oath to support this Constitution.[39]

At the Virginia ratifying convention, Madison said that the guarantee clause requires the militia of other states to be called "on application by the legislature or executive, as the case may be." Maintaining this clear-cut distinction was standard usage for the period, and is of Lockean pedigree.[40]

   Article V's omission of any reference to the executive compels the inference that the governor's assent is not required for submission of a convention application. Some states expressly authorized the governor to fill vacancies in their delegations to the Philadelphia Convention, and the executives of Virginia and North Carolina did exercise that power, but the petitions from Virginia and New York accepted by Congress in 1789 both lack the governor's signature.[41]

   Although submission of state ratification acts to the governor has been common since the twelfth amendment, the governor cannot veto the ratification of an amendment to the federal Constitution by a state convention or legislature, nor veto the enabling legislation setting up a ratifying convention. Article V says only that amendments are valid "when ratified by the Legislatures . . . or by Conventions" in three fourths of the states.[42]

Agreement of Subject Matter

Twenty-four applications for a balanced-budget convention, and ten for a convention to consider school busing, will impose no duty on Congress; the showdown is likely to come when applications on a single topic vary in detail. Some balanced-budget convention proponents have argued that the convention's scope may be expanded to include such "budget" matters as federal funding of abortion.[43]

   If applications on a single topic are judged to vary too widely among themselves, they can probably be altered to conform with one another.

Rhode Island's delegates to the 1776 Providence convention received amended instructions, including a direction to ask the other commissioners "to agitate in their respective Legislatures the necessity of laying an Embargo." Virginia enlarged by new resolutions the authority of its Mount Vernon Conference commissioners, so as to involve Pennsylvania in the compact. At Philadelphia, William Paterson said: "If the confederacy [is] radically wrong, let us return to our States, and obtain larger powers, not assume them of ourselves." It seems, therefore, that delegates may acquire additional powers subsequent to filing of the applications, or even in mid-convention.[44]

The 1789 applications of Virginia and New York, in style rhetorical and discursive, ask the same deliberative scope. Virginia applied for a convention "with full power to take into their consideration the defects of this constitution that have been suggested by the State Conventions"—suggesting a convention of the "limited" variety—"and to report such amendments thereto as they shall find best suited to promote our common interests"—this, the operative part, may be construed as requesting a plenary convention. New York followed this wording somewhat, yet omitted the limitation: the convention is to have "full powers to take the said Constitution into their consideration, and to propose such amendments thereto, as they shall find best calculated to promote our common interests." The New York senate, in its answer to Governor Clinton's address opening the session, declared that "we shall without hesitation, recommend a submission of the system, to a general convention." Since both may be classified as plenary applications, the issue of agreement on particular issues would not have arisen.[45]

Yet in the petitions' supporting documents, a plenary convention did not seem to be the goal. "For their sense on this subject," said the Virginia application, speaking of the legislature's constituents, "we beg leave to refer you to the proceedings of their late Convention," in short the amendments approved by the ratifying convention at its close. As for New York, the Clinton circular stated: "we desire nothing more than that the amendments proposed by this or other states be submitted to the consideration and decision of a general convention."[46]

Several New York amendments follow exactly or nearly so the text of their Virginia models; others address the same subject but offer different solutions. (Each application, too, has amendments in areas not covered by the other.) Virginia's proposed amendment to what was then perpetual eligibility to the presidency limited tenure to eight years out of any sixteen-year period, a throwback to the requirement in the Articles of Confederation that no delegate could serve in Congress for more than three years out of any six. New York specified a limit of two terms, the solution adopted in the twenty-second amendment. Hence the varying texts of the Virginia and New York applications, and of the amendments proposed by the respective state ratifying assemblies, indicate (but do not conclusively prove) that suggested amendments need not agree in detail.[47]

Some applications, including those in the balanced-budget campaign, recite the text of an amendment and require the convention to adopt that language only. But no similar document from the founding age exists, and it is most unlikely that article V contemplates such applications. The conventions of the 1770s and 1780s consulted on common problems and hammered out solutions acceptable to the parties represented. The delegates were invited by circular letter, and if a specific result had been intended the circular would have set out the proposal for the simple decision whether or not to subscribe—the method in fact used to ratify the Articles of Confederation. Since it is not clear whether the specific text of an amendment was imposed to avoid a runaway convention or to foreclose other approaches, the states would probably amend their resolutions accordingly.[48]

Other applications, in a subtler variation, declare that they are not to be counted toward a convention if limits cannot be imposed. The anxiety is that a convention on (say) the budget may decide that the entire government must be overhauled to reform the appropriations process—four-year terms for Representatives, a line-item veto for the President, and so on. If a convention wanders that far afield, it must get additional powers from the states, as the Annapolis commissioners did. That prospect does not negate the specificity requirement; article V presupposes a definite procedure, not a phantom the states can never employ. "If, with a show of reason, almost any topic can be linked with any other topic, a limited Convention is never possible," wrote Judge (then Professor) John Noonan. "But this conclusion, contra Hamilton and Madison, would leave the states helpless to mandate action by Congress on the specific grievances."[49]

In 1786, the significant extension of powers given by New Jersey to its commissioners did not prohibit the Annapolis Convention from meeting. Nor did the unique restriction in Delaware's commission, prohibiting assent to any plan diluting the equal vote of each state in Congress,

halt the Philadelphia Convention. Minor and perhaps even major variations in wording or substance, then, will not stand in the way of a
convention call. Applications for a plenary convention, however, are
probably not to be aggregated with petitions requesting specific amendments; a state desiring a balanced federal budget may not, and likely
does not, want the Constitution changed in any other respect.

Withdrawing Applications

The ability of states to withdraw their applications has been at issue in
past convention drives, an issue that when raised is a sign that the
campaign has lost steam, but Congress has never officially decided the
question. Yet the power to retract a ratification was accepted by the
founders, suggesting that the same holds true for applications.

On February 3, 1781, Congress approved an amendment to the
Articles of Confederation permitting it to levy a duty on certain imports.
The proposed amendment was ratified by all the state legislatures except
those of Georgia, which gave no reply, and Rhode Island, which rejected it. The uncertain status of Georgia—often occupied by the British and rarely represented in Congress—might have allowed Rhode
Island's approval to put the amendment into operation. [50] An independent source of revenue for Congress would have made it less reliant on
the states, which is why the amendment unraveled. Virginia's 1781
ratification was later suspended, pending approval of the impost by
every state, and ultimately repealed outright in the first week of December 1782. [51] New York rescinded on March 15, 1783, South Carolina followed the next day, and for a time it looked as though Massachusetts and Maryland would join them. [52]

On the constitutionality of the repeal, Edmund Randolph asked
Madison, then a Virginia delegate in Congress, whether Virginia's initial ratification "did not deprive this state of the power of revocation."
Madison replied: "Your doubt as to her power of revoking her accession, would I think have been better founded, if she had not been
virtually absolved by the definitive rejection by Rho: Island." The rescission power was recognized generally, for as Virginia delegate Theodorick Bland said, "it was in the power of the States to repeal their
grants." On January 28, 1783, Madison told Congress that "with the
same knowledge of public affairs which his station commanded, the

Legislature of Va would not have repealed the law in favor of the impost & would even now rescind the repeal." The rescissions stood, accepted by Congress. In 1783, Congress passed an amendment limiting the impost to a twenty-five-year period, specially revised to accommodate the rejecting states.[53]

The Confederation had been ratified by the state legislatures, giving rise to the contention that the legislatures could also repeal what they had passed; this feature would be avoided in the new Constitution. Nonetheless, the Rhode Island affair was still a fresh memory at Philadelphia. When the framers deliberated on the Constitution's ratification provision and recalled the Confederation's unanimity requirement, Nathaniel Gorham of Massachusetts demanded: "will any one say[ ] that all the States are to suffer themselves to be ruined, if Rho. Island should persist in her opposition to general measures[?]" The fiasco led the delegates to reduce the Confederation's unanimity requirement for both ratification of the Constitution and the addition of amendments to it.[54]

At Virginia's ratifying convention, Edmund Randolph announced his change of heart from opposition to support of the Constitution: "as I think those eight states which have adopted the Constitution will not recede, I am a friend of the Union."[55] Before the convention Madison had advised Randolph: "it could not be a very easy matter to bring about a reconsideration and recision of what will certainly have been done in six and probably eight States." These comments, independently of the Rhode Island affair, presuppose the ability of states to withdraw their ratification notices and imply that the same is true of their applications. Rhode Island's revision of its delegates' commission in 1776 provides further confirmation, since amending an application implies rescinding the original submission. In September 1791, Pennsylvania approved one of the amendments it had originally rejected when proposed by Congress in 1789—suggesting as well that states can apply or ratify after a prior negative vote.[56]

This learning was ignored or forgotten when rescissions were submitted during the adoption of the fourteenth and fifteenth amendments with the result that the effect of rescission has been treated by Congress and the Supreme Court not as dependent on constitutional principle but as subject to determination by Congress alone. When the requisite number of states had ratified the fourteenth amendment, the Senate and House in January 1868 passed resolutions declaring that the amendment was adopted as part of the Constitution. Ohio and New Jersey subsequently withdrew their ratifications.[57]

The Secretary of State's proclamation of July 20 listed Ohio and New Jersey among the twenty-nine ratifying states, but noted that they had rescinded and that it was uncertain "whether such resolutions are not irregular, invalid, and therefore ineffectual." With thirty-seven states both loyal and reconstructed then in the Union, twenty-eight were needed to adopt. On July 21, 1868, Georgia ratified the amendment; Congress, receiving word of the ratification by telegram the same day, passed a concurrent resolution declaring the amendment's adoption into the Constitution. The Secretary of State issued another proclamation on July 28, listing Georgia as well as New Jersey and Ohio among the thirty ratifying states, and stating that the amendment had been ratified by "more than" three fourths of the states.[58]

Before the fifteenth amendment had been ratified by three fourths of the states, New York passed a resolution of withdrawal in January 1870. After two more states ratified, the Secretary of State issued a proclamation that included New York in the roster of approving states, but mentioned the "resolutions claiming to withdraw" its ratification. The two additional ratifying states mooted the question of New York's rescission, and, as with the promulgation of the fourteenth amendment, Congress left open the legal status of withdrawing assent to a proposed amendment. Yet even if Congress had decided the issue, that determination would not have been binding on future Congresses.[59]

The weight of the evidence, then, supports the power of states to rescind an application as well as a ratification, and to submit an application or ratification after a prior rejection,[60] although this conclusion is not uncontroversial.[61]

Timeliness

Currently there is no deadline by which states must submit their convention applications. None is provided in the Constitution, and Congress has never made a determination on the subject. Many framers hoped that the Constitution would, as Madison said, "last for ages," and it was this concern that prompted Franklin's celebrated epigram: "Our new Constitution is now established, and has an appearance that promises permanency; but in this world nothing can be said to be certain, except death and taxes." In theory an application could remain effective, that is, could be aggregated toward a convention call, indefinitely.[62]

Not until the twentieth century was a time limit imposed by Congress on the ratification of amendments. In 1873 the Ohio legislature passed a resolution ratifying one of the amendments proposed unsuccessfully by Congress in 1789. Perhaps to avoid similar events, Congress, beginning with the eighteenth amendment in 1917, has specified a time certain within which ratification must occur. Traditionally the ratification period has been seven years, although the deadline for the proposed equal rights amendment was extended by three years. Using something like Ohio's reasoning, Wisconsin in 1929 requested Congress to call an article V convention on the ground that a total of thirty-five states, more than two thirds, had filed applications since 1789. Congress ignored the request, probably on the same assumption that allowed it to impose deadlines on the ratification of amendments: consent to any change in fundamental law must be contemporaneous, and must be addressed to the same issue compelling resort to the amendment process.[63]

This contemporaneity principle was endorsed by the Supreme Court in the 1921 case of *Dillon v. Gloss*, which upheld the power of Congress to fix a "reasonable" time for the ratification of constitutional amendments. J.J. Dillon was convicted of importing liquor in violation of the Prohibition amendment. His defense was that the amendment had not been validly adopted because Congress could not limit the time for the states to decide on amendments. Justice Van Devanter's opinion for the Court stated that "proposal and ratification are . . . succeeding steps in a single endeavor" and cannot be "widely separated in time."[64] Ratification must be "sufficiently contemporaneous" in the requisite three fourths of the states "to reflect the will of the people in all sections at relatively the same period." As-yet-unadopted amendments proposed in 1789, 1810, and 1861 are not still pending; their effective ratification and adoption would now be "quite untenable."[65] Hence "ratification must be within some reasonable time after the proposal." A constitutional amendment "proposed today has relation to the sentiment and felt needs of today, and . . . if not ratified early while sentiment may fairly be supposed to exist, it ought to be regarded as waived." The amendment's seven-year deadline was upheld because Congress, "keeping within reasonable limits, [may] fix a definite period for the ratification" of amendments "as an incident of its power to designate the mode of ratification."[66]

This principle was further elaborated a decade and a half later in *Coleman v. Miller*, the Supreme Court's last major pronouncement on article V. In 1924 Congress had proposed an amendment forbidding interstate commerce in the products of child labor, but did not provide a time limit for ratification. The Kansas legislature rejected the amendment in 1925, but in 1937 voted to ratify. The Court let the ratification stand and concluded, regarding the thirteen-year span, that "Congress has the power under Article V to fix a reasonable limit of time for ratification in proposing an amendment," and that the congressional determination of what is a reasonable time is not subject to review by the courts.[67]

Several applications for a balanced-budget convention declare that they are "continuing" applications unless Congress itself proposes the amendment by a specified date, in which case the applications lose force. Since the applications are integral to the proposal stage, the legislatures can probably affix a definite time period, on analogy to the contemporaneity element of the ratification stage emphasized in *Dillon*. The states may, then, control the period in which their applications stay effective; they can, indeed, rescind them entirely.[68]

Ancillary to accepting convention applications and determining when a convention must be called, Congress (in the absence of a state-imposed deadline) probably has the power to establish a period within which applications remain in effect. An application deadline chosen for one convention campaign would not necessarily be used for subsequent campaigns, any more than a seven-year ratification deadline imposed by Congress on a particular amendment fixes that limit for all amendments to come. Most state legislatures meet annually, though seven state constitutions provide only for sessions held every other year. A period of less than two years might prevent every state from considering an application at least once and be judicially invalidated on the theory that it denied the states' application power guaranteed by the Constitution. Applications sent before a deadline is established may be deemed, on the authority of *Coleman*, to have lapsed at some "reasonable" point, for the states cannot expect that decade-old applications will satisfy the contemporaneity requirement.[69] "A case can be made," Paul Freund of Harvard Law School has written, "for allowing a relatively

long period for ratification after the Congress or a convention has performed the solemn deliberative act of proposing an amendment, while
the call for a convention should stress more strongly the element of a
contemporaneously felt need."[70]

At a forum held on May 23, 1979, under the auspices of the American
Enterprise Institute of Washington, D.C., Antonin Scalia declared:

Instead of displaying utter confusion and an inability to do anything about the
calls from the states, Congress could simply decide that they constitute a call for
a constitutional convention on the broad issue of fiscal responsibility and control at the federal level. . . . [Congress] could leave the call open for six
months. And during those six months, any of the thirty-four states that have
made a call could revoke it if they found the issue [as defined by Congress] too
broad for their liking. But in the absence of such revocation, Congress would go
ahead.

Justice Scalia assumed that the call of Congress determines the scope of
the convention, but in all likelihood he is incorrect since only the
states, not Congress, can define the convention's agenda. John Jay said
of the contemplated Philadelphia Convention: "their authority is to be
derived from acts of the State legislatures."[71]

Madison wrote in 1830 that "in case of an experienced inadequacy of
[the Constitution's] provisions, an ulterior resort is provided in amendments attainable by an intervention of the States, which may better
adapt the Constitution for the purposes of its creation." Madison's statement is consistent with his remark in *Federalist* 43 half a century earlier
that article V "equally enables the general and the state governments to
originate the amendment of errors as they may be pointed out by the
experience on one side or on the other." There is no evidence, and it is
contrary to plausible inference, that Congress has the power to ex-
pand—or contract—the scope of the convention. It was under the
recommendation of the Annapolis report that the Philadelphia Convention assembled, said Charles Pinckney, "for most of the appointments
had been made before the recommendation of Congress was formed or
known." In the South Carolina legislature Edward Rutledge, brother of
delegate John, endeavored to prove "from the act passed last session,
appointing delegates . . . that they had not exceeded their powers." It is
therefore legally immaterial how Congress frames the call, although its
drafting would be symbolically important as an indication of respect.[72]

Justice Scalia is probably right, however, that Congress would give the states a certain amount of time to revise applications. The parties could then adjust strategy, the states deciding if they wanted to continue pressing for an amendment, and if so whether from Congress or a convention; Congress examining the applications to see how many could be repelled. A major altercation would be likely to occur regarding the length of time applications stay effective, since a faction in Congress might favor the amendment and advocate a long period to include as many applications as possible. The committee reporting Senator Ervin's convention legislation in 1971 recommended a seven-year effectiveness period for applications, on the model of the traditional ratification deadline, while the committee minority, comprising liberals opposed to a convention and the amendments espoused in the conservative agenda, recommended four years. Since the amendment has by definition lost in Congress by the time thirty-four applications arrive, sufficient votes for a period longer than six or seven years would probably be lacking, unless a simple majority in each house favored the amendment sufficiently to extend the deadline in hopes of eventually reaching the two thirds necessary to carry the amendment itself, or of obtaining the convention demanded in the applications. Yet even the committee recommending the Ervin bill rejected "a much longer time, say, 15 years" because it "would not satisfy the reasoned desire for consensus."[73]

With guidelines for validity and deadlines for effectiveness established, and with at least one application found defective or stale, pressure would shift back to the states whose petitions were rejected, and the cycle would resume. The applying states would by no means automatically resubmit corrected applications, since the legislatures in the early states would have had major changes in personnel, and might have voted on the applications originally with little realization of their possible impact.

6

Congress, the Courts, and the President

"Congress Will Be Obliged . . ."

If the states return with thirty-four valid, effective applications on the same subject, Congress will be faced with the choice of calling the convention, proposing its own amendment, or hoping the pressure will recede. Convention calls have been pushed back in several states whose constitutions required that the legislature hold a referendum on calling a convention, and upon approval of the voters to call one. New Hampshire's legislature in 1861 and 1864, and Iowa's legislature in 1920, refused to call conventions after the voters had approved them in mandatory referenda. The legislature of New York, after a convention had been voted in the referendum of 1886, delayed holding one for eight years. In 1930 and 1950, the Maryland General Assembly refused to pass an enabling act despite pro-convention majorities in the referenda, the 1950 returns favoring a convention by four to one. Apparently Maryland's malapportioned legislature declined a call both times because it feared that a convention might change the state constitution to require equitable apportionment in at least one house of the Assembly.[1]

Congress will naturally resist calling a convention. In the midst of Senator Dirksen's antireapportionment campaign, his Illinois colleague

Paul Douglas opined that "there is little real expectation that the Congress will call a convention even if two-thirds of the State legislatures pass the applications. It cannot, I believe, be forced to do so."[2] A few writers agree that even if the requisite applications were filed, Congress may refuse a call, but most scholarly opinion finds an inescapable obligation. Senator Charles Mathias wrote that "the choice is not mine. It is clear that if two thirds of the states submit valid applications to the Congress, then we'll have no choice but to call a convention."[3]

Once Congress has determined that the requisite number of valid and effective applications has been submitted, the duty is plain. Congress "*shall* call a Convention," says article V, or as paraphrased by the Supreme Court, "Congress . . . *must* call a convention." The convention clause is, after all, descended from Resolution 13 of the Virginia Plan, declaring that "the assent of the National Legislature ought not to be required" to obtain amendments. The Morris-Gerry motion to "require" a convention at the instance of two thirds of the states appears meant to exclude any third party's discretion. John Marshall, a staunch federalist at the Virginia ratifying convention, later wrote that the state legislatures "may require Congress to call a convention of the people to propose amendments."[4]

The founding generation spoke with one voice on this duty. In *Federalist* 85 Hamilton, arguing against the Randolph-Lee plan for amendments before ratification, maintained that article V is a bona fide guarantee. Whenever two thirds of the state legislatures concur, the federal government "will have no option upon the subject. By the fifth article of the plan the congress will be *obliged*" to call a convention. "The words of this article are peremptory. The congress '*shall* call a convention.' Nothing in this particular is left to the discretion of that body. And of consequence all the declamation about their disinclination to a change, vanishes in air."[5]

A month after Essay 85 appeared James Innes, federalist attorney general of the commonwealth, said at Virginia's ratifying convention: "By the paper before you, if two thirds of the states think amendments necessary, Congress are obliged to call a convention to propose amendments." At the North Carolina convention, Andrew Bass contended that "the introduction of amendments depended altogether on Congress." Thereupon James Iredell, shortly an Associate Justice of the United States Supreme Court, answered

that it did not depend on the will of Congress; for that the legislatures of two thirds of the states were authorized to make application for calling a convention to propose amendments, and, on such application, it is provided that Congress *shall* call such convention, so that they [Congress] will have no option.

Framer John Dickinson, in a newspaper essay, agreed: "whatever their sentiments may be, they *must* call a convention for proposing amendments, on applications of two-thirds of the legislatures of the several states."[6]

In a published letter, Madison wrote: "the question concerning a General Convention, does not depend on the discretion of Congress. If two thirds of the States make application, Congress cannot refuse to call one; if not, Congress have no right to take the step."[7] On May 5, 1789, when Virginia's convention application was presented to Congress, Madison informed his colleagues in the House of Representatives that when "two-thirds of the State Legislatures concurred in such application, . . . it is out of the power of Congress to decline complying, the words of the Constitution being express and positive relative to the agency Congress may have in case of applications of this nature." From the words of article V "it must appear, that Congress have no deliberative power on this occasion."[8]

Form and Content

Any convention call issued would contain the bare essentials of the convention's operation, and therefore would be the main forum of contest between Congress and the states for control of the procedure. By 1787 the convention calls issued by Congress had become relatively standardized, for they all specified the scope and purpose of the convention, the parties to attend, and (in the 1777 and 1787 examples) the time and place the convention was to be held. The calls issued by the state legislatures during ratification specified additionally the date and manner of electing delegates, the apportionment of delegates, the qualifications of delegates and electors, and the compensation given to the delegates.[9]

The calls issued by the state legislatures for the ratifying conventions of 1787–1790, as well as the convention applications of Virginia and New York, were in the form of concurrent resolutions, not statutes. Every convention call issued by the Continental Congress from 1775 to 1787 was contained in a resolution of recommendation, not a statute or ordinance. When Congress legislated on matters within its competence it used ordinances, the equivalent of statutes. When a matter depended on state action, Congress used resolves, which were couched as recommendations. The February 21 resolve calling the Philadelphia Convention declared only that "it is expedient" that the states attend. The same arrangement, it appears, was kept in article V: a convention call by resolution, with no direct legislative power on the part of Congress. The minimal congressional discretion written into article V dovetails precisely with the history of conventions as bodies independent of the regular legislatures. [10]

It is often assumed in congressional and scholarly studies that Congress may regulate the convention's operation through the necessary and proper clause of article I. According to a Senate report recommending the Ervin bill, "Congress unquestionably has the authority to legislate about the process of amendment by convention, and to settle every point not actually settled by article V of the Constitution itself." But the necessary and proper clause grants legislating power to Congress to execute only those "Powers vested by this Constitution in the Government of the United States." A delegated power, as Dr. Charles Jarvis said at the Massachusetts ratifying convention, "must be in its nature discretionary with that body to which this power is delegated," but discretion whether to issue a call is precisely what Congress does not have. Article I and article V, in fact, seem designed to govern different types of action: article I throughout uses "pass" for the power to enact legislation, while article V consistently uses "propose" for the amending procedure. [11]

Congress is therefore limited to decisions on the "housekeeping" provisions of the call—the time and place of the convention, the apportionment and qualifications of the delegates. A simple majority in each house of Congress on these details, appropriately in the form of a concurrent resolution, is sufficient for approval. When the House of Representatives (as resolved into a committee of the whole) was considering the amendments that became the Bill of Rights, Representative Samuel Livermore of New Hampshire asked whether a two-thirds majority was needed to carry a motion in committee. Chairman Elias Boudinot of New Jersey ruled that "a majority of the committee were sufficient to form a report." The ruling was confirmed by the House. [12]

Congress has sought to control the representation at a convention— the total number of delegates attending, the method of their selection, the manner of voting (by state or by individual member), and the majority vote needed to propose an amendment—by defining those features in its proposals. Only the total number of delegates, however, may be handled by Congress: the method of selection is up to each state, and voting matters are entirely within the discretion of the convention itself.

Congress, as a central clearinghouse, is the logical choice to recommend the total number of delegates. There is, however, no power to prescribe; in the regional and national conventions held up to and including 1787, each state sent as many delegates as it liked. Virginia appointed seven deputies to the Philadelphia Convention, New York three.

Ervin's original bill provided for a convention modeled after the House of Representatives, and he has some historical support. In the pre-Revolutionary era, the state lower house represented the colonists in the defense of their rights against the governor. The upper house, usually not elected, began as an adjunct to the governor and hence was allied to the Crown. The pre-1787 state constitutions that specify the apportionment of an amending convention—the Massachusetts Constitution of 1780, the New Hampshire Constitution of 1784, and Jefferson's 1783 draft for Virginia—all require the convention to have the same number of delegates as the respective state lower house. The Hatch bill, however, allocates for each state the number of delegates equal to the senators as well as representatives it sends to Congress (even though the convention would meet in one rather than two chambers). The purpose is to afford smaller states a weighted influence in proposing amendments, as they have in Congress. Precedent exists here as well: the state conventions of the Revolutionary era were generally bicameral, since the framing bodies were often the existing legislatures.[13]

A modern article V convention might therefore have as many as 435 or 535 members, if the convention has at least one delegate from each state and delegates are allotted by population, as opposed to the fifty-five who attended (at various times) the Philadelphia Convention. As of 1787 appointment by state legislature was the only method ever used to select members of a regional or national assembly, but since the Constitution does not specify the method of selecting convention delegates, currently the states may decide the matter for themselves. Congress cannot appoint itself the convention, since it has no power over choosing the delegates.[14]

If the states establish election procedures, the constitutional guarantees pertaining to congressional elections will likely apply. Only the Delaware and Pennsylvania ratifying conventions could have satisfied the Supreme Court's one-person, one-vote standard, and article I's characterization of Representatives as "chosen . . . by the People" does not apply to national convention delegates. Nevertheless, the one-person, one-vote rule would likely govern convention elections through the fourteenth amendment, under which no state can "deny to any person within its jurisdiction the equal protection of the laws." If a malapportioned convention were specified in the call issued by Congress, an applying state could probably obtain an injunction to have the call modified or set aside pending issuance of a call that met constitutional standards. The principle underlying reapportionment cases, wrote one commentator, "seems to be that a state may not create or tolerate a political structure which gives any group in the electorate disproportionate weight in influencing the outcome of vital political decisions."[15]

The first of the standing rules reported by George Wythe's committee and approved by the Philadelphia Convention provided: "A House, to do business, shall consist of the Deputies of not less than seven States; and all questions shall be decided by the greater number of these which shall be fully represented." The convention originally considered weighting the votes to favor the more populous states, but dropped the idea when Virginia's delegation argued that the scheme "might beget fatal altercations between the large & small States." Hence the convention decided its own quorum, approving vote, and manner of casting ballots (by state). Elbridge Gerry assumed that a second convention would vote by states in remarking that two thirds of the states could obtain a convention, "a majority of which can bind the Union."[16]

Sam Ervin's original 1967 bill provided that a simple majority of the total number of delegates would suffice to propose an amendment, but in 1971 liberals in the Senate amended it to require a two-thirds vote. The difference between a simple majority and a supermajority is often the difference between adoption and defeat; the Dirksen amendment in 1965 would have passed at least the Senate on a simple majority rule, as would have the balanced-budget amendment in 1986. If Congress were able to raise the convention's majority vote, it could choke the convention and thereby do indirectly what article V forbids it to do directly.[17]

Parliament from its earliest days observed the principle of simple majority rule, which Sir William Holdsworth traced to canon law.

Locke extolled the rule, which was transported to the colonies as a chief tenet of their legal culture. The principle was enshrined by Franklin at the Philadelphia Convention as "the common practice of Assemblies in all Countries and Ages," and Gerry worried that "a majority of" the states at an article V convention would bind the Union. Deploring the antifederalists' drive, John Jay argued that any new plan from a second convention "carried by a slender majority, must expect numerous opponents" and risk rejection.[18]

Accordingly, where the Constitution does not specify a vote—as it does not for a national convention—a simple majority is sufficient to decide the issue, and Congress may not raise the figure.[19] Since the convention decides its own approving vote, it could, by a simple majority, determine that proposing an amendment requires a supermajority, for example two thirds or three fifths. But this hurdle can be imposed only by the convention itself, not from without by Congress.[20]

As part of the housekeeping chores attached to issuing the convention call, Congress probably can set the qualifications for delegates and the electorate eligible to vote for them; the constitutional requirements for electing members of Congress need not be strictly duplicated. The resolution calling New York's 1788 ratifying convention relaxed the qualifications for voters by omitting the state constitution's property requirement for participating in general elections.[21]

Some proposals exclude members of Congress, on the theory that members should not be eligible for a body designed to circumvent them. Exclusion is based on article I, section 6, which provides that "no Person holding any Office under the United States, shall be a Member of either House during his Continuance in Office." The incompatibility clause was taken from a similar provision in article V of the Confederation, and was to prevent the corruption resulting from a small group's exerting control through holding multiple offices. When the Philadelphia delegates—ten of whom were sitting members of the Confederation Congress—surveyed federal offices incompatible with a seat in Congress, discussion was confined to those positions filled by appointment of the President. An office under the United States in article II of the Constitution, said John Marshall, is a "continuing" duty. The delegates at the Annapolis Convention, wrote James Monroe, "assembled . . . for a temporary purpose."[22]

In the Confederation Congress, Madison said that one reason for holding the Philadelphia Convention was so that "persons might be admitted wthr. or not they be in Congs." Tench Coxe, Annapolis delegate and prominent federalist author, argued in December 1788 that amendments to the new Constitution should be proposed by Congress, not another convention. One major consideration was that "it is highly probable that a new convention would contain many members of the new Congress." Nothing, it should be added, bars election of a sitting president, cabinet member, or federal judge as a delegate.[23]

Assuming a congressional majority set against, for instance, a balanced-budget measure, Congress can call the applying states' bluff by agreeing to issue the call in lieu of proposing the amendment. Congress can then sit back, for it is under no duty to provide any funds or other assistance. It has been contended that a convention has the inherent power to appropriate all necessary expenses, but under article I monies may be drawn from the Treasury only "in Consequence of Appropriations made by Law."[24]

Congress has the discretion to finance the convention under article I's spending clause, or to leave the expenses to the states—as it did with the Philadelphia Convention, which asked Congress to pay only the salaries of "the Secretary and other officers of this Convention" and "the incidental expenses of this convention." Congress is permitted to attach conditions to the federal benefits it disburses, but only an independent source of revenue can ensure the financial and hence political independence of the delegates. Even if Congress passes an appropriation, it is subject to the President's veto. A serious hidden danger of inadequate public funding is that political action committees and other special-interest groups could step in to finance the delegates' campaigns and salaries, eliminating except for the affluent service not beholden to outsiders.[25]

Ultimately, the Constitution does guarantee a convention, so that an assembled national convention is protected against premature dissolution for lack of funds. The states would carry a heavy burden, however, in showing that they cannot support their delegates at even a modest gathering. According to a recent estimate by the Congressional Budget Office, total expenses for a national convention lasting one month, excluding the costs of delegate elections, would come to about $4.8 million, and $4.5 million for each additional month.[26]

A modern national convention would likely proceed in much the same fashion as its ancestors: after swearing in the delegates, the convention would select officers, appoint committees—on elections, on rules, and on amendments—and then as a body vote on disputed elections, proposed rules, and the amendments in the applications. The Philadelphia Convention elected its president, George Washington, and its secretary, William Jackson. The convention's internal management would be within its province, and not that of Congress. Referring to the Pennsylvania ratifying convention, George Logan declared in the legislature that "the business of forming rules belongs to that body alone."[27]

The conventions that framed the Revolution-era state constitutions established their own rules of proceeding, as did the regional conventions of the time. One rule of Delaware's 1776 convention stipulated "That no Member of this Convention shall, whilst in the House and during the Sitting thereof, read any Book or printed Paper, on Penalty of a Check from the President."[28] The Philadelphia Convention adopted the rules drawn up by Wythe's rules committee.[29] The ratification conventions as well adopted their own rules and passed on the qualifications of attending delegates.[30] In one notable case, the North Carolina convention threw out two sets of returns from Dobbs County because the elections had been disrupted by violence, and ordered the Dobbs delegates to vacate their seats.[31]

Since conventions possessed inherent rights of self-protection, delegates were accordingly held entitled to the immunities necessary for carrying out their duties freely and without disturbance. These immunities, or parliamentary privileges—derived from the rights claimed by the House of Commons against the Crown and established by the sixteenth century—are also concerned with an assembly's power of self-government. These powers are of the kind bestowed on Congress in article I: "Each House shall be the Judge of the Elections, Returns and Qualifications of its own Members, . . . may determine the Rules of its Proceedings, punish its Members for disorderly Behaviour, and, with the Concurrence of two thirds, expel a Member."[32]

By the middle of the eighteenth century, parliamentary privileges were "antient" and "undoubted" rights well entrenched in colonial government.[33] Privilege from arrest had been confirmed for members of Parliament and brought over to the colonial, later state, assemblies; the privilege was established for Congress under the Articles of Confederation as well as its successor under the Constitution in the speech or debate clause of article I.[34] Incorporating parliamentary privileges into written law was deemed an abundance of caution, for the privileges inhered in all representative assemblies.[35]

In the 1788 case of *Bolton v. Martin*, the Philadelphia Common

Pleas court heard a suit arising from a summons issued to James Martin, a delegate to the Pennsylvania ratifying convention, while Martin was attending. The court, relying on English precedents, dismissed the action on the ground that the delegates had "the same or equal immunities" as members of the legislature. The members of Pennsylvania's General Assembly "are legally and inherently possessed of all such privileges, as are necessary to enable them, with freedom and safety, to execute the great trust reposed in them." Equivalent privileges for delegates to a national convention are therefore not dependent on congressional largess. [36]

Incident to the convention's power to determine its membership, vacancies created after the convention begins can probably be filled at its own request rather than, as some bills provide, according to procedures set by Congress. On the evening of November 9, 1779, the Massachusetts framing convention sent a letter to the town of Brookfield, asking its inhabitants to elect, "if they see meet," a replacement for Judge Jedediah Foster, who had died. [37]

Although Congress would likely "regulate the time and place of holding the Convention," as Representative William Loughton Smith said in 1796, deciding on the meeting site is another key prerogative belonging to the convention. Should Congress specify a locale that the delegates immediately or after a time find unsuitable, the convention may adjourn to another site. William Findley, a member of the Pennsylvania ratifying convention as well as of the state legislature, said that "the House on a former occasion did direct the [ratifying] Convention as to the time when they should meet and the place where; yet I can't think any penalty could arise, if they were to make alterations in these particulars." After the first session of the Rhode Island ratifying convention, held in March 1790 at South Kingstown, failed to adopt the Constitution, it voted to adjourn to Newport, at which session the state finally ratified. [38]

During the founding era, deliberative assemblies were held to possess the intrinsic power of excluding the public, in the name of protection against intruders and political pressures. Parliament had long conducted its business with doors closed, and the colonial assemblies likewise held their sessions in secret, partially to avoid interference from the royal governor. As is well known, the Philadelphia Convention adopted a rule providing that "nothing spoken in the House be printed, or otherwise published, or communicated without leave." [39]

Secrecy—"a proper precaution," George Mason thought—enabled the Philadelphia delegates to consider ideas without public commitment to any position and "to prevent mistakes and misrepresentation until the business shall have been completed." Although Jefferson and Henry spoke their displeasure afterward, there was little public complaint. In 1830, Madison left a visitor the impression that "no Constitution would ever have been adopted by the convention if the debates had been public." Spectators from the general public did attend the ratifying conventions, and today a national convention would be the subject of intense scrutiny. Pressure for open doors would emerge both externally, from an intrigued populace, and internally, from delegates in a position to achieve a national reputation overnight. While in theory a convention may shut out the public, this parliamentary privilege has, in modern times, been in practical terms abrogated.[40]

Though it has done so in proposed legislation, Congress cannot prescribe a time limit for the session: the framers assuredly did not intend to grant Congress life-and-death power over a convention. The Philadelphia delegates were "altogether uncertain when the Convention will rise," Washington drily noting that if "*some* good does not proceed from the Session, the defects cannot, with propriety, be charged to the hurry with which the business has been conducted." The convention demanded by the antifederalists would have met for a period unknowable in advance, a fact Jay exploited to urge ratification. If the states were to reject the Constitution "some time must pass before the measure of a new Convention, can be brought about," he wrote. "What time they may expend when met, cannot be divined."[41]

The power to define the session's length, then, belongs to the national convention exclusively. Although a national convention could in theory remain in session forever, practical constraints render that prospect all but impossible. As a convention dragged on past the limits of public support, the prestige of attending for delegates would diminish, as well as that of any amendment submitted for ratification. The Missouri constitutional convention of 1922–1923 lasted seventeen months, and saw most of its proposed amendments rejected by the voters out of disgust with the protracted term and expense. A Rhode Island convention, its draft constitution rejected at the polls, sat for fifty months, with adjournments, beginning December 8, 1964. On January 23, 1969, a senate resolution was sent to its officers requesting the convention to "terminate forthwith its ineffectual existence with its ever-increasing useless expenses to the state," and threatening to "invite the determination of the voters to put an end to said convention." The assembly dissolved on February 17, 1969.[42]

Delegate elections for a limited-issues national convention, for example a convention to propose a balanced-budget amendment, may be less like those for the conventions held to frame state constitutions than like those for the conventions authorized by Congress to decide on ratifying the amendment to repeal Prohibition. For the first and so far only time since the Constitution itself was ratified, Congress in 1933 specified that ratification was to be accomplished by state conventions rather than by the state legislatures. Twenty-five states elected delegates on a statewide or "at large" basis (the repealers or "wets" wanted to avoid gerrymandered districts that might favor "drys"), fourteen by districts, and four by a combination of the two. The number of delegates ranged from 3 in New Mexico's convention to 329 in Indiana's.[43]

Delegates were generally listed on the ballots according to their position, either "For Ratification" or "Against Ratification," although eight states provided for a third column listing uncommitted candidates, and two made no mention of positions. Five states required candidates to take a pledge that, if elected, they would vote consistently with the positions specified in their petitions of candidacy. Arizona's enabling act provided that a delegate failing to vote in accordance with that position would be guilty of a misdemeanor, with the errant vote thereupon voided and the office deemed vacant.[44]

Although the repeal conventions were theoretically independent of popular referenda, a feeling of obligation prevailed on the part of the delegates to register faithfully the declared sentiment of the electorate. Since there was no extended debate on the merits of repeal, the conventions were brief. None lasted more than a day, with New Hampshire's the shortest at seventeen minutes.[45] The deliberative latitude of a limited-issues national convention probably lies between the yes-or-no vote of the ratifying conventions and the unbounded sessions of the Revolution's plenary framing assemblies—rather close to that of the Annapolis Convention.

Preempting the Convention

Convention proponents like Everett Dirksen have assumed that an amendment proposed by Congress can be substituted for a convention when thirty-four petitions arrive. But if thirty-four applications are filed, the convention mechanism could theoretically be locked in with no brakes to be applied. Article V's requirement that Congress call a convention "on the Application of the Legislatures of two thirds of the several States" seems parallel to the final stage, in which amendments are "valid . . . when ratified by . . . three fourths of the several States." The apposite history and case law suggest that Congress, upon receipt of the necessary valid and timely applications, must go through with a convention call. An application cannot be withdrawn after the constitutional number have been submitted, just as a ratification cannot be rescinded after three fourths of the states have approved an amendment, because amendments then become "Part of this Constitution."[46]

Two kinds of circumstances only can defeat the obligation to hold a convention. First, if no more than the necessary number of applications has been submitted, and some applications give Congress the alternatives of calling a convention or itself proposing an amendment on the same subject, Congress may take advantage of the offer and propose the amendment, rendering the petitions obsolete. When Madison, in his *Report on the Virginia Resolutions*, referred to the states' power to obtain "a Convention for the same object," that object was *proposal* of an amendment to counter the Alien and Sedition Acts.[47]

Congress might, without waiting for the full complement of applications, propose the amendment and preempt the applications in that manner. This was the strategy when Congress proposed the Bill of Rights and (possibly) the seventeenth amendment. Congress's own proposal will obviate the applications only if the amendment represents a simple proposition. If the issue is complex and admits of many different approaches, as was true of slavery, a convention could be held even after Congress submitted an amendment. Nobel economics laureate James M. Buchanan and his associates have advocated a convention as the most plausible way to obtain a budget amendment: "if the convention route materializes, there is every reason why the states should block a congressional pre-emptive strike. Congress, logrolling across its special interests . . . , would provide the weakest possible version of a balanced budget amendment." Enacting a *statute* on the same subject as the pertinent amendment, however, would not dispose of the applications. A federal statute, unlike a constitutional amendment, can be repealed by Congress or voided by a court as unconstitutional. While a statute might defuse the convention campaign politically, the applications as a constitutional matter remain effective.[48]

Second, even if the requisite valid and effective applications are filed, a convention need not (to be sure, cannot) be held if the states decline to attend. The Constitution requires only that a convention be *called*, not that one actually be *held*. New York's 1789 convention application declared that the Constitution had been ratified by that state "in confidence that certain powers in [the Constitution] would not be exercised, until a Convention should have been called *and convened*." Framer Thomas FitzSimons said in the Pennsylvania legislature that "a [ratifying] convention was only recommended to the choice of the people, and if any of the counties had declined appointing deputies and disregarded the recommendation of the legislature, they might have done so without censure."[49]

There is ample precedent for refusal by the states. Of the five regional conventions on trade proposed by Congress in 1777, only two, in York and New Haven, were held. The Annapolis Convention was not well attended, and Rhode Island sent no delegates to Philadelphia. Not many states would turn down the opportunity to be represented at a national convention, but if for some reason each state agreed not to send delegates, all obligations to proceed further along the convention route would be terminated.

Suppose Congress, before or during a convention's session, proposes an amendment to discourage the convention from submitting one of its own. If the convention approves an amendment, may Congress retract its amendment after submission to the states? Congress's sole brush with the issue was inconclusive. In 1864, Senator Henry Anthony of Rhode Island proposed a joint resolution to repeal the Corwin amendment, sent out in 1861. No other action was ever taken, except that the Senate Judiciary Committee was discharged from its consideration, and the proposal died at the end of the Thirty-eighth Congress.[50]

If Congress could withdraw an amendment, the retraction would nullify the ratification of any state that had assented. Since the retraction would deny the states' ratifying power, which is secured by article V, the retraction would be invalid under the supremacy clause. Congress is therefore probably barred from rescinding an amendment it proposes after the first state has ratified; perhaps it is effectively barred after dispatch of the amendment to the states.[51]

An applicable parallel is the transmission of bills to the President for signing into law: an enrolled bill officially leaves the possession of Congress when it is delivered to the Office of the Executive Clerk at the

White House.[52] Certainly Congress may not withdraw a proposed amendment after the requisite number ratify, for amendments are "valid . . . as Part of this Constitution" when three fourths approve. For similar reasons Congress most likely can extend an application deadline in mid-course, but cannot significantly shorten a deadline once promulgated.

If Congress and the convention propose rival amendments on the same subject, the states have the option of ratifying both, either, or none. The Confederation Congress tried to add amendments to the Constitution before distribution to the states, but Madison explained that submitting two drafts, one the act of Congress and the other of the convention, would engender confusion because "Some States might ratify one & some the other of the plans." In the extremely unlikely event that both rival amendments were approved by the states, the courts probably have the competence to decide whether both can stand as harmonious provisions in the same Constitution.[53] Rival amendments are not that farfetched in view of the nation's history: the scenario was envisioned by Lincoln in his first inaugural address, when he gave a halfhearted blessing to a convention for a compromise amendment on slavery, while Congress's own Corwin amendment was already circulating among the states.

The Judicial Power

Whether courts may entertain cases involving convention procedures is critical to the operation of the process, for some bills give sole power of review to Congress, making it the judge in its own case. Senator Ervin's 1967 bill forbids court review of any congressional determination of whether a convention-proposed amendment came within the call, and makes each state the final arbiter of its own application's validity. The Hatch bill, however, does provide for judicial review in the Supreme Court. Probably a convention-related suit would come under the Supreme Court's appellate jurisdiction, to which Congress has the power to make exceptions. The Court, however, can generally construe statutory curbs to get around jurisdictional limitations, if necessary to vindicate constitutional rights.[54]

Even granting the Court's jurisdictional competence, exclusion may be urged on the authority of *Coleman v. Miller*, which relied heavily on the political question doctrine to acknowledge Congress's claimed power to determine an amendment's seasonable ratification. The concurring opinion of Justice Black, joined by Justices Roberts, Frankfurter, and Douglas, went further than that of the Court in ceding dominion of article V, insisting that the article gives "[u]ndivided control" of the amending process to Congress.[55]

The political question doctrine counsels judicial abstention when the issue presented is appropriately resolved by the political departments of the federal government, either Congress or (especially in foreign affairs) the President. It is a determination that an issue is not, as Justice Felix Frankfurter said, "appropriate for disposition by judges," either because of constitutional factors militating in favor of resolution by another branch of government, or because the problem is by nature intractable to the methods of judicial decisionmaking—a "lack of judicially . . . manageable standards."[56]

Some of the founders, with no dissent recorded, expected the courts to aid in maintaining the integrity of the amending process. At Philadelphia, Gouverneur Morris advised: "If the Confederation is to be pursued no alteration can be made without the unanimous consent of the Legislatures: Legislative alterations not conformable to the federal compact, would clearly not be valid. The Judges would consider them as null & void."[57] In *Hollingsworth v. Virginia* a decade later, the Supreme Court pronounced the eleventh amendment "constitutionally adopted," rejecting the allegation that it "has not been proposed in the form prescribed by the Constitution, and, therefore, it is void." Present to hear the case, according to the minutes, were four Associate Justices: William Paterson, New Jersey's wartime attorney general and Philadelphia delegate; William Cushing, vice president of the Massachusetts ratifying convention; James Iredell, the North Carolina ratifier; and Samuel Chase, an antifederalist at Maryland's ratifying convention.[58]

The court system established by article III of the Constitution is in marked contrast to the virtual absence of an effective judiciary in the pre-adoption era. Wrote Oliver Ellsworth, Connecticut delegate, ratifier, and third Chief Justice of the United States: "Congress under the old Confederation had power to ordain and resolve, but having no judicial or executive of their own, their most solemn resolves were totally disregarded." During the Revolution, Congress created standing committees of its members to hear appeals from admiralty cases decided in the state courts, and article IX of the Confederation authorized

Congress to appoint tribunals for deciding piracy cases as well as boundary disputes between the states. The fate of this first experiment in a federal judiciary was sealed when the states refused to enforce judgments that reversed their own courts' decisions.[59]

Judicial review is of special value when convention procedures are involved, as Laurence Tribe has observed, since the convention method was intended to bypass Congress. Judicial enforcement of the amendment process furthers the main purpose of the clause, which is to ensure orderly political change, or "establishing good government from reflection and choice," as Hamilton wrote in the opening number of *The Federalist*, rather than from "accident and force." In his famous *Marbury v. Madison* opinion, Chief Justice John Marshall rhetorically asked: "To what purpose are powers limited, and to what purpose is that limitation committed to writing, if these limits may, at any time, be passed by those intended to be restrained?"[60]

Sensibly, Tribe argues that the courts would not be bound to treat an amendment as part of the Constitution if Congress determined that thirty-five ratifying states sufficed as the three fourths of the fifty states required by article V, or if Congress decided that senators from nonratifying states could vote as the functional equivalents of the state legislatures. Hence while courts will not review a state legislature's certification that it has in fact applied, the question whether the state— and Congress in accepting or rejecting the application—followed procedures recognized by article V is, Justice Stevens has suggested, "a question the Court will answer."[61]

The *Coleman* retreat from the judicial obligation, as Marshall put it, "to say what the law is," moreover, is an aberration in the long history of article V questions that have been presented to and decided by the Court. That history begins as early as 1798, with *Hollingsworth*, and despite hints that the validity of adopted amendments may be unreviewable,[62] the Supreme Court has consistently upheld the fifteenth amendment against charges that it was illegally coerced as a war measure.[63] The Court affirmed the eighteenth amendment's validity "by lawful proposal and ratification" in the face of arguments that its subject matter was beyond the amending power of Congress, and that it was constitutionally required to be ratified by state conventions.[64] Another case stemming from adoption of the eighteenth amendment invalidated a state provision that made ratification dependent on a popular referendum.[65] Justice Brandeis framed the issue for the Court in *Leser v.*

Garnett: "Whether the Nineteenth Amendment has become part of the Federal Constitution is the question presented for decision."[66]

The lower federal courts also have ruled on the validity of amendments to the Constitution,[67] and held justiciable (subject to court review) other article V questions, including those pertaining to the convention route.[68] State courts likewise have held judicially reviewable issues presented by the application stage,[69] having long held justiciable questions relating to amendment of their respective state constitutions.[70] One federal court decided that a provision of Louisiana's constitution, a constitution that had been adopted by convention, went beyond the terms of the convention call and on that basis invalidated the provision.[71]

The hands-off posture of the four concurring justices in *Coleman* has never been adopted by a majority of the Supreme Court, and so is not binding precedent. The backers of the initiative requiring the California legislature to submit an application for a balanced-budget convention had argued that the state court lacked authority to decide the issue since the question related to amending the federal Constitution and was therefore, on the authority of *Coleman*, a political question. Noting that the *Coleman* concurrence did not speak for a majority, Justice Rehnquist answered: "however this Court would presently resolve the issues raised in the *Coleman* case, I do not think a majority would subscribe to applicants' expansive reading of the 'political question' doctrine in connection with the amending process."[72]

The fallacy of the *Coleman* justices was in lumping together two different kinds of amending issues and pronouncing them both nonjusticiable. One kind is timeliness: since a multiplicity of social, political, and economic factors will determine whether a proposal is still viable, the answer will differ from amendment to amendment, and seems peculiarly suited for legislative consideration. The other kind is procedural correctness. Thus, whether seven years is a reasonable ratification deadline is a question of the first type; whether Congress in fact has the power to set the deadline is a question of the second. "Where the alteration purports to be made along the lines of a procedural method" specified in a constitution, wrote Melville Fuller Weston, "there is a standard which the court can apply and, by so doing, it can perceive judicially whether or not the change has followed the prescribed lines. If it has, there is no difficulty in pronouncing as a matter of law its accomplishment."[73] The congressional determinations of timeliness have been left alone by the courts, but the procedural issues—the majority needed to ratify, whether an application may be compelled by initiative—the courts have properly reclaimed.

If Congress Refuses

The duty of Congress to call a convention may be viewed alternatively as the right to have a convention called. In the event of congressional noncompliance with the obligations of article V, that right may be vindicated in the courts. Suit would be brought after Congress determined that the conditions for a call had not been met: one or more applications were incorrect in form, or stale, or did not agree in subject matter with the rest. Or, equally likely, Congress would have ignored the petitions entirely. The suit would probably ask the federal court to order Congress to make the necessary determinations and, upon ascertaining that all requirements have been satisfied, to call a convention or in the alternative to propose the amendment.[74]

Article V's reference to the state legislatures as the applying agents would be construed to endow them with standing—that is, eligibility to bring suit because of injury traceable to the defendant's unlawful conduct, a requirement inferred by the courts from article III—and to exclude other possible litigants such as the governors, the President, members of the general public, or a faction of Congress.[75] No pro-convention member of Congress willing to bring suit against the majority could surmount the barriers erected by the courts, and individual members of the public would be ineligible as well.[76] Only the state legislatures, specifically those that had filed applications, would have standing to sue: only they could allege that their constitutionally guaranteed amending powers had been infringed by the inaction of Congress.[77] The defendants in a suit against a recalcitrant Congress would be the officers charged with tabulating the applications and possibly members of Congress themselves.[78]

In *Powell v. McCormack*, Adam Clayton Powell, Jr., elected to the House of Representatives, was barred by the House from taking his seat in response to allegations of crime and corruption. The House claimed the right to exclude Powell under its power to judge the qualifications of its members. Rejecting the contention that the case presented a nonjusticiable political question, a unanimous Supreme Court (including

Justice Black, thirty years after *Coleman*) declared Powell's exclusion unconstitutional. With *Powell* as precedent in a convention suit, relief might well be available against Congress itself, since the speech or debate clause protects only "legitimate legislative activity," where congressional deliberation proper is involved.[79] That protection does not extend to nondiscretionary duties, which by definition do not require, in fact forbid, congressional judgments on the merits. Even if the courts dismissed the suit against members of Congress, relief issued against ministerial officials (such as the Clerk of the House) would likely force Congress to act, since it is unimaginable that Congress would not want a say in drafting a convention call.[80]

If Congress refused to obey a court order, further judicial relief probably would be unobtainable, although the Supreme Court has pronounced the suggestion of such disobedience "inadmissible." Senator Roman Hruska was of the opinion that if Congress ignored an order to issue a call, the Supreme Court "could itself order the Convention." Yet article V says that "*Congress . . .* shall call a Convention," and a definite procedure was envisaged. If "a convention should not be obtained," said Representative Thomas Tucker in August 1789, the government would lose "the confidence and support of the people." The sole remaining, yet probably most decisive, recourse would be public opinion, in particular as demonstrated at the polls. At the point where voting for a convention is seen as essential to an incumbent's survival, a call or proposal would seem near certain.[81]

The President's Veto

Presidents have been involved in major convention campaigns ever since Washington, in his first inaugural address (ghostwritten by Madison), asked Congress to deflect the antifederalists' drive by proposing amendments that manifest "a reverence for the characteristic rights of freemen" but do not "endanger the benefits of an United and effective Government." Andrew Jackson fought a two-pronged war against nullification and a convention; Buchanan bequeathed the dilemma to Lincoln. State legislators, ordinarily receptive to presidential gratitude, have tended to act independently of the White House; New Hampshire snubbed Carter by filing a budget application, while Michigan defied Reagan's wishes by voting one down.[82]

A president hostile to the idea or subject matter of a prospective convention might threaten to veto any call, secure in the knowledge that most scholarship supports that position.[83] Yet the constitutional text and history show that the President remains outside the convention, indeed the entire amendment, route. What may be the only surviving contemporary analysis of the issue appeared in a federalist newspaper essay:

It is provided, in the clearest words, that Congress shall be *obliged* to call a convention on the application of two thirds of the legislatures . . . . It must therefore be evident to every candid man, that two-thirds of the states can *always* procure a general convention for the purpose of amending the constitution, and that three-fourths of them can introduce those amendments into the constitution, although the President, Senate and Federal-House of Representatives, should be *unanimously* opposed to each and all of them.

It does not seem to have been alleged during ratification that the convention clause was a sham on the ground that the President could block desired amendments. George Mason's published pamphlet, listing his "Objections to this Constitution of Government," does not include that charge.[84]

In the leading case, *Hollingsworth v. Virginia* (1798), the Supreme Court held the eleventh amendment "constitutionally adopted," although the amendment had not been presented for President Washington's approval. The Court's terse, unanimous opinion gives no hint of the reasoning behind the result, but Attorney General Charles Lee remarked during oral argument that

the same course [has] been pursued relative to all the other amendments, that have been adopted[.] And the case of amendments is evidently a substantive act, unconnected with the ordinary business of legislation, and not within the policy, or terms, of investing the President with a qualified negative on the acts and resolutions of Congress.[85]

At this point Justice Chase interjected his agreement: "The negative of the President applies only to the ordinary cases of legislation: He has nothing to do with the proposition, or adoption, of amendments to the Constitution." While *Hollingsworth* turned on the necessity of presidential approval for a proposed amendment rather than for a convention call, Chase's broad labeling of the "case of amendments" as distinct from "the business of legislation" brings the convention call under the *Hollingsworth* umbrella.[86]

Hollingsworth's critics maintain that a convention call is a statutory measure and therefore subject to the veto. Under the presentment clauses of article I:

> *Every Bill which shall have passed the House of Representatives and the Senate, shall, before it become a Law, be presented to the President of the United States;* If he approve he shall sign it, but if not he shall return it, with his Objections to that House in which it shall have originated. . . .
>
> *Every Order, Resolution, or Vote* to which the Concurrence of the Senate and House of Representatives may be necessary (except on a question of Adjournment) *shall be presented to the President of the United States; and before the Same shall take Effect, shall be approved by him,* or being disapproved by him, shall be repassed by two thirds of the Senate and House of Representatives.

Both clauses, as the italicized words show, cover measures intended to become laws, binding enactments of statutory force. Their origin lies in the eighth resolution of the Virginia Plan, which provided for a council of revision empowered "to examine every act of the National Legislature before it shall operate." The evolution of the presentment clauses at the convention illustrates the delegates' consistent understanding that the presidential negative—"veto" occurs nowhere in the Constitution—applies only to measures that would be of legal effect immediately upon passage by Congress. [87]

The second presentment clause was added at Madison's suggestion in order to prevent evasion of the executive veto for laws that might be proposed not as bills but "under the form and name of Resolutions, votes &c." The clause, said Madison, would put "votes, Resolutions &c. on a footing with Bills." As has been shown, the resolution of Congress issued to call a convention is not a statutory enactment. Since the presentment clauses are restricted to statutes, they do not apply to the convention call, which is therefore not subject to the President's veto. [88]

Similarly, amendments proposed by Congress or a convention are not subject to the veto. Amendments are intended to become legally binding, but as issued by Congress remain proposals until ratified by the states. In *The Federalist* Hamilton wrote that the President's veto "furnishes an additional security against the enaction of improper laws," but constitutional amendments become effective only with the states' approval: "three fourths must ratify." Justice Chase's remark in *Hollingsworth* is therefore to the point, and *Hollingsworth* itself rightly decided. [89]

To be sure, presentment to the President literally applies to all resolutions requiring the concurrence of both houses, but this reading must be outweighed by the foregoing considerations and the distinct use of "pass" in article I (including the presentment clauses) versus the use of "propose" in article V (suggesting an incomplete activity). The amending provision was worked out for the most part at the end of the convention, which, as Madison wrote long afterward, "was not exempt from a degree of the hurrying influence produced by fatigue and impatience in all such Bodies."[90]

After *Hollingsworth*, as before, Congress held the President's signature unnecessary for proposal. The twelfth amendment was submitted in 1803 without President Jefferson's signature, and an amendment unsuccessfully proposed in 1810, providing that acceptance of a foreign title would cause forfeiture of United States citizenship, was not transmitted to President Madison. In the first widely used systematic treatise on the Constitution, William Rawle wrote that the President "has even less to do in respect to alterations of the Constitution than the two houses have. . . . [I]f the two houses resolve to submit one of them, his concurrence in their so doing is not required, and perhaps would not be allowed." Rawle cites *Hollingsworth*, and as counsel for the defeated side was specially qualified to explain its significance.[91]

A convention campaign is only as strong as the public opinion behind it, and members of Congress survive by being sensitive to the depth and direction of that opinion. Congress will respond to a drive in its end stages after it determines the least radical, nonalienating, step: inaction (as in 1929 and 1963), rejection of applications, a statute or amendment, or a convention call. In the various decision points along the route, whether to press for an amendment, how long the applications stay effective, even whether delegates will attend if a call is indeed issued, the convention process is revealed not as an uncontrollable monster that acts unthinkingly, but as a mechanism that, like the others created by the Constitution, is alive to public support and will not operate without it. John Marshall said, "The people made the constitution, and the people can unmake it. It is the creature of their will, and lives only by their will." Nothing of the first constitutional magnitude will happen if a considerable majority of the American nation, after publicized and extended debate in the state and national capitals, remains opposed.[92]

7

The Convention's Proposing Agenda

By far the most controverted article V issue, the issue at the core of the ability of Congress or the states to control the procedure—and consequently of the leverage the states actually have against Congress—is whether a national convention is limited to proposing the amendments described in the state applications. Extensive commentary has grown around the issue of the convention's proposing agenda; the ABA committee concluded that "a convention could be convened for a specific purpose and that, once convened, it would have no authority to exceed that purpose."[1] The Massachusetts supreme court, alone among courts in looking at the issue, has said: "It is for Congress or for the convention to decide whether and to what extent to limit the agenda of the convention." The illimitability theory currently holds the edge among constitutional scholars.[2]

Somewhere in the middle is Justice Scalia, who has endorsed a balanced-budget convention. Denying he seeks "an open convention for its own sake, to expose the whole system to possible change," Scalia was "willing to run the risk of an open convention to get the changes that are wanted . . . , even with respect to the limited proposal of financial responsibility at the federal level. I think that risk is worth taking. It is not much of a risk. Three-quarters of the states would have to ratify whatever came out of the convention."[3]

Contemporary Testimony

Little concerning the scope of a national convention survives from the ratification debates. The only directly pertinent remarks are those of Wilson Cary Nicholas at the Virginia convention. Answering Patrick Henry's criticism that article V is overly difficult to use, Nicholas maintained that even if Congress withheld an amendment, another method is available:

> The conventions which shall be so called will have their deliberations confined to a few points; no local interest to divert their attention; nothing but the necessary alterations. They will have many advantages over the last Convention. No experiments to devise; the general and fundamental regulations being already laid down.[4]

It is not clear whether Nicholas is asserting that future conventions will be limited to "the necessary alterations" as a constitutional requirement or simply as the most realistic course of events.

In a 1788 letter Silas Lee, a critic-turned-supporter of the Constitution, declared that the commission of the Philadelphia Convention was a legal check on the delegates' powers:

> I hope the precedent of the late federal Convention will not be followed by the next that may be appointed; viz instead of revising or amending this in certain parts, which may be found inconvenient, they will not with one Stroke wipe the whole away, as was the fate of the old Confederation, & propose a new one . . . . [Y]ou seem to think . . . that every General Convention will propose a plan of their own—notwithstanding, I suppose you must mean, their commission impowers them only to amend—This I have ever understood was the fact in the late federal convention[.] But altho compossd of the first characters in the Continent I, by no means, think it the *less unwarrantable* on that account.[5]

In Maryland just after ratification, two federalist writers argued for Congress as the agent to introduce amendments, rather than the convention sought by critics of the new government. "A Federalist" wrote:

> The *antifederals* are for the different assemblies *applying* to congress to call a convention to propose amendments.
>
> The *federals* are opposed to this mode of obtaining amendments as improper, unnecessary and hazardous. *Improper*, because neither the state assemblies nor congress can confine the deliberations of the convention to certain enumerated amendments. A convention, whenever called, will have a general power to alter every part of the system, and, if they please, to propose the old articles of confederation. *Unnecessary*, because amendments can be [o]btained in an *easier* and *less expensive mode. Hazardous*, from our not knowing what amendments or changes in the constitution may be proposed.

Similar perils were depicted by "A.B." a few days later:

The first mode [proposal by Congress] is the gentlest and most rational . . . . The second mode, from its very nature, can only be intended to be used when the constitution shall be found, by experience, to be so defective as to require a thorough and radical reform. It seems moreover to be particularly meant to guard the *rights* of the state-assemblies, by vesting them with a power to defend themselves from the encroachments of Congress, by means of a convention, which they cannot be denied. The first mode therefore seems established to remedy partial evils, the last to remedy general defects.

Should a general convention be called, neither the legislatures, nor Congress, can limit their powers or define the amendments for their deliberation. But, besides the risk of creating a body of men who may new-model the constitution, years would be consumed in the experiment [between the application and ratification stages].[6]

Possibly the two Maryland essayists confused, unintentionally or otherwise, the federal article V convention with the plenary (and revolutionary) convention that had framed Maryland's charter in 1776. Both writers were criticizing particular amendments favored by the antis.

From Paris on Christmas Day 1788, Jefferson described the status of the campaign for amendments:

Virginia and Massachusets had preferred this method of amendment, that is to say, desiring Congress to propose specific amendments to the several legislatures, which is one of the modes of amendment provided in the new constitution. In this way nothing can be touched but the parts specifically pointed out. New York has written circular letters to the legislatures to adopt the other mode of amendment, provided also by the constitution that is to say to assemble another federal convention. In this way the whole fabric could be submitted to alteration.[7]

As with Wilson Nicholas, it is not clear whether Jefferson is predicting the likely outcome ("could be submitted . . .") or giving article V a legal interpretation.

On July 21, 1789, Elbridge Gerry pressed the House of Representatives to consider the various proposals of the state ratifying conventions for amendments to the Constitution. Fisher Ames "was sorry to hear an intention avowed by his colleague, of considering every part of the frame of this constitution. It was the same as forming themselves into a convention of the United States."[8] The contemporary discussion that has come down oscillates between the view that conventions are limitable to specific topics (Silas Lee) and that they are plenary (Fisher Ames) or may ignore restrictions (the Maryland writers and Jefferson). But the fullest analysis of amendments proposed by a convention acting *ultra vires*, beyond its allotted powers, came from the federalists in defending the Constitution itself.

The Philadelphia Precedent

The action of the Philadelphia Convention in producing a new constitution despite having been called by Congress "for the sole and express purpose of revising the Articles of Confederation" is the most cited precedent for adding *ultra vires* amendments issued by an article V convention. The February 21 call anticipated amendments to the Confederation ratified pursuant to article XIII (probably a cluster of amendments like those of the 1786 "Grand Committee"), for it proclaimed that "there is provision in the Articles of Confederation and perpetual Union for making alterations therein," and all amendments were to be "agreed to in Congress" as well as the state legislatures. This was the understanding, with varying degress of explicitness, of all the appointing states.[9]

The Constitution was first read in Congress, meeting in New York, on September 20, 1787, and in the week before issuance of the transmittal order the reach of the Philadelphia Convention's powers was centrally in issue. As Nathan Dane observed, the new Constitution "appears to be intended as an entire system in itself, and not as any part of, or alteration in the Articles of Confederation." The compromise of September 28, to send a brief resolution to the states expressing neither approval nor disapproval, was a federalist victory, for the Constitution's advocates knew that the simple fact of transmission by Congress would be considered a mark of assent. "The people do not scrutinize terms," wrote Edward Carrington, a stout federalist representing Virginia; "the unanimity of Congress in recommending a measure to their consideration, naturally implies approbation."[10]

Opposition premised on the Constitution's *ultra vires* aspects continued. The objections were twofold: first, that the convention had been empowered only to propose amendments to the existing Confederation, not create an entire new Constitution; second, that adoption required the approval of Congress and all thirteen state legislatures, and would not be satisfied by substituting nine conventions. "The federal Convention ought to have amended the old system," Patrick Henry argued, because "for this purpose they were solely delegated; the object of their mission extended to no other consideration." In a widely read pamphlet, Mercy

Otis Warren fulminated: "the article which declares the ratification of nine states sufficient . . . is a subversion of the union of the confederated states."[11]

The federalists rebutted the charges with three defenses. Each was capsulized in Madison's *Federalist* Essay 40, which considered "whether the Convention were authorised to frame and propose this . . . Constitution." First, the Constitution was within the Confederation: the credentials issued to the delegates by their home legislatures authorized them "to frame a national government, adequate to the exigencies of government and of the Union." Second, the Confederation could not have been violated, for it was no longer in existence or else not legally binding (although even the first argument implied that the Articles were dispensable if need be). At the Virginia convention Randolph said: "The Confederation is gone; it has no authority."[12]

Third, even if the Confederation were binding and violated, ratification by the "supreme authority," the people as assembled in state ratifying conventions, would, said Madison, "blot out all antecedent errors and irregularities." Edmund Pendleton, federalist and chief judge of Virginia's chancery court, said while president of the state ratifying convention: "Suppose the paper on your table dropped from one of the planets; the people found it, and sent us here to consider whether it was proper for their adoption; must we not obey them?"[13]

It is this third argument, that subsequent ratification cures antecedent irregularities, which suggests *ultra vires* amendments proposed by an article V convention, if ratified by three fourths of the states, would become ensconced as part of the Constitution. This is exactly what concerned Madison about "the project of another general Convention," for an antifederalist convention would attract delegates "of insidious views, who under the mask of seeking alterations popular in some parts but inadmissible in other parts of the Union might have a dangerous opportunity of sapping the very foundations of the fabric." Another convention, even if nominally limited to amendments specified in the applications, could at that time easily have ridden roughshod over its commission, as the Philadelphia Convention had just done. "If we should accede to this system," said antifederalist William Lenoir, "it may be thought proper, by a few designing persons, to destroy it, in a future age, in the same manner that the old system is laid aside."[14]

The decision to provide for ratification of the Constitution by specially elected conventions rather than by the state legislatures was in part an admission by the Philadelphia Convention that it had gone outside its powers and required uncontestable sanction. "The people," said Madison, were "the fountain of all power, and by resorting to them, all difficulties were got over." Hence "the Constitution is to be founded on the assent and ratification of the people of America, given by deputies elected for the special purpose."[15]

With Essay 40's concession that in the ratification clause, article VII, "the Convention have departed from the tenor of their commission," Madison blandly admitted the unconstitutionality of the proposal. Even if "the Convention were neither authorised by their commission, nor justified by circumstances, in proposing a Constitution," rejection was not warranted: "The prudent enquiry" is "not so much *from whom* the advice comes, as whether the advice *be good*." In so counseling disregard for article XIII of the Confederation, Madison also counseled disregard for all enacted law. "There is no position which depends on clearer principles," wrote Hamilton in Essay 78, "than that every act of a delegated authority, contrary to the tenor of the commission under which it is exercised, is void."[16]

But Madison's appeal is not to legality or constitutionality; it is rather to extraconstitutional legitimacy. The federalists would have agreed with Clinton Rossiter's assessment of the delegates' work: "Their actions were, in the narrow sense, illegal under the terms of the Articles of Confederation; they also were, in the broad sense, legitimate under the principles of the American Revolution—and were in fact sparked by a desire to bring it to fruition." Rejecting the Constitution merely because it was *ultra vires*, said Madison, quoting the Declaration of Independence, "would render nominal and nugatory, the transcendent and precious right of the people to 'abolish or alter their governments as to them shall seem most likely to effect their safety and happiness.'"[17] Quoting the Declaration (Jefferson wrote "alter or abolish") signaled the Constitution's revolutionary character insofar as it breached the existing legal order. That which is transcended is the positive law: the Constitution was to supersede the Confederation, just as the Declaration announced the end of Parliament's jurisdiction over the colonies.[18]

The decade between the Confederation and the Constitution was one of experimentation, when the American concept of constitutionality itself was still being defined. Oliver Ellsworth said at Philadelphia that "a new sett of ideas seemed to have crept in since the articles of Confederation were established. Conventions of the people," instead of the regular state legislatures, "were not then thought of" as competent to effect constitutional change. Virginia's 1776 constitution, wrote Jefferson in the 1780s, "was formed when we were new and unexperienced in the science of government."[19] Consequently, Madison could point to a long list of unconstitutional, *ultra vires* actions allowed by Congress during the Confederation era, and reasonably expect that the same factors that countenanced a breach then would do so once more:

First, strictly considered, the 1785 Mount Vernon Conference results were unconstitutional, for (aside from the defective representation) article VI of the Confederation prohibited two or more states from entering into "any treaty, confederation, or alliance, whatever, between them, without the consent of . . . Congress." The Mount Vernon compact, never submitted to Congress for approval, was given an impeccable imprimatur by Washington's attendance, a service he performed again at Philadelphia.[20]

Second, as Madison broadly hinted in *Federalist* 40 by referring to the revolutionary origins of the Continental Congress, the new Constitution was no less legitimate than the federal charter then in effect, whose strictures the Philadelphia delegates stood accused of violating.[21] The Continental Congress, Madison reminded his readers, had issued "*informal and unauthorised propositions* . . . to the people . . . for their safety and happiness." The Continental Congress had arisen out of opposition to royal authority, and most delegates to the First and Second Continental Congresses were chosen by self-constituted—revolutionary—assemblies and conventions, or by polling freeholders, rather than appointed by the regular colonial legislatures. The resolutions of Congress in 1775 and 1776 had led to the formation of the early state constitutions; the Confederation itself, as a result, was proposed as well as ratified by legislatures that were technically unconstitutional. Ratification of the Articles of Confederation did indeed "blot out . . . irregularities" relating to the establishment of the Confederation. Henry Knox, to be President Washington's Secretary of War, wrote in January 1787: "Should the Convention agree on some continental constitution and propose the great outlines" without congressional approval but "directly to . . . the respective Legislatures . . . , would not this to all intents and purposes be a government derived from the people and assented to by them as much as they assented to the confederation?"[22]

Third, Congress itself had acted *ultra vires* on numerous occasions.

Shortly after the Philadelphia Convention ended, Madison complained that "Congress had never scrupled to recommend measures foreign to their Constitutional functions, whenever the Public good seemed to require it; and had in several instances . . . exercised assumed powers of a very high & delicate nature, under motives infinitely less urgent than the present state of our affairs." Madison was referring to "the establishment of the new Western Governments" by measures such as the Northwest Ordinance of 1787. Nothing in the Articles allowed Congress to organize the territories into self-governing entities or admit them into the Union.[23]

Finally, even prior to 1787, the Confederation's amending procedure had been unconstitutionally altered. Congress had reduced the unanimity requirement of article XIII to excuse Georgia from acting on the 1781 impost amendment, having determined that "the war may prevent the legislatures of some of these states from assembling," and resolved that the amendment would become effective "so soon as all the states, whose legislatures shall and may assemble, shall consent." Virginia briefly considered empowering Congress to implement the 1783 impost amendment on the ratification of twelve states, to excuse Rhode Island. In January 1787, Jay told Washington of his preference for a convention to "make such alterations" in the Confederation "as to them should appear necessary and proper, and which being by them ordained and published should have the same force and obligation which all or any of the present articles now have."[24]

It was therefore not outlandish to think of Congress and the states as permissibly effecting a change in the Confederation's amending procedure. Before the Philadelphia Convention sat, Stephen Higginson became the first to recommend that the new Constitution be ratified by conventions in nine states. Higginson knew his proposal violated the letter of article XIII: "By the conformity of the States to such a recommendation, in appointing their separate [ratifying] Conventions . . . they will implicitly and clearly, if not in a sense explicitly consent to an alteration, and particularly such as may be agreed to by nine of those Conventions." Higginson knew that he advocated a sharp practice: "the consent of the States . . . may possibly be obtained in this way when they may not intend it, and perhaps without their knowing it at the time; but having in any way gained it, and the Constitution reported being ratified by Congress, a small minority may then clamour . . . in vain."[25]

Complicating matters was the fact that insistence on adhering to the letter of the Confederation was itself politically motivated. William Paterson's biographer concedes that the stress laid on following the Confederation at Philadelphia was not only an argument from legal principle but also a bargaining ploy by small-state delegates to ensure that equality of state representation was kept in at least one house of the legislature. Once he achieved his goal, Paterson ceased his technical objections and signed the Constitution.[26]

The Checking Power of Congress

A national convention, like its Annapolis predecessor, would not necessarily propose any amendments at all. Randolph assured an apprehensive Madison that the delegates at a second convention "may not concur in any particular correction of the new theory," in which case "the constitution remains as it is." But it is likelier that a convention would seek to exercise power to the utmost, Senator Patrick Leahy has written, inasmuch as "it would plausibly be a body with a greater sense of urgency to effect changes in the Constitution, because of its limited life, and a greater sense of mission" among the members, who "need not stand for reelection." And it is just as likely that Congress would seek at every turn to curb the convention's influence out of antipathy to a rival power center and disapproval of a remedy so distasteful that it acceded to an unprecedented convention rather than proposal.[27]

Of the South Carolina nullification convention's 1833 session, a state judge the next year addressed modern concerns when he

observed, that the Convention was convened for definite objects, expressed and designated in the act which authorised it, and all who are familiar with its history know, that the convocation of it was long and successfully opposed, on a doubt suggested that its powers could not be limited—apprehensions were entertained that the unequal parish Representation in the Legislature would be corrected, and it was not until this doubt was removed that the powers of a Convention might be limited, that the Legislature could be prevailed on to pass an act calling a convention.

But as Theodore Sorensen said at the Ervin bill hearings in 1967:

No matter how many and how sincere are the assurances from the backers of a new Convention that their sole concern is reapportionment, no one can safely assume that the delegates to such a Convention, once seated and in action, would wish to go home without trying their hand at improving many parts of this delicately balanced document. All of us know of the pressures that will then build up to amend the Bill of Rights, to halt supposed pampering of the criminally accused, to stop so-called abuses of the fifth amendment, to limit free speech for the disloyal, to reopen the wars between church and state, to limit the Supreme Court's jurisdiction or the President's veto power or the congressional warmaking authority.

It is the Sorensen view that animates discussions of article V, and indeed the South Carolina court decided that the convention had strayed from its mandate, the consideration of means of redress against the tariff, in prescribing for militia officers an oath of "true allegiance" to South Carolina and only "obedience," a less exacting duty, to the federal government. [28]

The trend toward aggrandizement of power at a convention is supported by modern experience in the states. When delegates are presented with the choice of writing a new constitution or submitting a number of amendments to the existing document, they have exhibited a desire to become a part of history by framing a new constitution. The proposed new charter for New York was defeated in 1967 because the voters rejected the whole package rather than accept several controversial provisions, notably a repeal of the ban on state aid to parochial schools. [29]

Any amendments that emerge from a national convention are proposals only, not binding until ratified by thirty-eight states. Whether a national convention is effectively limited to the amendments specified in the triggering applications, assuming the Constitution is otherwise followed, depends on the fate *ultra vires* amendments meet at the hands of Congress and the courts.

Congress has the power to check *ultra vires* amendments by refusing to select for them "one or the other Mode of Ratification," either legislature or special convention. Congress alone is charged with determining the mode of ratification of all proposed amendments, by settled (and probably correct) practice with a two-thirds vote. The framers did not, as far as the record shows, debate the propriety of having Congress determine the ratification method for amendments proposed by a convention, but the arrangement did not likely go unnoticed by the strong nationalists, including Hamilton and Madison, on the Committee of Style. [30]

Congress need not make the selection if the amendment is *ultra vires*, or if it requires no ratification or ratification by a reduced number of states, for submission would lack constitutional sanction. Hence Congress, though not expressly required to pass on the validity of convention-sponsored amendments, would surely make technical validity a de facto prerequisite for ratification.[31]

Under no circumstances does Congress decide the content of the amendments. The Constitution was sent by the delegates to the Confederation Congress not "for their approbation" (the convention in fact deleted that language) but, as Madison explained, "merely as a matter of form and respect." Wrote North Carolina delegate Hugh Williamson to James Iredell on the ratifying conventions: "Congress can have nothing to do with it but put the question—pass or not pass." The convention clause was predicated on getting around a Congress that, as George Mason suspected, would "refuse their consent." For Congress to alter materially an amendment would be to transform a convention-proposed amendment into a Congress-proposed amendment. The revised measure would require a two-thirds vote of each house for submission to the states, not the simple majority used for determinations of technical validity.[32]

Congress cannot thwart the adoption of duly proposed amendments by assigning a prohibitively short ratification deadline. Contrary to the assertion in *Dillon v. Gloss* that Congress's power to fix a ratification time limit was "an incident of its power to designate the mode of ratification," the framers regarded the deadline-setting power as distinct from that of choosing the mode of ratification; hence a grant of one power to Congress does not automatically include a grant of the other. A draft James Wilson prepared at Philadelphia while on the Committee of Detail distinguishes under separate headings "The Manner of Ratification" from "What Day shall be appointed for the States to give an Answer." Since the power to set the deadline is not mentioned in the Constitution, that power, for convention-originated amendments, belongs not to Congress but to the convention. The Revolution-era constitutional conventions of Massachusetts and New Hampshire, which employed ratification procedures, set their own deadlines.[33]

If Congress delayed or refused to select a ratification mode, an attending state could bring suit to compel performance. The court would order Congress to determine the amendment's validity if that had not been done. If the reason offered by Congress for nonselection was that the amendment was nonconforming, quite possibly the court would make the determination itself and, if it upheld the amendment, direct Congress to choose a mode and submit the measure for ratification. For its part, if a convention should try to force an amendment through the states without obtaining a congressional decision on the mode of ratification, the amendment—whether within the convention's mandate or not—would remain invalid. Likewise invalid would be an amendment requiring no ratification, or ratification by a reduced number of states. If a convention submitted a measure purporting to be legislation binding without passage by Congress, Congress would be able to obtain an injunction to prevent enforcement, since it could allege injury to its lawmaking powers. At the first session of the 1790 Rhode Island ratifying convention, delegate Henry Marchant, later a federal judge, said: "If we look into the Act by which we met we shall find why & how we met here. We have no Legislative Power. Have no other Powers than as Trustees for the Busin[ess]."[34]

The Amendments in the Courts

Congress may be expected to keep an eye on the proceedings, taking the narrowest possible view of what a validly proposed amendment would be. Still, an *ultra vires* amendment favored by a majority but less than two thirds of Congress might slip through under an excessively lenient interpretation of the convention's mandate. (An amendment to allow organized spoken prayer in public schools was defeated recently in the Senate, 56 to 44.) Another possibility, Gerald Gunther maintains, is that Congress, "despite its initial belief that it could impose limits, and despite its effort to impose such limits, would ultimately find it to be the course of least resistance to submit all of the proposals emanating from a convention of delegates elected by the people to the ratification process, where the people would have another say."[35]

Without crystallized knowledge of the roles of Congress and a convention, the prospects for treacherous misunderstandings multiply. If it is seen that amendments on nonconforming topics have a chance at ratification, delegates will have to campaign and be chosen for their positions not only on the topic that spurred the convention, but also on a variety of unrelated yet divisive issues like school prayer and abortion. The deliberations in the convention on legitimate amendments will be distorted, since delegates almost certainly will have to compromise on one amendment to achieve satisfaction on another. Finally, as Paul J. Mishkin of Berkeley has written, if Congress refuses to send an *ultra vires* amendment to the states, the rejection may be misinterpreted by the amendment's supporters "as a subterfuge, a tactic for continued opposition on the substance of the issue and, even more, as a betrayal of trust by their opponents, Congress, and 'the system.'" And there is "likely to be enough substance in their view to persuade large numbers of their followers, at least." Likewise, if Congress did submit the questioned amendment for ratification, its opponents would resent the delegates for exceeding their limits and Congress for failing to enforce them. The upshot might well be grave tension within "the network of trust on which a free democratic society depends."[36]

In cases from *Hollingsworth v. Virginia* (1798) to *Coleman v. Miller* (1939), the Supreme Court has tacitly accepted the premise that proposal and adoption of amendments must satisfy all constitutional requirements, and hence by implication that mere ratification by three fourths of the states, if Congress or a convention exceeded its powers, would be insufficient. A challenge to the eighteenth amendment as invalid on the theory that Congress could not propose an amendment banning the sale of liquor—in other words, invalid because Congress exceeded its proposal powers—was taken up, and rejected on its merits, by the Court.[37] An amendment proposed by the President and sent directly to the states, bypassing a vote of Congress, even if ratified would be an *ultra vires* exercise of the President's power and void.[38]

An amendment attacked as unconstitutional because improperly proposed or adopted could not be challenged in the courts until ratified by three fourths of the states, and then only by a party with standing. If the adopted amendment created a civil or criminal cause of action, the invalidity of the amendment would be asserted as a defense (as was the case with J. J. Dillon). If the amendment abolished the cause of action, the plaintiff would bring suit alleging the rights existing before the amendment's adoption, and assert the invalidity of the amendment after the amendment had been put forward as a defense. Imagine an amendment abolishing the right to attend racially integrated public schools. A black plaintiff could allege a violation of the fourteenth amendment's equal protection clause, as elaborated in *Brown v. Board of Education*. The court would then determine whether the new amendment was valid and abrogated *Brown*. If the amendment were adjudged valid, the plaintiff's suit would have to be dismissed; if invalid, the plaintiff would be entitled to relief.[39]

A disputed amendment will not necessarily stand or fall in its entirety. A court may strike down an invalid portion, even if it is just one part of one sentence, if the rest of the amendment can stand on its own. The edited measure will then be sustained as constitutionally acceptable.[40] Violations of the mandate may well be considered analogous to violations of the one-subject rule in state law. State courts have long adjudicated suits arising under constitutional provisions requiring that each amendment deal with only one subject, and the United States Supreme Court has decided cases arising under state constitutional provisions forbidding any statute to embrace more than one subject. The purpose of these provisions, the Court has said, "is to prevent the practice, common in all legislative bodies where no such provision exists, of embracing in the same bill incongruous matters, having no relation to each other, . . . by which measures are often adopted without attracting attention, which, if noticed, would have been resisted and defeated." But the courts will not lightly interfere; they will "disregard mere verbal inaccuracies, resolve doubts in favor of validity, and hold that . . . the violation must be substantial and plain."[41]

The first court to consider the question decided that a challenged amendment's purpose was to change from annual to biennial the legislature's sessions, and so let stand an increase in the lower house term of office from one to two years as well as alterations in the compensation of all members of the legislature. "In order to constitute more than one amendment," said the court, "the propositions submitted must relate to more than one subject, and have at least two distinct and separate purposes not dependent upon or connected with each other."[42]

In another prominent case, a single amendment proposed by the legislature, ratified by the electorate, and adopted into the Mississippi constitution made elective the judges of the state's supreme, circuit, and chancery courts; it also provided for the nomination of judges by districts, who would then be voted for by the entire state. The amendment repealed five sections of the existing constitution, three of them relating to the appointment of supreme court judges and the other two dealing with the establishment of circuit and chancery court districts in the state. The court held that "there were at least four amendments submitted to the people in this proposition" in violation of the constitution's single subject requirement, "and, notwithstanding the action of the legislature in inserting them in the constitution, [they] are null and void, and form no part of said constitution." As a court recently phrased the criterion: "The test of whether an Act or a constitutional amendment violates the multiple subject matter rule is whether all of the parts . . . are germane to the accomplishment of a single objective."[43]

Ordinarily the courts defer, or give the benefit of the doubt, to Congress when the validity of a federal statute is challenged, but the situation is reversed and deference is unnecessary when Congress determines that a convention-proposed amendment is invalid. Congress as the embodiment of popular consensus has been temporarily displaced by the convention; far from being the sponsor of the amendment, Congress is presumptively hostile, and the courts are therefore likely to be highly respectful of the convention.[44]

A convention called exclusively for a balanced-budget amendment in all likelihood cannot add an abortion ban, either as a provision in the budget amendment or as a separate measure; they are different social goals, as evidenced by, among other things, the two separate application drives. It is, still, possible to think of circumstances where two objectives are not so easily separated, and where a court might decide the case differently with different personnel.[45]

Conceivably, some amendments would survive the judicial gauntlet simply because no one is eligible to bring suit. The Supreme Court has said: "The assumption that if respondents have no standing to sue, no one would have standing, is not a reason to find standing." No private citizen could challenge an amendment like the twenty-fifth, defining the presidential succession, or one granting the President a line-item veto, or regulating the appointment of federal judges. (Of course, to the extent that Congress can propose the same amendments, it too may be considered a "runaway.") *Ultra vires* amendments proposed by a convention, however, can be withheld from the states by congressional refusal to assign a mode of ratification. But the amendments most often feared (or touted) as *ultra vires* candidates relate to social policy—abortion, school busing, school prayer—and since these amendments affect personal rights, they can produce plaintiffs eligible to contest the validity of their adoption. Congress, seeing an *ultra vires* amendment head toward inevitable adoption, could preserve formalities by itself submitting the identical measure for state ratification.[46]

An *ultra vires* amendment might also survive merely if suit is not brought for a considerable period and the government has acted on the assumption of its validity. On such facts courts have sometimes refused to invalidate an irregularly added provision under the rubric of acquiescence. "It is confessedly the assent of the people which gives validity to a Constitution," said a judge in 1793 of Virginia's Revolution-era charter, and this "subsequent acquiescence and assent" gives a constitution "as much validity . . . as if it had been previously expressly authorized." Acquiescence, at bottom, represents judicial deference to a political fait accompli, and reluctance to disrupt public order far more by invalidating the provision than by leaving it undisturbed. The Supreme Court has never endorsed this doctrine as regards constitutional amendments, but Justice Brandeis did say that the fifteenth amendment's validity "has been recognized and acted on for half a century."[47]

Generally, legal challenges to a convention-proposed amendment might be expected long before the acquiescence doctrine could be invoked, since any amendment that necessitated a convention call would have generated enough hostile parties en route to ensure swift action. Yet an amendment can have implications totally unforeseen at the time of its adoption. The fourteenth, as a prime example, was originally interpreted narrowly, but decades later found to incorporate most of the federal Bill of Rights, making those protections applicable to the states.[48]

"Having witnessed the difficulties and dangers experienced by the first Convention which assembled under every propitious circumstance," Madison wrote in 1788, "I should tremble for the result of a Second, meeting in the present temper of America." It is essential to see that Madison's apprehension of an uncontrolled convention differs from the apprehensions of later times. There was, for example, in 1788 no article III judiciary with teeth to enforce the limits ascribed to each and every governmental body. The first case in article V jurisprudence was ten years away, and the Court did not have sufficient clout to back up its rulings until the accession of John Marshall. Last, the method of amendment Madison assumed for another convention, resubmission of the whole document as modified, was dropped for separate provisions added at the end of the Constitution.[49]

In short, Madison could not at that time have visualized the machinery to guarantee the bounds imposed on a convention. Representative Abraham Baldwin, a Georgia framer, thought

it was not to disparage the instrument, to say that it had not definitely, and with precision, absolutely settled everything on which it had spoke. . . . It was a great thing to get so many difficult subjects definitely settled at once. . . . The few that were left a little unsettled might, without any great risk, be settled by practice or by amendments in the progress of the Government.[50]

State constitutions and amendments have in the past resulted from *ultra vires* conventions. A number of the primitive constitutions lacked any method of amendment whatsoever, with the result that popular referenda on the question of revision were needed to legitimize the conventions. Members of the Pennsylvania legislature in this manner justified a convention to decide on ratifying the federal Constitution, even though the state constitution gave the legislature no such power. "Calling a convention," said Richard Peters, "was recommended by the legislature, and the sovereignty of the people has decided upon that recommendation; it is not [by] an act of the legislature that the Convention exists, it is the act of the people." Notable framing conventions unauthorized by state constitution were held in Pennsylvania (1789–1790), Georgia (three conventions in 1788–1789), Massachusetts (1820–1821), New York (1801, 1821), and Virginia (1829–1830, 1850–1851).[51]

State experience suggests that the electorate will judge submissions on their merits, although there is no precedent to allow estimating what extra prestige an article V convention might bestow. Two of the amendments drafted by Madison and refined by the likes of Sherman, Gerry, and Ellsworth in the First Congress were, nonetheless, refused. By the same token, *ultra vires* amendments from a national convention might doom even bona fide valid amendments, causing rejection of the entire package—as evidenced by the negative reaction to the constitution proposed by the Illinois convention of 1862 and the amendments offered by Missouri's marathon convention of 1922–1923. The Kentucky legislature, despite a constitutional provision requiring that a new charter be proposed by a convention called by the legislature, appointed a commission to draft a new constitution. The state courts upheld submission of the draft for ratification, content that the vote would "be an expression of the inalienable right of the ultimate sovereign to reform the government," but the draft was resoundingly defeated at the polls in November 1966.[52]

Although the Kentucky voters made their judgment on the basis of substance rather than procedure, the public may well be outraged at any attempted assault on the federal Constitution, for on a certain scale public veneration of the Constitution, as a symbol and embodiment of impartiality on the highest levels of our political existence, is likely to take precedence over any one result or political movement committed to that result. The convention route is not risk-free; a misstep during the final stages of a campaign or beyond may cost public support for the convention, together with the amendment and the political cause associated with it.

To Alter or Abolish

It should be remembered that the federalists were defending an entirely new government in the 1787 Constitution, not an *ultra vires* amendment to an existing constitution. In the First Congress, Madison said: "My idea of the sovereignty of the people is, that the people can change the constitution if they please; but while the constitution exists, they must conform themselves to its dictates." The Philadelphia Convention defended its work as a needed new constitution, superseding the old Confederation; an article V convention proposing *ultra vires* amendments still professes to act within the Constitution. The standards of the Confederation were discarded at Philadelphia, but the standards of the Constitution must govern any non-plenary article V convention. In the words of a state court, "The Constitution may be set aside by revolution but it can only be amended in the way it provides."[53]

When the Pennsylvania convention of 1873 proposed a new constitution, along with changes in the bill of rights that went beyond what was sanctioned in the enabling act, suit was filed to prevent submission of the constitution for popular ratification. The Pennsylvania supreme court admitted that the convention had acted *ultra vires*, but before the case was decided the constitution had been submitted to the voters and approved by a large majority. Said the court: "The change made by the people in their political institutions, by the adoption of the proposed Constitution . . . forbids an inquiry into the merits of this case. The question is no longer judicial."[54]

A state court invalidated an *ultra vires* provision of the constitution framed by the Louisiana convention of 1913, but was criticized at the time by a commentator who maintained that "by the enactment of the new constitution the old government has been displaced" and invalidating a part of the new constitution was illogical, since the authority to invalidate existed solely under the old constitution, which was no longer in operation. In his *Treatise* Judge Jameson held that "courts may pass upon the validity of a supposed amendment," but disapproved of courts' adjudicating the validity of a constitution: "when the political power has spoken upon the question, the judicial department ought . . . to follow its decision."[55]

It is much easier in any event for a court to decide that the amending procedure of a constitution has been respected or violated than to reject a new constitution that has been ratified by the electorate and command that the old charter be restored. In particular, federal courts owe their existence to article III of the federal Constitution, which vests "[t]he judicial Power of the United States" in "one supreme Court, and in such inferior Courts" as Congress decides to establish. The Constitution, in turn, draws its sanction from ratification by the states. The proposed Constitution, said Madison, was "nothing but a dead letter, until life and validity were breathed into it by the voice of the people, speaking through the several State Conventions." On this reasoning, if a new constitution were ratified by state conventions, the judicial system would be bound to respect it, no matter how irregularly proposed or adopted. To date, the Supreme Court's decisions have taken the politically less risky route of vindicating all challenged amendments, though *Dillon v. Gloss* intimates that an amendment proposed in 1789 and completely ratified a hundred or more years later would not be upheld.[56]

Article V provides that adopted amendments become "Part of *this* Constitution," a phrase that (as Nathaniel Gorham said at Philadelphia) refers exclusively "to the existing Constitution." Congress and a convention are alike limited by article V to amendments respecting this, and not some other, new, frame of government. One reason why the Constitution could not be amended by interweaving the proposals within the text to create a totally new draft, said Representative Livermore in 1789, was that "neither this Legislature, nor all the Legislatures in America, were authorized to repeal a constitution." Roger Sherman agreed:

by the present constitution, we, nor all the Legislatures in the Union together, do not possess the power of repealing it. All that is granted us by the 5th article is, that whenever we shall think it necessary, we may propose amendments to the constitution; not that we may propose to repeal the old, and substitute a new one.

Nevertheless, a virtually new instrument might be adopted in the guise of a series of amendments. "I will not undertake to define the extent of the word amendment, as it stands in the fifth article," said Representative Gerry, but "if we proposed to change the division of the powers given to the three branches of the Government, and that proposition is accepted and ratified . . . , it will become as valid, to all intents and purposes, as any part of the constitution."[57]

The difference between "this Constitution" and a successor would have been blunted two hundred years ago if a second convention had interwoven its proposals into the existing instrument. Nothing, indeed, prohibits applications from specifying a plenary convention to draft an entirely new constitution; this was, after all, demanded in so many words by the Virginia and New York applications delivered to the First Congress. Washington vouchsafed to Abraham Baldwin during the convention that he did not expect the Constitution to last more than twenty years. Madison and others of the founding age never denied the option of a complete change of government, whether peacefully or by the "ultima ratio," force of arms. The first constitutions of New Hampshire, South Carolina, and New Jersey, adopted in 1776, were expressly declared to be temporary, and before 1800 the original thirteen states had adopted completely new constitutions eight times. Madison's amendments to the Constitution were originally prefaced by a declaration in the Jeffersonian style affirming that "the people have an indubitable, unalienable, and indefeasible right to reform or change their Government, whenever it be found adverse or inadequate to the purposes of its institution."[58]

In sum, a national convention is in all likelihood constitutionally limited to proposing amendments described in the state applications that generated the call. *Ultra vires* amendments dealing with personal freedoms—abortion, school busing, school prayer—can produce plaintiffs eligible to contest the validity of their adoption, but may become part of the Constitution through acquiescence or if never challenged in court. *Ultra vires* amendments dealing with overarching issues of governmental structure rather than personal rights may survive to become part of the Constitution, if the courts find no party eligible to bring suit. Yet these elusive amendments may not succeed to adoption if Congress declines to choose a mode of ratification and withholds them from ratification by the states. An entirely new constitution might be instituted only in the remote event that a plenary national convention is authorized by applications from two thirds of the states, or if it is proposed by an ostensibly limited convention and ratified by conventions in the states.

Replacing the Constitution has not been unthinkable in the past two centuries. A new constitution almost certainly would have been proposed at a second convention if Congress had not put the Bill of Rights before the states. Jefferson may have contemplated the possibility in 1801; Senator Lane in 1860 and Senator Ingalls in 1876 offered serious proposals. Yet as the dates suggest, a new constitution will not be adopted in times of tranquility but only, if ever, as the result of civil war, revolution, or holocaust. Timothy Farrar, Daniel Webster's law partner and an ardent Unionist, wrote just after Appomattox that a national convention "without limit and without landmark, is a measure not likely to be resorted to for any other purpose than to destroy the government. Whenever so large a proportion of the American people become imbued with that purpose, it is safe to predict that they will march to their object by a more direct route than by procuring an amendment of the Constitution in this circuitous manner."[59]

Conclusion

The Politics of Uncertainty

The article V convention is the last resort of a disaffected minority, just as the colonial conventions were ranged against the Crown, their constitutional irregularity a sign that action was being taken outside the established channels of government. The meetings at Annapolis and Philadelphia were only a second choice for nationalists who could not obtain their desired constitutional reforms from Congress. The strongest convention drives, both before and after 1787, have accordingly represented sizable factions whose agendas posed a threat to the mainstream political orthodoxy. The antifederalist campaign for a second convention was a rematch of states' righters against nationalists to cancel the Philadelphia result, netting a compromise in the Bill of Rights.

Patrick Henry no doubt felt he was battling against a large and distant government that was capable of eviscerating personal liberties, just as he had twenty years earlier during the Stamp Act crisis. Madison understood and anticipated this reaction to unpopular initiatives from the central government, writing in *The Federalist* that

ambitious encroachments of the Foederal Government, on the authority of the State governments, would not excite the opposition of a single State or of a few States only. They would be signals of general alarm. . . . A correspondence would be opened. Plans of resistance would be concerted. . . . The same combination in short would result from an apprehension of the foederal, as was produced by the dread of a foreign yoke.

159

This is why the history of the convention clause has paralleled that of nullification, for both are state strategies to repel policies of the central government; both were used to resist the tariff of abominations and federally mandated racial integration of public schools.[1]

In Shays's Rebellion, Madison saw the "leveling spirit" that would greet oppressive "interested co-alitions," and presciently warned the Philadelphia delegates that the United States would be characterized by "different classes havg. a real or supposed difference of interests," including "creditors & debtors, farmers, merchts. & manufacturers." The prominent drives indeed have emanated from the agrarian regions of the country, from the first under Virginia's leadership in 1787–1788. The petitions resulting from the nullification crisis of the 1830s reflected the economic distress and alienation of the South, continuing earlier rivalries, to culminate in the Civil War. With the nation transformed into an industrial, urban power, the stimulus for reform has even more pronouncedly come from the South and West: direct election of senators, Prohibition, restoring prayer in schools, abolishing the one-person, one-vote rule, balancing the federal budget. The convention to permit United States participation in a world government was a rare example of applications submitted for a national and even international, rather than a sectional, purpose.[2]

Like the Loch Ness monster, convention drives emerge for a while into the national spotlight and cause havoc when the public is stunned by the "unprecedented" action, previous campaigns and conventions before Philadelphia all but forgotten. They invariably resubmerge into obscurity to begin the cycle again, in this century one serious drive every twenty years. The modern convention strategy has often been bifurcated, because amendment proponents are at a loss to know which theory will be more effective—selling the convention as a limitable, or as an illimitable, body. State legislators who are lobbied to approve an application must be reassured that the measure is perfectly responsible and safe, but the more respectable the measure, the less threatening it is to Congress, who will be unimpressed except by the prospect of Armageddon. President Reagan hinted to Congress that it might be faced with a runaway balanced-budget convention, while Vice President Bush, campaigning in Michigan, held for a limited assembly.

Nothing would surprise the framers more than the confusion surrounding the convention method of amendment, for it was common and accepted in their time. The convention route had been built with familiar materials; it was not intended to be, nor did it start out as, an especially clandestine procedure. Virginia's application, authored by Henry, was as much a manifesto to enlist the support of other states as it was a legal instrument, and was reprinted in the newspapers of the day.[3] The antifederalists' drive for a second convention was widely discussed in the press and in the ratifying conventions.

While publicity was essential for Henry's scheme, the opposite was true for Everett Dirksen's. Modern drives have followed a pattern, beginning quietly as grass-roots movements until a substantial number of states file applications and attract national figures and organizations to coordinate efforts in the remaining states. At about the thirtieth state the campaigns tend to slow, either because the conditions giving rise to them have changed or because Congress has proposed something of its own. Amendment opponents inevitably raise the specter of a runaway convention proposing unwanted amendments (school prayer to a liberal audience, the equal rights amendment to a conservative group), slowing the campaign further.

Probably we are also intimidated by the luster of the Philadelphia delegates, and whisper of a decline in our country's leadership. Madison was the first to admit that the Constitution would never have been adopted without Washington and Franklin to commend it, although Washington himself believed that "the People (for it is with them to Judge) can as they will have the advantage of experience on their Side, decide with as much propriety on the alterations and amendments which are necessary [as] ourselves. I do not think we are more inspired, have more wisdom, or possess more virtue, than those who will come after us."[4]

Congress in modern times has by and large maintained that a convention cannot be limited. This view, however sincerely arrived at, happens also to be useful in dissuading states from submitting applications, thereby leaving Congress in exclusive control of the amendment process. For the same reason Congress, especially the liberal establishment concentrated for the last thirty years in the House of Representatives, has an interest in leaving the route undefined. Don Edwards, chair of a House Judiciary subcommittee, finds "no assurance" that a national convention "could not be a runaway," and opposes a procedures bill on the ground that it would aid the drive for a convention: "Anything that encourages this sort of utilization of Article V is unwise." The more obscure the process, the easier it is for Congress to discourage pressure by rejecting applications on technical grounds—a phenomenon that has been aptly called the "politics of uncertainty."[5]

For this reason Congress has never established a procedure for receiving and verifying applications, never promulgated guidelines for applications or for the convention itself. Congress could have done so long ago, Justice Scalia has said, by amending article V if necessary. "But the Congress is not about to do that. It likes the existing confusion, because that deters resort to the convention process. It does not want amending power to be anywhere but in its own hands."[6]

It is no coincidence that the sponsors of congressional legislation purporting to limit a convention to specific issues have generally favored the amendment that is, at the time, the subject of a convention drive. Making the convention workable makes it more appealing to the holdout states and increases the chance of a showdown and capitulation by Congress in proposing the amendment. The Republican Senate has passed convention legislation and a balanced-budget amendment; both measures have foundered in the Democratic House.

The same countervailing forces between the central and local governments that produced the article V convention in the first place, then, have also operated to render it perilously obscure. Yet obscurity is not always to the advantage of convention opponents: if the balanced-budget amendment garners a thirty-third application, partisans are sure to recite as a precedent the seventeenth amendment's proposal in 1912 with one fewer than the required number of applications. Clarifying that amendment's history, seeing that the applications were more a symbol than the actual instrument of change, makes it less rather than more likely that Congress will be panicked into approving a budget amendment.

Some, like Gerald Gunther, fear that a convention, once held, would pave the way for a barrage of national conventions on other issues, with the result that "the solemnity and seriousness of the process would be trivialized." Madison in *The Federalist* also was "against a frequent reference of constitutional questions, to the decision of the whole society," yet even the Constitution's friends did not object to a convention in and of itself. They were instead of the opinion that a convention, at that time sure to be dominated by antifederalists bent on dismantling the entire structure, would have been held too soon for changes of any consequence to be introduced safely. After ratification and within months of his appointment as the first Chief Justice, John

Jay wrote: "The measure of a new convention to consider and decide on the proposed amendments will, I think, be expedient to terminate all questions on the subject. If immediately carried, its friends will be satisfied, and if convened three years hence, little danger, perhaps some good, will attend it."[7]

A series of conventions—envisioned, certainly, by Elbridge Gerry and Gunning Bedford at Philadelphia and Wilson Nicholas at the Virginia ratifying convention—would be no more trivializing, in any case, than the record of the other mode. Ten thousand amendments, some wise, many not, have been introduced in Congress in the past two centuries, but only twenty-six have been added to the Constitution. In accordance with Madison's declaration in *Federalist* 43 that article V "equally enables" the origination of amendments by the states and by Congress, neither method was conspicuously favored during the Constitution's first hundred years. Certainly the Supreme Court's 1831 opinion in *Smith v. Union Bank of Georgetown* and the convention proposals of the Civil War prove that the two methods were considered on a par. As of 1865 only twelve amendments had been added, on just three separate occasions, the last in 1804; those twelve had become, said the Court in mid-century, "historical and of another age." Congressional exclusivity did not become a settled expectation until the 1900s, with the adoption of the seventeenth amendment.[8]

It is far more dangerous to allow a convention drive to progress to its final stages with many crucial questions left unanswered than to provide minimal guidance. The acrimonious disputes and damage to the public's faith in its government that would ensue at thirty-four applications would overshadow by far any differences relating to the proposed amendment itself. Solving the enigma of article V can dispel extraneous apprehensions regarding a convention, and so permit undistracted debate on the amendment's merits. St. George Tucker, who predicted that a national convention "will probably never be resorted to," observed also that "senators are at present limited to thirty-two," and in the year of the Louisiana Purchase prophesied, "it is not probable that they will ever exceed fifty."[9]

Appendix

Convention Applications of Virginia and New York, 1788–1789[1]

Virginia

VIRGINIA, *to wit:*

IN GENERAL ASSEMBLY, Nov. 14, 1788.

Resolved, That an application be made in the name and on behalf of the Legislature of this Commonwealth to the Congress of the United States, in the words following, to wit:

"The good People of this Commonwealth, in Convention assembled, having ratified the Constitution submitted to their consideration, this Legislature has, in conformity to that act, and the resolutions of the United States in Congress assembled, to them transmitted, thought proper to make the arrangements that were necessary for carrying it into effect. Having thus shown themselves obedient to the voice of their constituents, all America will find that, so far as it depended on them, that plan of Government will be carried into immediate operation.

"But the sense of the People of Virginia would be but in part complied with, and but little regarded, if we went no farther. In the very moment of adoption, and coeval with the ratification of the new plan of Government, the general voice of the Convention of this State pointed to objects no less interesting to the People we represent; and equally entitled to our attention. At the same time that, from motives of affection to our sister States, the Convention yielded their assent to the ratification, they gave the most unequivocal proofs that they dreaded its operation under the present form.

"In acceding to the Government under this impression, painful must have been the prospect, had they not derived consolation from a full expectation of its imperfections being speedily amended. In this resource, therefore, they placed their confidence, a confidence that will continue to support them, whilst they have reason to believe that they have not calculated upon it in vain.

"In making known to you the objections of the People of this Commonwealth to the new plan of Government, we deem it unnecessary to enter into a particular detail of its defects, which they consider as involving all the great and unalienable rights of freemen. For their sense on this subject, we beg leave to refer you to the proceedings of their late Convention, and the sense of the House of Delegates, as expressed in their resolutions of the thirtieth day of October, one thousand seven hundred and eighty-eight.

"We think proper, however, to declare, that, in our opinion, as those objections were not founded in speculative theory, but deduced from principles which have been established by the melancholy example of other nations in different ages, so they will never be removed, until the cause itself shall cease to exist. The sooner, therefore, the public apprehensions are quieted, and the Government is possessed of the confidence of the People, the more salutary will be its operations, and the longer its duration.

"The cause of amendments we consider as a common cause; and, since concessions have been made from political motives, which, we conceive, may endanger the Republic, we trust that a commendable zeal will be shown for obtaining those provisions, which experience has taught us are necessary to secure from danger the unalienable rights of human nature.

"The anxiety with which our countrymen press for the accomplishment of this important end, will ill admit of delay. The slow forms of Congressional discussion and recommendation, if, indeed, they should ever agree to any change, would, we fear, be less certain of success.

Happily for their wishes, the Constitution hath presented an alternative, by admitting the submission to a convention of the States. To this, therefore, we resort as the source from whence they are to derive relief from their present apprehensions.

"We do, therefore, in behalf of our constituents, in the most earnest and solemn manner, make this application to Congress, that a convention be immediately called, of deputies from the several States, with full power to take into their consideration the defects of this constitution that have been suggested by the State Conventions, and report such amendments thereto as they shall find best suited to promote our common interests, and secure to ourselves and our latest posterity the great and unalienable rights of mankind.

"JOHN JONES, *Speaker Senate.*
"THOMAS MATHEWS, *Speaker Ho. Del.*"

New York

STATE OF NEW YORK,
In Assembly, February 5, 1789.

Resolved, If the honorable the Senate concur therein, that an application be made to the Congress of the United States of America, in the name and behalf of the Legislature of this State, in the words following, to wit:

The People of the State of New York having ratified the Constitution agreed to on the seventeenth day of September, in the year of our Lord one thousand seven hundred and eighty-seven, by the Convention then assembled at Philadelphia, in the State of Pennsylvania, as explained by the said ratification, in the fullest confidence of obtaining a revision of the said Constitution by a General Convention; and in confidence that certain powers in and by the said Constitution granted, would not be exercised, until a Convention should have been called and convened for proposing amendments to the said Constitution: In compliance, therefore, with the unanimous sense of the Convention of this State, who all united in opinion that such a revision was necessary to recommend the said Constitution to the approbation and support of a numerous body of their constituents; and a majority of the members of which conceived several articles of the Constitution so exceptionable, that nothing but such confidence, and an invincible reluctance to separate from our sister States, could have prevailed upon a sufficient number to assent to it, without stipulating for previous amendments: And from a conviction that the apprehensions and discontents which those articles occasion, cannot be removed or allayed, unless an act to revise the said Constitution be among the first that shall be passed by the new Congress: we, the Legislature of the State of New York, do, in behalf of our constituents, in the most earnest and solemn manner, make this application to the Congress, that a Convention of Deputies from the several States be called as early as possible, with full powers to take the said Constitution into their consideration, and to propose such amendments thereto, as they shall find best calculated to promote our common interests, and secure to ourselves and our latest posterity, the great and unalienable rights of mankind.

By order of the Assembly:

JOHN LANSING, Junior, *Speaker.*

IN SENATE, *February* 7, 1789.

By order of the Senate:

PIERRE VAN CORTLANDT, *President.*

Works Frequently Cited

Books

ABA Study: American Bar Association Special Constitutional Convention Study Committee, *Amendment of the Constitution by the Convention Method Under Article V* (1974).

W. Adams, *First American Constitutions:* W. Adams, *The First American Constitutions: Republican Ideology and the Making of the State Constitutions in the Revolutionary Era* (1980).

Adams Diary: L. Butterfield, ed., *Diary and Autobiography of John Adams* (4 vols., 1961).

American Archives: P. Force, ed., *American Archives* (9 vols., Washington, D. C., 1837–1853).

B. Bailyn, *Ideological Origins:* B. Bailyn, *The Ideological Origins of the American Revolution* (1967).

W. Blackstone, *Commentaries:* W. Blackstone, *Commentaries on the Laws of England* (4 vols., 1st ed., Oxford, 1765–1769).

S. Bloom, *Formation of the Union:* S. Bloom, ed., *History of the Formation of the Union* (1941).

E. Burnett, *The Continental Congress:* E. Burnett, *The Continental Congress* (1941).

E. Burnett, *Letters:* E. Burnett, ed., *Letters of Members of the Continental Congress* (8 vols., 1921–1936).

Collected Works of Lincoln: R. Basler, ed., *The Collected Works of Abraham Lincoln* (9 vols., 1953).

Elliot: J. Elliot, ed., *The Debates in the Several State Conventions on the Adoption of the Federal Constitution* (2d ed., Philadelphia, 1836) (1st ed., n. p., 1830).

The Federalist: J. Cooke, ed., *The Federalist* (1961).

J. Goebel, *Antecedents:* J. Goebel, *Antecedents and Beginnings to 1801* (1971) (vol. 1 of the Oliver Wendell Holmes Devise History of the Supreme Court of the United States).

Hamilton Papers: H. Syrett, J. Cooke, et al., eds., *The Papers of Alexander Hamilton* (26 vols., 1961–1979).

G. Haynes, *Senate of the United States:* G. Haynes, *The Senate of the United States: Its History and Practice* (2 vols., 1938).

G. Hunt, *Writings of Madison:* G. Hunt, ed., *The Writings of James Madison* (9 vols., 1900–1910).

J. A. Jameson, *Treatise:* J. A. Jameson, *A Treatise on Constitutional Conventions: Their History, Powers, and Modes of Proceeding* (4th ed., 1887) (1st ed., n. p., 1866).

JCC: W. Ford et al., eds., *Journals of the Continental Congress 1774–1789* (34 vols., 1904–1937).

Jefferson Papers: J. Boyd et. al., eds., *The Papers of Thomas Jefferson* (22 vols. to date, Princeton, N. J., 1950–   ).

M. Jensen, *The New Nation:* M. Jensen, *The New Nation: A History of the United States During the Confederation 1781–1789* (1965).

Letters of Delegates: P. Smith et al., eds., *Letters of Delegates to Congress 1774–1789* (13 vols. to date, 1976–   ).

Madison Papers: W. Hutchinson, R. Rutland, et al., eds., *The Papers of James Madison* (15 vols. to date, 1962–   ).

New Hampshire Collections: 9 I. Hammond, ed., *Collections of the New Hampshire Historical Society* (1889).

1979 Hearing: *Constitutional Convention Procedures: Hearing on S. 3, S. 520, and S. 1710 Before the Subcommittee on the Constitution of the Senate Committee on the Judiciary,* 96th Congress, 1st Session (1979).

1967 Hearings: *Federal Constitutional Convention: Hearings on S. 2307 Before the Subcommittee on Separation of Powers of the Senate Committee on the Judiciary,* 90th Congress, 1st Session (1967).

L. Orfield, *Amending the Federal Constitution:* L. Orfield, *The Amending of the Federal Constitution* (1942).

Popular Sources: O. Handlin and M. Handlin, eds., *The Popular Sources of Political Authority: Documents on the Massachusetts Constitution of 1780* (1966).

W. Pullen, "The Application Clause of the Amending Provision": W.

Pullen, "The Application Clause of the Amending Provision of the Constitution" (dissertation, University of North Carolina, Chapel Hill, 1951).

J. Rakove, *Beginnings:*   J. Rakove, *The Beginnings of National Politics: An Interpretive History of the Continental Congress* (1979).

Ratification History: M. Jensen et al., eds., *The Documentary History of the Ratification of the Constitution* (6 vols. to date, 1976–   ).

Records: M. Farrand, ed., *The Records of the Federal Convention of 1787* (4 vols., rev. ed., 1937) (1st ed., 1911).

Virginia Delegate Journal: Journal of the House of Delegates of the Commonwealth of Virginia (printed by Thomas W. White, Richmond, 1828).

Washington Writings: J. Fitzpatrick, ed., *The Writings of George Washington* (39 vols., 1931–1944).

G. Wood, *Creation of the Republic:*   G. Wood, *The Creation of the American Republic 1776–1787* (1969).

Articles

Black, "Threatened Disaster":   Black, "The Proposed Amendment of Article V: A Threatened Disaster," 72 *Yale Law Journal* 957 (1963).

J. F. Jameson, "Early Uses":   J. F. Jameson, "The Early Political Uses of the Word Convention," 3 *American Historical Review* 477 (1898).

Smith, "Movement Towards a Second Constitutional Convention":   Edward P. Smith, "The Movement Towards a Second Constitutional Convention in 1788," in John Franklin Jameson, ed., *Essays in the Constitutional History of the United States in the Formative Period 1775–1789,* at 46 (1889).

Notes

Preface

1. Goldberg, "The Proposed Constitutional Convention," 11 *Hastings Constitutional Law Quarterly* 1, 2 (1983); *New York Times*, Dec. 20, 1985, at A22; United Press International news release, May 24, 1987.

2. Rovere, "Affairs of State," *New Yorker*, March 19, 1979, at 136, 137; Kean, "A Constitutional Convention Would Threaten the Rights We Have Cherished for 200 Years," 1986 *Detroit College of Law Review* 1087, 1090.

3. Tribe, "Issues Raised by Requesting Congress to Call a Constitutional Convention to Propose a Balanced Budget Amendment," 10 *Pacific Law Journal* 627, 638 (1979); Black, "The Proposed Amendment of Article V: A Threatened Disaster," 72 *Yale Law Journal* 957, 964 (1963).

4. Kurland, "Article V and the Amending Process," in D. Boorstin, ed., *An American Primer* 148, 152 (1968).

5. T. Jefferson, *A Manual of Parliamentary Practice for the Use of the Senate of the United States* (1st ed., Washington, D. C., 1801), reprinted in *House Document No. 271*, 97th Congress, 2d Session 111–12 (1983).

6. Council of State Governments, *The Book of the States 1986–87*, at 5 (1986). For tables summarizing the amending procedures in the current state constitutions, see id. at 16–20. See also P. Schrag, *Behind the Scenes: The Politics of a Constitutional Convention* (1985) (account of 1982 District of Columbia constitutional convention held in preparation for statehood, by a delegate to the convention); E. Cornwell, Jr., J. Goodman, and W. Swanson, *Constitutional Conventions: The Politics of Revision* (1974); A. Sturm, *Thirty Years of State Constitution-Making: 1938–1968* (1970); J. Wheeler, *The Constitutional Convention: A Manual on Its Planning, Organization and Operation* (1961); Adrian, "Trends in State Constitutions," 5 *Harvard Journal on Legislation* 311 (1968).

7. *Reports of the Proceedings and Debates of the Convention of 1821*, at 199 (Albany, 1821); A. Cole, ed., *The Constitutional Debates of 1847*, at 27, 32 (1919); *Report of the Debates and Proceedings of the Convention for the Revision of the Constitution of the State of Kentucky* 862–64 (Frankfort, 1849) (remarks of delegate William D. Mitchell); *Official Report of the Debates and Proceedings in the State Convention* 78 (Boston, 1853) (delegate Benjamin F. Butler).

8. J. Cornelius, *A History of Constitution Making in Illinois* 37–39 (1969); O. Dickerson, *The Illinois Constitutional Convention of 1862*, at 10–15, 32–41 (1905).

9. *Journal of the Constitutional Convention of the State of Illinois, Convened at Springfield, January 7, 1862*, at 19, 20–21 (Springfield, 1862).

10. J. A. Jameson, *A Treatise on Constitutional Conventions: Their History, Powers, and Modes of Proceeding* §312 at 309 n.1 (4th ed., 1887) (hereinafter J. A. Jameson, *Treatise*). See Bragg v. Tuffts, 49 Ark. 554, 561 (1887) (Arkansas 1861 secession convention "usurped all legislative and executive functions and its ordinances were the acts of a provisional government resting on a revolutionary basis") (citing Jameson's *Treatise*).

11. J. A. Jameson, *Treatise* §316 at 312–13; T. Cooley, *A Treatise on the Constitutional Limitations Which Rest upon the Legislative Power of the States of the American Union* 32 (1st ed., Boston, 1868); see H. Hyman, *A More Perfect Union* 371–79 (1975) (on Farrar, Cooley, and other commentators of the period); Cummings v. Missouri, 71 U.S. (4 Wall.) 277 (1867).

12. W. Dodd, *The Revision and Amendment of State Constitutions* 92–93 (1910); R. Hoar, *Constitutional Conventions: Their Nature, Powers, and Limitations* 108, 120–24 (1917).

13. *Congressional Globe*, 40th Congress, 3d Session 855 (1869); M. Kammen, *A Machine That Would Go of Itself: The Constitution in American Culture* 390 (1986).

14. James Madison to Samuel Harrison Smith, Feb. 2, 1827, in 9 G. Hunt, ed., *The Writings of James Madison* 269 (1910) (hereinafter G. Hunt, *Writings of Madison*); H. Gilpin, ed., *The Papers of James Madison* (3 vols., Washington, D.C., 1840).

15. E. Wright, *Fabric of Freedom 1763–1800*, at 174 (rev. ed., 1978); Hutson, "The Creation of the Constitution: The Integrity of the Documentary Record," 65 *Texas Law Review* 1, 34 (1986).

16. J. Goebel, *Antecedents and Beginnings to 1801*, at 325–26 (1971) (vol. 1 of the Oliver Wendell Holmes Devise History of the Supreme Court of the United States) (hereinafter J. Goebel, *Antecedents*). For an admirable discussion of the sources for this period, see 1 M. Jensen, ed., *The Documentary History of the Ratification of the Constitution* 30–38 (1976) (hereinafter *Ratification History*).

17. 12 C. Hobson, R. Rutland, et al., eds., *The Papers of James Madison* 62–64 (1979) (hereinafter *Madison Papers*); C. Hyneman and C. Carey, eds., *A Second Federalist* vii–x (1967).

18. On the current practice of Congress respecting the receipt and retention of applications, see Stasny, "State Applications for a Convention to Amend the Federal Constitution January 1974–September 1977: Compilation and Comment," in 123 *Congressional Record* 36534, 36535 (1977); Stasny, "A Federal Constitutional Convention: Anomalies in the Application Process," 124 *Cong. Rec.* 31423 (1978).

19. A list of state applications to Congress for a national convention filed between 1789 and 1963 is in Graham, "The Role of the States in Proposing Constitutional Amendments," 49 *American Bar Association Journal* 1175, 1179–83 (1963). See also American Bar Association Special Constitutional Convention Study Committee, *Amendment of the*

Constitution by the Convention Method Under Article V, at 59–69 (1974) (hereinafter *ABA Study*) (table of applications listed by state and subject, prepared by Barbara Prager and Gregory Milmoe); C. Brickfield, *Problems Relating to a Federal Constitutional Convention* 84–96 (85th Congress, 1st Session, Committee Print 1957); *Senate Document No. 78,* 71st Congress, 2d Session 2–3 (1930) (Senate compilation of applications filed through 1930); *Senate Report No. 135,* 99th Congress, 1st Session 49–58 (1985) (updated through July 1985); W. Pullen, "The Application Clause of the Amending Provision of the Constitution" (dissertation, University of North Carolina, Chapel Hill, 1951).

20. For a sound overview of the current debate see Brest, "The Misconceived Quest for the Original Understanding," 60 *Boston University Law Review* 204 (1980).

21. James Madison to Martin Luther Hurlbert, May 1830, in 9 G. Hunt, *Writings of Madison* at 372; 5 *Annals of the Congress of the United States* 776 (Gales & Seaton edition, Washington, D.C., 1849) (proceedings of April 6, 1796) (remarks of Rep. Madison); J. Cooke, ed., *The Federalist* No. 83 at 560 (1961); Powell, "The Original Understanding of Original Intent," 98 *Harvard Law Review* 885, 903–4 (1985). Yet on occasion the members, even Madison, invoked their recollections of Philadelphia to bolster political positions they took while in Congress. Clinton, "Original Understanding, Legal Realism, and the Interpretation of 'This Constitution,'" 72 *Iowa Law Review* 1177, 1197–98 (1987) (collecting instances).

22. Black, "Amendment by National Constitutional Convention: A Letter to a Senator," 32 *Oklahoma Law Review* 626, 642–43 (1979); similarly, Dellinger, "The Recurring Question of the 'Limited' Constitutional Convention," 88 *Yale Law Journal* 1623, 1634 n.47 (1979).

23. 6 *Madison Papers* at 425.

24. James Madison to Thomas Jefferson, Dec. 4, 1786, in 9 *Madison Papers* at 189. Framer Richard Dobbs Spaight said that the Confederation's unanimity requirement for amendment, which gave a single state the veto, showed "how impolitic it would be to put the general welfare in the power of a few members of the Union." 4 J. Elliot, ed., *The Debates in the Several State Conventions on the Adoption of the Federal Constitution* 207 (2d ed., Philadelphia, 1836) (1st ed., n.p., 1830) (hereinafter *Elliot*).

25. *The Constitution of the State of Georgia* 1–2 (Savannah, 1777).

26. James Madison to Charles Jared Ingersoll, June 25, 1831, in 8 Va. (4 Call) 127 (1833 ed.); *ABA Study* at 7–8; Alexander Hamilton to Rufus King, July 25, 1792, in 12 H. Syrett, J. Cooke, et al., eds., *The Papers of Alexander Hamilton* 99 (1967) (hereinafter *Hamilton Papers*).

1. Prelude to the Grand Convention

1. W. Adams, *The First American Constitutions: Republican Ideology and the Making of the State Constitutions in the Revolutionary Era* 139–40 (1980) (hereinafter W. Adams, *First American Constitutions*); L. Orfield, *The Amending of the Federal Constitution* 1 (1942) (hereinafter L. Orfield, *Amending the Federal Constitution*); Dodd, "The First State Constitutional Conventions, 1776–1783," 2 *American Political Science Review* 545, 557 (1908).

2. H. St. John (Viscount Bolingbroke), *A Dissertation upon Parties* 108 (3d ed.,

London, 1735); 1 W. Blackstone, *Commentaries on the Laws of England* * 50–52 (1st ed., Oxford, 1765).

3. H. Vane, *A Healing Question Propounded and Resolved upon Occasion of the Late Publique and Seasonable Call to Humiliation* (1st ed., London, 1656), in 6 W. Scott, ed., *The Somers Collection of Tracts* 303, 312 (2d ed., London, 1811). A similar plan appears in a proposal of 1648. A. McLaughlin, *A Constitutional History of the United States* 109–10 n.8 (1936).

4. 7 W. Browne, ed., *Archives of Maryland* 61 (1889) (proceedings of Maryland lower house, Oct.-Nov. 1678).

5. 2 L. Butterfield, ed., *Diary and Autobiography of John Adams* 130 (1961) (hereinafter *Adams Diary*).

6. B. Bailyn, *The Ideological Origins of the American Revolution* 175–98 (1967) (hereinafter B. Bailyn, *Ideological Origins*); G. Wood, *The Creation of the American Republic 1776–1787*, at 261–62 (1969) (hereinafter G. Wood, *Creation of the Republic*); 1 H. Commager, ed., *Documents of American History* 45–47 (9th ed., 1973); J. Gough, *Fundamental Law in English Constitutional History* 160–213 (1955); Corwin, "The Progress of Constitutional Theory Between the Declaration of Independence and the Meeting of the Philadelphia Convention," 30 *American Historical Review* 511 (1925).

7. Bayard v. Singleton, 1 N.C. (Mart.) 42, 45 (1787); *The Federalist* No. 22 at 145 (Hamilton), No. 39 at 254 (Madison); James Madison to Thomas Jefferson, March 19, 1787, in 9 *Madison Papers* at 318.

8. J. F. Jameson, "The Early Political Uses of the Word Convention," 3 *American Historical Review* 477, 479–80, 484 (1898) (hereinafter J. F. Jameson, "Early Uses"). John Franklin Jameson, a historian who taught at Johns Hopkins, Brown University, and the University of Chicago, does not use the term to refer to periodical gatherings that nominate candidates for elective office, or to multilateral agreements among countries.

9. George Washington to the President of Congress (Elias Boudinot), March 18, 1783, in 26 J. Fitzpatrick, ed., *The Writings of George Washington* 229 (1938) (hereinafter *Washington Writings*); R. Hoar, *Constitutional Conventions: Their Nature, Powers, and Limitations* 2 (1917); J. F. Jameson, "Early Uses" at 485–86.

10. 1 W. Blackstone, *Commentaries* * 50–51, * 150; J. Pocock, *The Machiavellian Moment: Florentine Political Thought and the Atlantic Republican Tradition* 361 (1975); J. F. Jameson, "Early Uses" at 482–83.

11. 12 Car. 2 ch. 1; 1 W. & M. ch. 1. See 6 W. Holdsworth, *A History of English Law* 194 (1924); H. Horwitz, *Parliament, Policy and Politics in the Reign of William III*, at 6–14 (1977) (the constitutional obstacles to convening Parliament after James's burning of the royal writs).

12. J. F. Jameson, "Early Uses" at 483–84; J. M[ilton], *The Readie and Easie Way to Establish a Free Commonwealth* 32 (2d ed., London, April 1660), in 7 R. Ayers, ed., *Complete Prose Works of John Milton* 431 (1980) (1st ed., London, Feb. 1660); *A Brief Collection of Some Memorandums: or, Things Humbly Offered to the Consideration of the Members of the Great Convention* 7, 13 (1689), in J. F. Jameson, "Early Uses" at 479 n.3.

13. 1 T. Hutchinson, *The History of the Colony of Massachusetts-Bay* 372–87 (Boston, 1764); R. Johnson, *Adjustment to Empire: The New England Colonies 1675–1715*, at 88–107 (1981); 3 J. Palfrey, *History of New England* 588–89 (Boston, 1864); *An Account of the Late Revolutions in New England by A.B.* (June 6, 1689), in M. Hall, L. Leder,

and M. Kammen, eds., *The Glorious Revolution in America: Documents on the Colonial Crisis of 1689*, at 48–53 (1964). The rebel conclave in Bacon's Rebellion (Virginia, 1676) was referred to as a "convention" by some contemporaries. J. F. Jameson, "Early Uses" at 478.

14. 3 C. Andrews, *The Colonial Period of American History* 124–37 (1937); 3 H. Osgood, *The American Colonies in the Seventeenth Century* 452–76 (1907); 1 W. Smith, Jr., *The History of the Province of New-York* 70–76 (M. Kammen, ed., 1972) (1st ed., London, 1757); Jacob Leisler to King William and Queen Mary, Aug. 20, 1689, in 3 E. B. O'Callaghan, ed., *Documents Relative to the Colonial History of the State of New-York* 615 (Albany, N.Y., 1853).

15. 13 *Archives of Maryland* at 231–47 (papers relating to the "Associators' Assembly"); 1 G. Chalmers, *An Introduction to the History of the Revolt of the American Colonies* 204–5 (Boston, 1845); M. Hall, L. Leder, and M. Kammen, *Documents on the Colonial Crisis* at 167–86; D. Lovejoy, *The Glorious Revolution in America* 257–70 (1974); 1 J. Scharf, *History of Maryland* 307–41 (1879).

16. 2 B. Carroll, ed., *Historical Collections of South Carolina* 169 (New York, 1836), reprinting [F. Yonge,] *A Narrative of the Proceedings of the People of South Carolina, in the Year 1719* (1st ed., London, 1726) (Francis Yonge was a member of the South Carolina upper house in 1719); 2 H. Osgood, *The American Colonies in the Eighteenth Century* 356–62 (1924); M. Sirmans, *Colonial South Carolina* 125–28 (1966).

17. M. Jensen, *The Founding of a Nation* 508–34 (1968); 4 W. Ford et al., eds., *Journals of the Continental Congress 1774–1789*, at 136 (1906) (hereinafter *JCC*) (address reported Feb. 13, 1776).

18. R. Brown, *Revolutionary Politics in Massachusetts* 29–31 (1976); Thomas Hutchinson to Richard Jackson, Oct. 5, 1768, in id. at 31. See B. Bailyn, *The Ordeal of Thomas Hutchinson* 123–24 (1974).

19. 1 *JCC* at 35 (1904); O. Handlin and M. Handlin, eds., *The Popular Sources of Political Authority: Documents on the Massachusetts Constitution of 1780, at* 7 (1966) (hereinafter *Popular Sources*); R. Bushman, *King and People in Provincial Massachusetts* 213–15 (1985); G. Wood, *Creation of the Republic* at 317–18.

20. 2 *JCC* at 76–77; 3 *Adams Diary* at 352; 2 *JCC* at 84.

21. 3 *JCC* at 319, 326–27, 403–4.

22. 4 id. at 342; 3 *Adams Diary* at 335.

23. Anonymous, *The Alarm; or, an Address to the People of Pennsylvania on the Late Resolve of Congress* 3 (Philadelphia, 1776), in 1 C. Hyneman and D. Lutz, eds., *American Political Writing During the Founding Era* 321, 326 (1983) (emphasis deleted); "Consideration," Remarks on the Proceedings and Resolutions of the Meeting in the State-House Yard . . . October 21 and 22, 1776 (Philadelphia, Oct. 30, 1776), in 2 P. Force, ed., *American Archives* 1154 (5th ser., Washington, D.C., 1851) (hereinafter *American Archives*).

24. On the drafting of state constitutions during the Revolutionary era, see W. Adams, *First American Constitutions* at 63–98; A. McLaughlin, *Constitutional History* at 106–17; J. Main, *The Sovereign States, 1775–1783*, at 143–221 (1973); A. Nevins, *The American States During and After the Revolution 1775–1789*, at 117–39 (1924); R. Simmons, *The American Colonies* 360–72 (1981); W. C. Webster, "Comparative Study of the State Constitutions of the American Revolution," 9 *Annals of the American Academy of Political and Social Science* 380 (1897). Many public and private records

describing the creation of the state constitutions are preserved in P. Force, ed., *American Archives* (9 vols. Washington, D.C., 1837–1853).

For accounts of individual state constitutions, see J. Daniell, *Experiment in Republicanism: New Hampshire Politics and the American Revolution, 1741–1794*, at 164–79 (1970); C. Erdman, *The New Jersey Constitution of 1776* (1929); F. Green, *Constitutional Development in the South Atlantic States, 1776–1860*, at 47–141 (1966); H. Grigsby, *The Virginia Convention of 1776* (Richmond, 1855); 9 W. Hening, ed., *The Statutes at Large; Being a Collection of All the Laws of Virginia, from the First Session of the Legislature, in the Year 1619*, at 53–57, 109–51 (Richmond 1821) (election of delegates and proceedings of Virginia convention); *Journal of the Convention for Framing a Constitution of Government for the State of Massachusetts Bay* (Boston, 1832) (proceedings of the 1779–1780 convention); 1 C. Lincoln, *The Constitutional History of New York* 471–595 (1906); B. Mason, *The Road to Independence: The Revolutionary Movement in New York, 1773–1777* (1966); J. Selsam, *The Pennsylvania Constitution of 1776* (1936); A. Saye, *A Constitutional History of Georgia* 96–116 (rev. ed., 1970); Morison, "The Vote of Massachusetts on Summoning a Constitutional Convention, 1776–1916," 50 *Proceedings of the Massachusetts Historical Society* 241 (1917); Morison, "The Struggle over the Adoption of the Constitution of Massachusetts, 1780," id. at 353.

25. M. Jensen, *The New Nation: A History of the United States During the Confederation 1781–1789*, at 332–33 (1965) (hereinafter M. Jensen, *The New Nation*); S. Williams, *History of the Lost State of Franklin* (rev. ed., 1933); F. J. Turner, "Western State-Making in the Revolutionary Era" (pts. 1 and 2), 1 *American Historical Review* 70, 251 (1895–1896).

26. W. Adams, *First American Constitutions* at 74–83; 1 D. Ramsay, *The History of the Revolution in South-Carolina* 133–35 (Trenton, 1785).

27. 3 J. Adams, *A Defence of the Constitutions of Government of the United States of America* 211 (1st ed., London, 1788); 3 *Adams Diary* at 358–59.

28. See B. Bailyn, *Ideological Origins* at 34–54; H. Colbourn, *The Lamp of Experience: Whig History and the Intellectual Origins of the American Revolution* (1965); I. Kramnick, *Bolingbroke and His Circle* (1968); P. Maier, *From Resistance to Revolution: Colonial Radicals and the Development of American Opposition to Britain, 1765–1776*, at 27–48 (1974); J. Pole, *Political Representation in England and the Origins of the American Republic* 7–26 (1966); C. Robbins, *The Eighteenth-Century Commonwealthman* (1959); G. Wood, *Creation of the Republic* at 14–36.

29. B. Bailyn, *Ideological Origins* at 35, 36. For a recent assessment of Locke's place in the development of American political theory, see Kramnick, "Republican Revisionism Revisited," 87 *American Historical Review* 629 (1982).

30. 3 [J. Trenchard and T. Gordon,] *Cato's Letters* 326 (1st book ed., London, 1724).

31. Corwin, "Progress of Constitutional Theory" at 513–14; T. Jefferson, *Notes on the State of Virginia* 120 (W. Peden, ed., 1955) (1st ed., Paris, 1785); James Madison to Thomas Jefferson, Oct. 24, 1787, in 10 *Madison Papers* at 212.

32. D. Lutz, *Popular Consent and Popular Control: Whig Political Theory in the Early State Constitutions* 78 (1980); *Popular Sources* at 153.

33. T. Jefferson, *Notes on Virginia* 122, 125.

34. N. Webster, "On Government" (1788), in *A Collection of Essays and Fugitiv[e] Writings on Moral, Historical, Political and Literary Subjects* 49, 54, 51 n.*, 52 (1st ed., Boston, 1790). See R. Rollins, *The Long Journey of Noah Webster* 40–44 (1980) (on

Webster's attitude toward the conventions of 1783 in Virginia, New Jersey, New York, and Connecticut, opposing the pensions voted by Congress to Continental Army officers). Admitted to the bar in 1781, Noah Webster through his books and essays promoted both a distinctive American literary idiom and a strong central government. In his *Dissertations on the English Language* 20 (1st ed., Boston, 1789), he wrote: "As an independent nation, our honor requires us to have a system of our own, in language as well as government." Webster's twin concerns culminated in the publication of *An American Dictionary of the English Language* (2 vols., New York, 1828).

35. The definition is based on W. Adams, *First American Constitutions* at 92; T. Cooley, *A Treatise on the Constitutional Limitations Which Rest upon the Legislative Power of the States of the American Union* 32–33 (1st ed., Boston, 1868); W. Dodd, *The Revision and Amendment of State Constitutions* 22, 72 (1910); F. Green, *Constitutional Development* at 60; R. Hoar, *Constitutional Conventions: Their Nature, Powers, and Limitations* 4 (1917); J. A. Jameson, *Treatise* §§11–15 at 10–15; A. McLaughlin, *Constitutional History* at 108–9, 112–13.

36. W. Adams, *First American Constitutions* at 87–88; *Popular Sources* at 99–166, 202–365 (collecting returns of the towns), 402–3.

37. W. Adams, *First American Constitutions* at 71–75, 79, 81–83, 86; 9 N. Bouton, ed., *Documents and Records Relating to Towns in New Hampshire* 842, 877, 895–96 (1875); C. Lobingier, *The People's Law or Popular Participation in Law-Making* 68–104 (1909); E. Oberholtzer, *The Referendum in America* 33 (1893); A. Nevins, *States During the Revolution* at 128.

38. *The Fundamental Constitutions of Carolina* of 1669, §120, in 2 B. Poore, ed., *The Federal and State Constitutions, Colonial Charters, and Other Organic Laws of the United States* 1408 (2d ed., 1878). See *Charter of New Plymouth Colony* of 1629, in 3 F. Thorpe, ed., *The Federal and State Constitutions* 1852 (1909); Heller, "Article V: Changing Dimensions in Constitutional Change," 7 *University of Michigan Journal of Law Reform* 71, 72–73 (1973).

39. 1 J. Trumbull, ed., *The Public Records of the Colony of Connecticut* 346–47 (Hartford, 1850); *Pa. Frame of Government* of 1682, §23; G. Wood, *Creation of the Republic* at 614; 1 M. Farrand, ed., *The Records of the Federal Convention of 1787*, at 202–3 (rev. ed., 1937) (hereinafter *Records*).

40. *Del. Const.* of 1776, art. 30; *Md. Const.* of 1776, art. 59; *S. C. Const.* of 1778, art. 44.

41. *Pa. Const.* of 1776, §47; R. Brunhouse, *The Counter-Revolution in Pennsylvania 1776–1790*, at 159 (1942); *Vt. Const.* of 1777, §44; J. A. Jameson, *Treatise* §155 at 141–42.

42. *Mass. Const.* of 1780, pt. 2, ch. 6, art. 10. The phrase "in order to" (e.g., as here, "amendments") is an archaic usage meaning "in regard to" or "for the purpose of obtaining."

43. *N.H. Const.* of 1784, pt. 2; Morison, "Vote of Massachusetts" at 246–47; J. Daniell, *Experiment in Republicanism* at 226–32.

44. 6 J. Boyd et al., eds., *The Papers of Thomas Jefferson* 304, 614 (1952) (hereinafter *Jefferson Papers*).

45. E. Williams, *The Eighteenth-Century Constitution* 3 (1960); Thomas Jefferson to Ralph Izard, July 17, 1788, in 13 *Jefferson Papers* at 373; 4 *Hamilton Papers* at 203 (emphasis deleted).

46. 5 *JCC* at 425, 433; 9 id. at 925; 2 id. at 198 (Franklin's art. XII).

47. M. Jensen, *The New Nation* at 313–26; 9 I. Hammond, ed., *Collections of the New Hampshire Historical Society* 245–71 (1889) (hereinafter *New Hampshire Collections*) (Providence convention proceedings).

48. Benjamin Rush's Notes of Debates, Feb. 4, 1777, in 6 P. Smith, ed., *Letters of Delegates to Congress 1774–1789*, at 217–18 (1980) (hereinafter *Letters of Delegates*); William Ellery to Nicholas Cooke, Feb. 15, 1777, in id. at 283.

49. Thomas Burke's Notes of Debates, Feb. 15, 1777, in id. at 279; 7 *JCC* at 124–25; 1 C. Hoadly, ed., *The Public Records of the State of Connecticut* 599–606 (1894) (Springfield convention proceedings).

50. 9 *JCC* at 956–57; 9 *New Hampshire Collections* at 272–95 (New Haven convention proceedings).

51. 11 *JCC* at 569–70; William Fleming to Thomas Jefferson, July 13, 1779, in 3 *Jefferson Papers* at 33; Samuel Adams to John Adams, April 16, 1784; Samuel Adams to Noah Webster, April 30, 1784, in 4 H. Cushing, ed., *The Writings of Samuel Adams* 296, 305, 306 (1908).

52. 2 C. Hoadly, ed., *The Public Records of the State of Connecticut* 562–71 (1895).

53. Id. at 572–79; 5 *The Acts and Resolves, Public and Private, of the Province of the Massachusetts Bay* 1264 (1886).

54. John Witherspoon to William Churchill Houston, Jan. 27, 1778, in 8 *Letters to Delegates* at 670; 5 *The Acts and Resolves, Public and Private, of the Province of the Massachusetts Bay* 1263 (1886); 16 *JCC* at 262–67. On the trade conventions of the 1770s, see R. Morris, *Government and Labor in Early America* 92–119 (2d ed., 1981); C. Nettels, *The Emergence of a National Economy 1775–1815*, at 28–29 (1962).

55. J. Rakove, *The Beginnings of National Politics: An Interpretive History of the Continental Congress* 380 (1979) (hereinafter J. Rakove, *Beginnings*); John Dickinson to Thomas Rodney, July 22, 1779, in M. Flower, *John Dickinson: Conservative Revolutionary* 237 (1983); A. McLaughlin, *Constitutional History* at 137–47; *The Federalist* Nos. 15–22 at 89–146 (Hamilton and Madison).

56. M. Farrand, *The Fathers of the Constitution* 52 (1921); T. Paine, *Common Sense* (1st ed., Philadelphia, 1776), in 1 M. Conway, ed., *The Writings of Thomas Paine* 98 (1902).

57. Alexander Hamilton to James Duane, Sept. 3, 1780, in 2 *Hamilton Papers* at 407–8; 3 id. at 426, 420 n.1.

58. F. Hough, ed., *Proceedings of a Convention of Delegates from Several of the New England States, Held at Boston, August 3–9, 1780*, at 50, 52 (Albany, N.Y., 1867).

59. 3 C. Hoadly, ed., *The Public Records of the State of Connecticut* 564–74 (1922); 3 *Hamilton Papers* at 113. A convention set for Providence in April 1781 disbanded when only two states were represented; two months later a convention of New England delegates met at Providence to agree on a schedule for sending monthly rations of beef, salt, rum, and clothing to the Continental Army. 3 C. Hoadly, *Public Records of Connecticut* at 574–76.

60. Richard Henry Lee to James Madison, Nov. 26, 1784, in 8 *Madison Papers* at 151; George Washington to the Rev. William Gordon, July 8, 1783, in 27 *Washington Writings* at 49.

61. *Resolves of the General Court of the Commonwealth of Massachusetts* 70 (Boston, 1785); The Massachusetts Delegates to the Governor of Massachusetts (James Bowdoin), Sept. 3, 1785, in 8 E. Burnett, ed., *Letters of Members of the Continental Congress* 208

(1936) (hereinafter E. Burnett, *Letters*); id. at 207–8, 479, 504. Julius Goebel, using principles of modern constitutional interpretation, argued that the source of an amendment under the Articles was immaterial, so long as the proposal was approved by Congress and the states. J. Goebel, *Antecedents* at 198–99. At the time, however, the point was not settled, Washington among others holding with the delegates. George Washington to the Secretary for Foreign Affairs (John Jay), March 10, 1787, in 29 *Washington Writings* at 177.

62. E. Burnett, *The Continental Congress* 636–37 (1941); East, "The Massachusetts Conservatives in the Critical Period," in R. Morris, ed., *The Era of the American Revolution* 349, 368–70 (1939).

63. R. Morris, *The Forging of the Union 1781–1789*, at 247–52 (1987); 1 G. Bancroft, *History of the Formation of the Constitution of the United States of America* 249–52 (1882); George Mason to James Madison, Aug. 9, 1785, in 2 R. Rutland, ed., *The Papers of George Mason* 827 (1970); Compact Between Maryland and Virginia, in id. at 818; George Mason and Alexander Henderson to the Speaker of the House of Delegates, March 28, 1785, in id. at 816.

64. 6 D. Freeman, *George Washington: A Biography* 30, 66 (1954); 2 I. Brant, *James Madison: The Nationalist* 375–76 (1948); James Madison to George Washington, Dec. 9, 1785, in 8 *Madison Papers* at 439.

65. *Journal of the House of Delegates of Virginia* 151 (printed by John Dunlap and James Hayes, Richmond, 1786) (proceedings of Jan. 21, 1786); Edmund Randolph to the Executives of the States, Feb. 19, 1786, in 1 *Ratification History* at 180; James Madison to Thomas Jefferson, Aug. 12, 1786, in 9 *Madison Papers* at 96.

66. James Madison to James Monroe, March 19, 1786, in 8 *Madison Papers* at 505; J. Rakove, *Beginnings* at 370; James Monroe to the President of New Hampshire (John Sullivan), Aug. 16, 1786, in 8 E. Burnett, *Letters* at 430.

67. James Madison to Thomas Jefferson, Aug. 12, 1786, in 9 *Madison Papers* at 95–96; F. Bates, *Rhode Island and the Formation of the Union* 151–52 (1898).

68. 1 *Ratification History* at 184, 183, 184; James Madison to Noah Webster, Oct. 12, 1804, in 7 G. Hunt, *Writings of Madison* at 165.

69. 8 E. Burnett, *Letters* at 323–24; William Grayson to James Madison, March 22, 1786, in 8 *Madison Papers* at 508–10.

70. 30 JCC at 230; Diary of Thomas Rodney, May 3, 1786, in 8 E. Burnett, *Letters* at 350; 30 JCC at 387 n.1; 31 id. at 495–98 (1786 amendments); 28 id. at 201–2 (committee submission March 28, 1785).

71. M. Jensen, *The New Nation* at 418–19.

72. James Monroe to James Madison, July 26, 1785, in 8 *Madison Papers* at 330; James Monroe to Gov. Patrick Henry, Aug. 12, 1786, in 1 S. Hamilton, ed., *The Writings of James Monroe* 149 (1898); M. Jensen, *The New Nation* at 420.

73. Stephen Higginson to Henry Knox, Nov. 25, 1786, in J. Franklin Jameson, ed., "Letters of Stephen Higginson, 1783–1804," in 1 American Historical Association, *Annual Report, 1896*, at 704, 743 (1897). See D. Szatmary, *Shays' Rebellion: The Making of an Agrarian Insurrection* (1980).

74. James Madison to Edmund Pendleton, Feb. 24, 1787, in 9 *Madison Papers* at 295; J. Rakove, *Beginnings* at 376; 32 JCC at 73–74; James Madison to George Washington, Feb. 21, 1787, in 9 *Madison Papers* at 285.

75. 1 *Records* at 113; George Washington to Henry Knox, Feb. 3, 1787, in 29 *Washington Writings* at 152, 153, 152.

2. Philadelphia and After

1. On article V in general or the convention clause in particular, see W. Edel, *A Constitutional Convention: Threat or Challenge?* 26–33 (1981); L. Orfield, *Amending the Federal Constitution*; Buckwalter, "Constitutional Conventions and State Legislators," 20 *Journal of Public Law* 543, 543–45 (1971); Rhodes, "A Limited Federal Constitutional Convention," 26 *University of Florida Law Review* 1, 3–8 (1973); Voegler, "Amending the Constitution by the Article V Convention Method," 55 *North Dakota Law Review* 355, 359–66 (1979); Wood, "The Origins of Article V of the Constitution," in W. Moore and R. Penner, eds., *The Constitution and the Budget* (1980); Kurland, Memorandum on S. 2307, in *Constitutional Convention Procedures: Hearing on S. 3, S. 520, and S. 1710 Before the Subcommittee on the Constitution of the Senate Committee on the Judiciary*, 96th Congress, 1st Session 1085–93 (1979) (hereinafter *1979 Hearing*).

2. 1 *Records* at 22, 202–3.

3. Id. at 237; 2 id. at 188; 4 *Elliot* at 230 (James Iredell at North Carolina ratifying convention).

4. 1 *Records* at 519, 532. See id. at 432, 439 (Gerry and Luther Martin); 2 id. at 93, 391, 642 (Morris, Pinckney, and Franklin).

5. 2 id. at 557–58.

6. Id. at 558, 559; 9 *JCC* at 925; 2 *Records* at 602.

7. Id. at 629.

8. Id. at 629–30.

9. *The Federalist* No. 85 at 593.

10. 2 *Records* at 558; John Jay to George Washington, Jan. 7, 1787, in 3 H. Johnston, ed., *The Correspondence and Public Papers of John Jay* 228 (1891).

11. 2 *Records* at 559.

12. 1 id. at 323, 324.

13. 2 id. at 559.

14. Id. at 629, 631.

15. *The Federalist* No. 43 at 296 (emphasis supplied); N. Webster, "On Government" (1788), in *A Collection of Essays and Fugitiv[e] Writings on Moral, Historical, Political and Literary Subjects* 49, 58 (1st ed., Boston, 1790). See Dodge v. Woolsey, 59 U.S. (18 How.) 331, 348 (1856) (equal suffrage limitation is "permanent and unalterable").

16. 13 *Annals of Cong.* 101 (1803) (remarks of Sen. Dayton).

17. 2 *Records* at 479. The best accounts of the second convention episode are: S. Bloom, ed., *History of the Formation of the Union* 280–328 (1941) (hereinafter S. Bloom, *Formation of the Union*); J. Goebel, *Antecedents* at 415–24; R. Rutland, *The Ordeal of the Constitution* 36–41, 279–300 (1966) (hereinafter R. Rutland, *Ordeal of the Constitution*); DePauw, "The Anticlimax of Antifederalism: The Abortive Second Convention Movement, 1788–89," 2 *Prologue* 98 (1970); Edward P. Smith, "The Movement Towards a Second Constitutional Convention in 1788," in John Franklin Jameson, ed., *Essays in the Constitutional History of the United States in the Formative Period 1775–1789*, at 46 (1889).

18. 2 *Records* at 564, 632.

19. Id. at 633.

20. Id. at 587–88; *The Federalist* No. 83 at 558–67, No. 84 at 575–81, No. 85 at 591.

On the ratification conventions, see L. DePauw, *The Eleventh Pillar: New York State and the Federal Constitution* (1966); H. Grigsby, *The History of the Virginia Federal Convention of 1788* (2 vols., 1891); S. Harding, *The Contest over the Ratification of the Federal Constitution in the State of Massachusetts* (1896); O. Libby, *The Geographical Distribution of the Vote of the Thirteen States on the Federal Constitution, 1787–8* (1894); J. McMaster and F. Stone, eds., *Pennsylvania and the Federal Constitution 1787–1788* (1888); C. Miner, *The Ratification of the Federal Constitution in New York* (1921); B. Peirce and C. Hale, eds., *Debates and Proceedings in the Convention of the Commonwealth of Massachusetts, Held in the Year 1788* (Boston, 1856); L. Trenholme, *Ratification of the Federal Constitution in North Carolina* (1932); J. Walker, *Birth of the Federal Constitution: A History of the New Hampshire Convention* (1888); Brooks, "Alexander Hamilton, Melancton Smith, and the Ratification of the Constitution in New York," 24 *William and Mary Quarterly* 339 (3d ser., 1967); Kaminski, "Controversy Amid Consensus: The Adoption of the Federal Constitution in Georgia," 58 *Georgia Historical Quarterly* 244 (1974); Newsome, "North Carolina's Ratification of the Federal Constitution," 17 *North Carolina Historical Review* 287 (1940); Pratt, "Law and the Experience of Politics in Late Eighteenth-Century North Carolina: North Carolina Considers the Constitution," 22 *Wake Forest Law Review* 577 (1987); Steiner, "Maryland's Adoption of the Federal Constitution" (pts. 1 and 2), 5 *American Historical Review* 22, 207 (1899–1900).

21. C. Rossiter, *1787: The Grand Convention* 281 (1966); R. Rutland, *Ordeal of the Constitution* at 36, 41, 213, 295 n.39, 313; 1 *Annals of Cong.* 759 (1789).

22. Edmund Randolph to the Speaker of the Virginia House of Delegates, Oct. 10, 1787, in 1 *Elliot* at 490; Richard Henry Lee to Edmund Randolph, Oct. 16, 1787, in id. at 505.

23. Thomas Jefferson to William Carmichael, Dec. 15, 1787, in 12 *Jefferson Papers* at 425–26; John Adams to Cotton Tufts, Feb. 12, 1788, in 2 P. Smith, *John Adams* 726 (1962); John Adams to Richard Price, April 19, 1790, in 9 C. F. Adams, ed., *The Works of John Adams* 564 (Boston, 1854).

24. James Madison to Edmund Randolph, Jan. 10, 1788, in 10 *Madison Papers* at 356; 1 *Annals of Cong.* 734–44, 795 (1789); 1 *Elliot* at 322 (Massachusetts ratification act recommended amendments to "be introduced into the said Constitution"); Richard Henry Lee to Samuel Adams, Oct. 5, 1787, in 13 *Ratification History* at 324. Madison's amendments, as introduced in the House of Representatives, were designed for insertion into the appropriate parts of the Constitution's text.

25. 1 *Annals of Cong.* 743, 736–37 (1789) (Reps. Smith and Livermore); James Madison to Edmund Randolph, Jan. 10, 1788, in 10 *Madison Papers* at 355.

26. *Journal of the House of Delegates of the Commonwealth of Virginia* 77 (printed by Thomas W. White, Richmond, 1828) (proceedings of Nov. 30, 1787) (hereinafter *Virginia Delegate Journal*); 12 W. Hening, *Statutes at Large* at 463.

27. Smith, "Movement Towards a Second Constitutional Convention" at 61, 90, 61.

28. R. Rutland, *Ordeal of the Constitution* at 106–7; Thomas Jefferson to James Madison, Nov. 18, 1788, in 14 *Jefferson Papers* at 188.

29. 3 *Elliot* at 627, 161.

30. Id. at 657–61, 652; James Madison to Tench Coxe, July 30, 1788, in 11 *Madison Papers* at 210; M. Tyler, *Patrick Henry* 355 (1899).

31. George Washington to James Madison, Nov. 17, 1788, in 11 *Madison Papers* at

351; George Lee Turberville to James Madison, Oct. 29, 1788, in id. at 323–24; *Virginia Delegate Journal* at 16 (proceedings of Oct. 30, 1788).

32. *Virginia Delegate Journal* at 16–17 (proceedings of Oct. 30, 1788); Francis Corbin to James Madison, Nov. 12, 1788, in 11 *Madison Papers* at 342; *Virginia Delegate Journal* at 42–44 (proceedings of Nov. 14, 1788) (the journal mistakenly records a 72–50 vote); *Journal of the Senate of the Commonwealth of Virginia* 31, 32 (Richmond, 1828) (proceedings of Nov. 19 and 20, 1788); James Monroe to Thomas Jefferson, Feb. 15, 1789, in 14 *Jefferson Papers* at 558. Like Henry, Monroe had voted against ratification at the Richmond convention.

33. 1 *Annals of Cong.* 258–61 (1789).

34. 2 *Elliot* at 413–14 (letter dated July 28, 1788).

35. George Washington to Benjamin Lincoln, Aug. 28, 1788, in 30 *Washington Writings* at 63; Timothy Pickering to John Pickering, Dec. 29, 1787, in 15 *Ratification History* at 177; 2 New York State, *Messages from the Governors* 289–90 (C. Z. Lincoln, ed., 1909); *Journal of the Assembly of the State of New-York (Twelfth Session)* 105–6 (Albany, 1788 [1789]) (proceedings of Feb. 5, 1789); *Journal of the Senate of the State of New-York (Twelfth Session)* 56 (Albany, 1788 [1789]) (proceedings of Feb. 7, 1789); 1 *Journal of the House of Representatives of the United States*, 1st Congress, 1st Session 29–30 (1789) (Gales & Seaton edition, 1826). 1 *Annals of Cong.* 282 (1789) omits the application, recording only its receipt. Modern edited texts of the Virginia and New York applications appear in L. DePauw, C. Bickford, and L. Hauptman, eds., *House of Representatives Journal* 47–48, 50 (1977) (vol. 3 of the Documentary History of the First Federal Congress of the United States of America, March 4, 1789–March 3, 1791).

36. R. Rutland, *Ordeal of the Constitution* at 124–27; I. Polishook, *Rhode Island and the Union* 198 (1969); 10 J. Bartlett, ed., *Records of the State of Rhode Island and Providence Plantations in New England* 275 (Providence, 1865).

37. 10 *Records of Rhode Island* at 309–10; R. Rutland, *Ordeal of the Constitution* at 291; 1 *Elliot* at 334–35. An application by Rhode Island for a national constitutional convention in 1790 is listed in C. Brickfield, *Problems Relating to a Federal Constitutional Convention* 87 (85th Congress, 1st Session, Committee Print, 1957), and Graham, "The Role of the States in Proposing Constitutional Amendments," 49 *American Bar Association Journal* 1175, 1179 (1963). Both writers cite the same source, *House Journal*, 1st Congress, 2d Session 148 (1790) (proceedings of Jan. 28, 1790), but this entry refers only to Rhode Island's enabling resolution for its ratifying convention.

38. John Brown Cutting to Thomas Jefferson, Oct. 6, 1788, in 13 *Jefferson Papers* at 660; 1 *Elliot* at 332; 20 W. Clark, ed., *The State Records of North Carolina* 527 (1902) (state senate proceedings of Nov. 20, 1788); 22 id. at 36–53 (journal of the Fayetteville convention). "North Carolina ratification convention" herein refers exclusively to the Hillsborough meeting.

39. 2 *Elliot* at 544; A. Gallatin, "Draft of a Report of the Harrisburg Conference" (Sept. 3, 1788), in E. Ferguson, ed., *Selected Writings of Albert Gallatin* 16–18 (1967). See P. Ford, *The Origin, Purpose and Result of the Harrisburg Convention of 1788* (1890) (collecting letters and other documents); J. McMaster and F. Stone, *Pennsylvania and the Federal Constitution* at 552–64.

40. J. Main, *The Antifederalists: Critics of the Constitution 1781–1788*, at 249 n.1 (1974); L. Orfield, *Amending the Federal Constitution* at 147. According to the first census, the population of the United States in 1790 totaled roughly 3,929,000. 7 Bureau of the Census, *Heads of Families at the First Census of the United States* 4, 8 (1908).

41. A. McLaughlin, *Constitutional History* at 220–21; Roll, "We, Some of the People: Apportionment in the Thirteen State Conventions Ratifying the Constitution," 56 *Journal of American History* 21, 35 (1969); Nettels, "The American Merchant and the Constitution," 34 *Publications of the Colonial Society of Massachusetts* 26 (1943) (mercantile class supported the Constitution by a ratio of 18 to 1); 3 *Elliot* at 654; 2 id. at 181; id. at 413.

42. R. Rutland, *Ordeal of the Constitution* at 299–300; Smith, "Movement Towards a Second Constitutional Convention" at 87, 91; Henry Lee to James Madison, ca. Dec. 20, 1787, in 10 *Madison Papers* at 339.

43. James Madison to Thomas Jefferson, March 29, 1789, in 12 id. at 38; "Plain Truth," To the FREEMEN of BALTIMORE-TOWN, *Virginia Independent Chronicle* (Richmond), Nov. 19, 1788, at 1; DeWitt Clinton to Charles Tillinghast, July 12, 1788, in I. Leake, *Memoir of the Life and Times of General John Lamb* 317 (Albany, N.Y., 1857); James Madison to Richard Peters, Aug. 19, 1789, in 12 *Madison Papers* at 347. DeWitt Clinton, nephew of George, later a United States senator and, like his uncle, Governor of New York, authored a series of essays opposing ratification under the title *Letters from a Countryman.*

44. 1 *Annals of Cong.* 448–59 (June 8, 1789); id. at 449, 787, 462 (1789) (Reps. Madison, Tucker, and Gerry). The major Jefferson-Madison correspondence is reproduced in 1 B. Schwartz, ed., *The Bill of Rights: A Documentary History* 592–623 (1971).

45. C. Miner, *Ratification of the Federal Constitution in New York* at 131–32; R. Rutland, *Ordeal of the Constitution* at 302–3, 306–7; Benjamin Franklin to the Duc de la Rochefoucauld, Oct. 22, 1788, in 9 A. Smyth, ed., *The Writings of Benjamin Franklin* 666 (1907).

3. The Nineteenth Century

1. James Madison to Thomas Jefferson, Sept. 21, 1788, in 13 *Jefferson Papers* at 624–25; S. Williams, *The Natural and Civil History of Vermont* 346 (1st ed., Walpole, New Hampshire, 1794), in 2 C. Hyneman and D. Lutz, eds., *American Political Writing During the Founding Era* 950, 966 (1983).

2. 1 United States Statutes at Large 571, 596 (1798).

3. 6 G. Hunt, *Writings of Madison* at 402, 403, 404.

4. D. Malone, *Jefferson and the Ordeal of Liberty* 491–505 (1962); M. Peterson, *Thomas Jefferson and the New Nation* 644–45 (1970).

5. Thomas Jefferson to Dr. Benjamin Barton, Feb. 14, 1801, in 7 P. Ford, ed., *The Writings of Thomas Jefferson* 490 (1896); Thomas Jefferson to James Monroe, Feb. 15, 1801, in id. at 491.

6. Thomas Jefferson to Joseph Priestley, March 21, 1801, in 8 id. at 22; Thomas Jefferson to Nathaniel Niles, March 22, 1801, in id. at 24.

7. D. Malone, *Jefferson the President: First Term, 1801–1805,* at 9–10 (1970).

8. E. Brown, ed., *William Plumer's Memorandum of Proceedings in the United States Senate 1803–1807,* at 47, 50 (1923) (emphasis deleted). Plumer's remarks as transcribed from the floor of Congress are at 13 *Annals of Cong.* 153 (1803).

9. L. Turner, *William Plumer of New Hampshire 1759–1850,* at 116–18 (1962).

Plumer gained "anonymous immortality" when, as a member of the 1820 electoral college, he cast the lone presidential vote for his friend John Quincy Adams, robbing James Monroe of a unanimous tally. His reasons, publicly stated and printed in contemporary newspapers, were dissatisfaction with the economic policies of the Monroe administration and the erratic performance of Vice President Daniel Tompkins—not, as has been dutifully but incorrectly repeated, a desire to preserve Washington's distinction as the only president to receive a unanimous electoral vote. Id. at 311–19.

10. 13 *Annals of Cong.* 158 (1803).

11. 1 St. G. Tucker, ed., *Blackstone's Commentaries: With Notes of Reference, to the Constitution and Laws, of the Federal Government of the United States; and of the Commonwealth of Virginia*, Appendix at 371, 171 (Philadelphia, 1803). A short biography appears at 8 Va. (4 Call) xxvi (1833 ed.). St. George Tucker, brother of Representative Thomas Tucker, succeeded his teacher George Wythe—framer, law tutor of Jefferson and Marshall—to the chair of law at the College of William and Mary. Tucker's edition of Blackstone's *Commentaries*, designed for American students and practitioners, contains annotations and essays on American federal and state legal topics. At his death in 1827 he had long been known as "the American Blackstone."

12. James Madison to George Lee Turberville, Nov. 2, 1788, in 11 *Madison Papers* at 331.

13. 30 U.S. (5 Pet.) 518, 524 (1831).

14. Id. at 521, 528. There is no further reference to article V in the files of the case preserved in the National Archives. Key, remembered for his lyrics to "The Star-Spangled Banner," appeared frequently before the Supreme Court, and from 1833 to 1841 was the United States Attorney for the District of Columbia.

15. J. Banner, Jr., *To the Hartford Convention* (1970); 6 I. Brant, *James Madison: Commander in Chief* 351–62 (1961); T. Dwight, *History of the Hartford Convention* (New York and Boston, 1833).

16. [J. Calhoun,] *Exposition and Protest Reported by the Special Committee of the House of Representatives of South Carolina on the Tariff*, in 1 T. Cooper, ed., *The Statutes at Large of South Carolina* 247 (Columbia, 1836). "In the Exposition, as in private letters," a leading historian has written, "Calhoun emphasized that the state aimed at reformation, not revolution. If its intimidating tactics proved successful, nullification would be unnecessary; indeed, putting the theory to the test of practice, incurring all the dangers of disunion, would constitute defeat in Calhoun's eyes." M. Peterson, *The Great Triumvirate: Webster, Clay, and Calhoun* 169 (1987).

17. 4 *Elliot* at 540 (emphasis deleted); Thomas Jefferson to Spencer Roane, June 27, 1821, in 15 A. Lipscomb, ed., *The Writings of Thomas Jefferson* 328–29 (1904); Thomas Jefferson to William Johnson, June 12, 1823, in id. at 451; similarly, Thomas Jefferson to John Cartwright, June 5, 1824, in 16 id. at 47. That a convention could meet "at the call of Congress," at that body's discretion, seems a slip of the pen, but Madison was not sure whether Jefferson had "alluded to a convention as prescribed by the Constitution, or brought about by any other mode." James Madison to John Townsend, Oct. 18, 1831, in 4 *Letters and Other Writings of James Madison* 199 (Philadelphia, 1865).

18. 1 T. Cooper, ed., *The Statutes at Large of South Carolina* 267 (Columbia, 1836); John C. Calhoun to James Hamilton, Jr., Aug. 28, 1832, in 11 C. Wilson, ed., *The Papers of John C. Calhoun* 639 (1978); James Madison to Nicholas P. Trist, Dec. 23, 1832, in 9 G. Hunt, *Writings of Madison* at 490–91; *Report*, 6 id. at 402.

19. James Madison to Robert Y. Hayne, April 3 or 4, 1830, in 9 id. at 386 n.2; R. Ketcham, *James Madison: A Biography* 642, 643 (1971).

20. James Madison to Edward Everett, Aug. 28, 1830, in 31 *North American Review* 537, 542, 543 (Oct. 1830); also in 9 G. Hunt, *Writings of Madison* at 398, 399. See 6 I. Brant, *James Madison: Commander in Chief* 479–85 (1961).

21. 31 *North American Review* at 539, 540; James Madison to Thomas Jefferson, June 27, 1823, in 9 G. Hunt, *Writings of Madison* at 140–41; J. Madison, "Genl. Remarks on the Convention" (ca. 1821), in 3 *Records* at 455.

22. *Acts and Resolutions of the General Assembly of the State of South Carolina, Passed in December 1831*, Appendix at 1–2 (Columbia, 1832 [1833]); 1 H. Commager, *Documents of American History* at 261–62; "Address to the People of the United States," in Massachusetts General Court, *State Papers on Nullification* 70 (Boston, 1834).

23. R. Ketcham, *James Madison: A Biography* 644–45 (1971); 9 *Register of Debates in Congress*, Appendix at 185 (Gales & Seaton edition, Washington, D.C., 1833).

24. *Acts and Resolutions of the General Assembly, of the State of South-Carolina, Passed in December, 1832*, at 28–29 (Columbia, 1832) (supplementary section, "Reports and Resolutions of 1832"); Massachusetts General Court, *State Papers on Nullification* 208, 256–57, 245 (Boston, 1834); *Journal of the Senate, of the Eighth General Assembly of the State of Illinois* 580, 631 (Vandalia, 1833); *Journal of the Senate of the United States of America*, 22d Congress, 2d Session 157 (Washington, D.C., 1832 [1833]).

25. *Acts and Resolutions of the General Assembly of the State of South-Carolina, Passed in December, 1827 and January, 1828*, at 72 (Columbia, 1828) (Reports and Resolutions December Session, 1827); Report of the Select Committee, in *Laws of the State of Mississippi, Passed at the Sixteenth Session of the General Assembly* 251–52 (Jackson, 1833).

26. *Acts of the General Assembly of the State of Georgia, . . . Passed in November and December, 1832*, at 248, 249–50 (Milledgeville, 1836); Massachusetts General Court, *State Papers on Nullification* 267, 280, 286 (Boston, 1834); *Laws of the State of New-Hampshire* 137 (Concord, 1833). The application originally passed by Georgia's lower house requested amendments in thirteen particulars; the senate deleted all but two. The lower house version, however, was inadvertently sent to Congress, and printed in the *Senate Journal*, 22d Congress, 2d Session 65–66 (1833). See W. Pullen, "The Application Clause of the Amending Provision" at 42–44.

27. *Acts Passed at the Extra and Annual Sessions of the General Assembly of the State of Alabama* 142, 141 (Tuscaloosa, 1833); *Message from His Excellency, Henry W. Edwards, to the Legislature of Connecticut, May, 1833*, at 11 (Hartford, 1833); 1 T. Cooper, ed., *The Statutes at Large of South Carolina* 390, 400–401 (Columbia, 1836). Since the Alabama act only "recommended" a convention rather than "applied" for one, it has been considered not a true article V application. W. Pullen, "The Application Clause of the Amending Provision" at 45. The intent, however, is plain, and there is no requirement that the word "apply" be used in an application.

28. W. Freehling, *Prelude to Civil War: The Nullification Controversy in South Carolina 1816–1836*, at 203–4 (1966); U. Phillips, *Georgia and State Rights* 131–32 (1902); 1 J. Davis, *The Rise and Fall of the Confederate Government* 191 (1881).

29. W. Wiecek, *The Guarantee Clause of the U.S. Constitution* 145–54 (1972); John C. Calhoun to Virgil Maxcy, Sept. 11, 1830, in 11 C. Wilson, ed., *The Papers of John C. Calhoun* 229 (1978); 1 A. Nevins, *Ordeal of the Union* 315–18 (1947); H. Ames, ed.,

State Documents on Federal Relations 262–69 (1906) (resolves adopted by Nashville convention).

30. D. Dumond, *The Secession Movement 1860–61*, at 216–17, 223 (1931); *Acts of the General Assembly of the State of Virginia, Passed in 1861*, at 337 (Richmond, 1861). The report of a separate article V application by Virginia in 1861 in H. Ames, *The Proposed Amendments to the Constitution of the United States During the First Century of Its History* 283 n.1 (1897), seems to be in error.

31. *Congressional Globe*, 36th Congress, 2d Session 112–14 (1860); Scott v. Sandford, 60 U.S. (19 How.) 393, 452 (1857).

32. *Acts of the General Assembly of the Commonwealth of Kentucky* 47 (Frankfort, 1861) (resolutions approved Jan. 25, 1861); *Virginia Acts* at 337 (passed Jan. 21, 1861); *Acts of the Eighty-Fifth Legislature of the State of New Jersey* 540–41 (Freehold, 1861) (resolutions passed Jan. 29, 1861); *Senate Miscellaneous Document No. 2*, Special Session (1861) (Indiana joint resolution passed March 11, 1861); *Public Laws of the State of Illinois, Passed by the Twenty-Second General Assembly* 281–82 (Springfield, 1861) (joint resolution passed before March 14, 1861); *58 Acts . . . Passed by the Fifty-Fourth General Assembly of the State of Ohio at Its Second Session* 181 (Columbus, 1861) (joint resolution passed March 20, 1861); *5 New York State, Messages from the Governors* 356 (C. Z. Lincoln, ed., 1909) (Arkansas resolution passed March 20, 1861); *Journal and Proceedings of the Missouri State Convention, Held at Jefferson City and St. Louis, March, 1861*, at 233 (St. Louis, 1861) (resolution passed March 20, 1861); 2 A. Stephens, *A Constitutional View of the Late War Between the States* 363–64 (Philadelphia, 1868).

33. L. Chittenden, ed., *A Report of the Debates and Proceedings in the Secret Sessions of the Conference Convention* 314, 57 (New York, 1864).

34. C. Wright, ed., *Official Journal of the Conference Convention, Held at Washington City, February, 1861*, at 24–25, 32, 63, 69 (Washington, D.C., 1861); *Cong. Globe*, 36th Congress, 2d Session 1254–55 (1861); D. Dumond, *The Secession Movement 1860–1861*, at 239–65 (1931); R. Gunderson, *Old Gentlemen's Convention: The Washington Peace Conference of 1861* (1961). Gunderson (p. 64) gives Chittenden's reporting a mixed review.

35. A. Kirwan, *John J. Crittenden: The Struggle for the Union* 366–421 (1962); S. Oates, *With Malice Toward None* 204–5 (1977).

36. *Cong. Globe*, 36th Congress, 2d Session 237, Appendix at 42 (1861); id. at 112, 183 (1860); id. at 1270 (Feb. 28, 1861); id. at 79 (1860); id. at 1030, 1236 (1861); *Cong. Globe*, 37th Congress, 1st Session 444 (1861) (Reps. Larrabee, Fenton, Burch, and Vallandigham). See Hyman, "The Narrow Escape from a 'Compromise of 1860': Secession and the Constitution," in H. Hyman and L. Levy, eds., *Freedom and Reform* 149, 164–66 (1967).

37. E. Pollard, *Lee and His Lieutenants* 792 (New York, 1867) (excerpting private diary of John B. Floyd, Secretary of War); *Cong. Globe*, 36th Congress, 2d Session, Appendix at 4 (1860).

38. Abraham Lincoln to Duff Green, Dec. 28, 1860, in 4 R. Basler, ed., *The Collected Works of Abraham Lincoln* 162 (1953). See P. Klein, *President James Buchanan* 358, 362–64, 382–87 (1962).

39. 4 *Collected Works of Lincoln* at 269, 270. See S. Oates, *With Malice Toward None* at 204, 218; J. Randall, *Constitutional Problems Under Lincoln* 350–51, 351–52 n.21 (rev. ed., 1951); Dowd, "Lincoln, the Rule of Law and Crisis Government: A Study of His Constitutional Law Theories," 39 *University of Detroit Law Journal* 633 (1962).

40. 4 *Collected Works of Lincoln* at 265; 1 J. Davis, *The Rise and Fall of the Confeder-ate Government* 678 (1881); *Cong. Globe*, 36th Congress, 2d Session 341 (1861); *House Report No.* 31, 36th Congress, 2d Session 20 (1861) (report of Rep. Taylor). Andrew Jackson had evidently shared Seward's position: "The people are the sovereigns, thay can altar and amend, and the people alone in the mode pointed out by themselves, can dissolve this union peacably." Andrew Jackson to John Coffee, Dec. 14, 1832, in 4 J. Bassett, ed., *Correspondence of Andrew Jackson* 500 (1929).

41. H. Ames, *Proposed Amendments to the Constitution During Its First Century* 283 and n.7; *Cong. Globe*, 37th Congress, 3d Session 4 (1862); H. Hyman, *A More Perfect Union* 119–20 (1975).

42. S. Fisher, *The Trial of the Constitution* 388, 387 (Philadelphia, 1862); *Laws of the State of Delaware* 382–83 (Wilmington, 1863) (adopted Jan. 29, 1863); *Acts of the General Assembly of the Commonwealth of Kentucky* 393 (Frankfort, 1863) (approved March 2, 1863; reaffirming Kentucky's 1861 application); *Special Laws of the State of Oregon* 10 (Salem, 1864) (adopted Oct. 17, 1864).

43. 2 H. Hockett, *The Constitutional History of the United States* 259–62 (1939); E. McPherson, ed., *The Political History of the United States of America, During the Great Rebellion* 2–11 (2d ed., Washington, D.C., 1865) (proceedings of state conventions); *Ordinances and Constitution of the State of South Carolina* 3, 7–36 (Charleston, 1861).

44. W. Yearns, *The Confederate Congress* 1–10, 22–30 (1960); Hull, "The Making of the Confederate Constitution," 9 *Publications of the Southern History Association* 272 (1905) (collecting letters of Georgia delegate Thomas R. R. Cobb); E. Thomas, *The Confederacy as a Revolutionary Experience* (1971); Alexander H. Stephens to Linton Stephens, Feb. 17, 1861, in C. Lee, *The Confederate Constitutions* 71 (1963); *C.S.A. Const.* (provisional) art. V, in J. Matthews, ed., *The Statutes at Large of the Provisional Government of the Confederate States of America* 8 (Richmond, 1864).

45. *C.S.A. Const.* (permanent) art. V, in id. at 21.

46. 1 J. Davis, *The Rise and Fall of the Confederate Government* 259 (1881); 1 *Journal of the Congress of the Confederate States of America, 1861–1865*, at 887 (1904) (proceed-ings of March 8, 1861); R. H. Smith, *An Address to the Citizens of Alabama, on the Constitution and Laws of the Confederate States of America* 15 (Mobile, 1861) (address given March 30, 1861).

47. C. Lee, *The Confederate Constitutions* 118–19, 146 (1963); J. Carpenter, *The South as a Conscious Minority 1789–1861* (1930); *C.S.A. Const.* (provisional) amend. I (May 21, 1861), in J. Matthews, *Confederate Statutes* at 9.

48. *Public Laws of the State of North Carolina* 225 (Raleigh, 1867) (resolutions "ratified" March 2, 1867); H. Hyman, *A More Perfect Union* at 442; C. Fairman, *Reconstruction and Reunion 1864–88*, at 253–399 (1971) (vol. 6 of the Oliver Wendell Holmes Devise History of the Supreme Court of the United States); E. McPherson, ed., *The Political History of the United States of America During the Period of Reconstruction* 18–28 (1871) (documents relating to establishment of state Reconstruction conventions); 1 W. Fleming, ed., *Documentary History of Reconstruction* 177–85, 449–53 (1906) (excerpts from proceedings of Reconstruction conventions).

49. P. Haworth, *The Hayes-Tilden Disputed Presidential Election of 1876*, at 168, 285 (1906).

50. 5 *Congressional Record* 2 (1876); P. Haworth, *Hayes-Tilden Disputed Presidential Election* at 242–44.

51. House Resolution No. 230, 48th Congress, 1st Session (1884); *House of Represen-*

tatives Report No. 2493, 49th Congress, 1st Session 5 (1886). See H. Ames, *Proposed Amendments to the Constitution During Its First Century* at 73, 284, 293.

52. J. Schouler, "A New Federal Convention," in *Ideals of the Republic* 291, 294, 295–96 (1908).

4. The Twentieth Century

1. C. Williamson, *American Suffrage: From Property to Democracy 1760–1860* (1960); *House Journal*, 19th Congress, 1st Session 258–59 (1826); H. Ames, *The Proposed Amendments to the Constitution of the United States During the First Century of Its History* 61 (1897). James Wilson had argued the idea at Philadelphia. 1 *Records* at 52, 151, 405–6.

2. 1 G. Haynes, *The Senate of the United States: Its History and Practice* 97 (1938) (hereinafter G. Haynes, *Senate of the United States*); 45 *Cong. Rec.* 7111–13 (1910); *New York Times*, April 27, 1911, at 8.

3. 1 G. Haynes, *Senate of the United States* at 86–88, 105–6.

4. Id. at 101–3.

5. Id. at 104; Stasny, "The Constitutional Convention Provision of Article V: Historical Perspective," 1 *Cooley Law Review* 73, 82 (1982); Phillips, "The Treason of the Senate," 40 *Cosmopolitan Magazine* 487, 628 (1906); 41 id. at 3, 267, 368, 525, 627 (1906).

6. 1 G. Haynes, *Senate of the United States* at 97; *Laws, Joint Resolutions, and Memorials Passed by the Legislative Assembly of the State of Nebraska* 466–67 (1893).

7. G. Haynes, *The Election of Senators* 104, 122–24, 275–76 (1906).

8. Graham, "The Role of the States in Proposing Constitutional Amendments," 49 *American Bar Association Journal* 1175, 1179–80 (1963); West, "American Politics," 37 *Forum* 155, 160 (1905); West, "Shall United States Senators Be Elected by the People?," 42 *Forum* 291, 298 (1909); West, "Proposed Amendments to the Constitution," 33 *Forum* 213, 215 (1902).

9. Clark, "The Next Constitutional Convention of the United States," 16 *Yale Law Journal* 65, 72, 73 (1906); G. Haynes, *Election of Senators* at 125.

10. M. Musmanno, *Proposed Amendments to the Constitution* 217 (1929); 47 *Cong. Rec.* 1485 (1911); 46 id. at 2769; 47 id. at 1741, 1743.

11. 1 G. Haynes, *Senate of the United States* at 111–12, 115–16, 108 and n.1; 46 *Cong. Rec.* 2647 (1911).

12. C. Haines, *The American Doctrine of Judicial Supremacy* 485–86 (2d ed., 1932); House Joint Resolution No. 95, 63d Congress, 1st Session (1913); National Legislative Reference Committee of the Progressive Party, *Progressive Congressional Program* 65–67 (1914).

13. "Proposals to Change the Constitution," 3 *Constitutional Review* 168, 173 (1919); J. Beck, *The Constitution of the United States* 280 n.* (1922).

14. 7 J. Richardson, ed., *A Compilation of the Messages and Papers of the Presidents 1789–1897*, at 151, 355 (1898); H. Ames, *The Proposed Amendments to the Constitution of the United States During the First Century of Its History* 272 (1897); Reynolds v. United States, 98 U.S. 145 (1878); *ABA Study* at 72–73.

15. M. Musmanno, *Proposed Amendments to the Constitution* 237–42 (1929); *Senate Report No.* 135, 99th Congress, 1st Session 53 (1985); "Asks Repeal Vote at One Convention," *New York Times*, Feb. 20, 1933, at 2; *Laws of the State of New York* 562 (1931).

16. Cuvillier, "The Need of a New Constitution," 77 *Forum* 321, 322 (1927).

17. Wheeler, "The Virtues of the Constitution," 77 *Forum* 326, 326–27, 328 (1927).

18. M. Kammen, *A Machine That Would Go of Itself: The Constitution in American Culture* 259 (1986); *New York Times*, May 24, 1932, at 11; id., June 28, 1932, at 6.

19. *Schechter*, 295 U.S. 495 (1935); *New York Times*, June 1, 1935, at 1, 6.

20. "Washington Studies Plan for a Quick Amendment of Federal Constitution," *New York Times*, June 2, 1935, §1 at 1, 29; "House Liberals Seek Constitution Change," id. at 29. On the desirability of a convention from the conservative standpoint, see Henry Hazlitt, *A New Constitution Now* (1942).

21. W. Elliott, *The Need for Constitutional Reform* 207, 206, 192, 207 (1935). Guided by similar centralizing impulses, FDR "Brains Trust" adviser Rexford G. Tugwell years later drafted a twenty-seven-page "Constitution for the Newstates of America" for the convention he thought would meet at the end of the century. R. Tugwell, *The Emerging Constitution* (1974).

22. W. Pullen, "The Application Clause of the Amending Provision" at 117–24.

23. 83 *Cong. Rec.* 9505 (1938); 90 id. at 8463 (1944); *Taxes on Incomes, Inheritances, and Gifts: Hearing on S.J. Res. 23 Before the Subcommittee on Constitutional Amendments of the Senate Committee on the Judiciary*, 84th Congress, 2d Session 60 (1956) (testimony of Frank E. Packard); Dresser, "The Case for the Income Tax Amendment: A Reply to Dean Griswold," 39 *American Bar Association Journal* 25, 25 (1953).

24. P. Martin, "The Application Clause of Article Five," 85 *Political Science Quarterly* 616, 623–24 (1970); 90 *Cong. Rec.* 8462, 8464 (1944); 97 id. at 10070 (1951); *Hearing on S.J. Res. 23* at 4.

25. Stasny, "The Constitutional Convention Provision of Article V: Historical Perspective," 1 *Cooley Law Review* 73, 91–92 (1982); Graham, "Role of the States" at 1176–77; *ABA Study* at 73.

26. Id. at 74; State of North Carolina, *Public Laws and Resolutions* 636 (1941); "Publius II" (O. Roberts, J. Schmidt, and C. Streit), *The New Federalist* 101–4 (1950); Streit, "Owen J. Roberts and Atlantic Union," 104 *University of Pennsylvania Law Review* 354, 365–67 (1955).

27. Graham, "Role of the States" at 1181; *Laws, Resolutions and Memorials of the State of Montana* 796–97 (1947).

28. Graham, "Role of the States" at 1177–78, 1182; Kefauver, "The Electoral College: Old Reforms Take on a New Look," 27 *Law and Contemporary Problems* 188 (1962).

29. *Brown*, 347 U.S. 483 (1954); 100 *Cong. Rec.* 8199 (1954); 102 id. at 1512, 2020–21, 3519–20, 4444–45 (1956); Orleans Parish School Bd. v. Bush, 365 U.S. 569 (1961); Bush v. Orleans Parish School Bd., 364 U.S. 500, 501 (1960); 107 *Cong. Rec.* 2154 (1961).

30. 101 *Cong. Rec.* 1532 (1955); 105 id. at 4398 (1959); *Swann*, 402 U.S. 1, 29–31 (1971); Stasny, "The Constitutional Convention Provision of Article V: Historical Perspective," 1 *Cooley Law Review* 73, 89–91 (1982).

31. *Roe*, 410 U.S. 113 (1973); American Enterprise Institute, *A Constitutional Convention: How Well Would It Work?* 23 (1979); Associated Press news release, Jan. 22,

1980; *Senate Report No.* 135, 99th Congress, 1st Session 13, 57–58 (1985). See Weiss, "Constitutional Convention Sought on Abortion Ban," 36 *Congressional Quarterly Weekly Report* 1677 (July 1, 1978).

32. 33 *Cong. Rec.* 219 (1899); 47 id. at 1873 (1911); 47 id. at 1298 (1911); 60 id. at 31 (1920); 69 id. at 455 (1927); 84 id. at 985 (1939); 89 id. at 8220 (1943); 122 id. at 16814 (1976); *General and Special Laws of the State of Texas* 1378 (1949); 98 *Cong. Rec.* 1057 (1952); 98 id. at 4003 (1952); 103 id. at 10863 (1957); 104 id. at 8085 (1958); 110 id. at 7371 (1964); 123 id. at 22002 (1977).

33. Almand, "The States Should Call a Constitutional Convention," 10 *Georgia Bar Journal* 437, 446 (1948).

34. *Baker*, 369 U.S. 186 (1962); *Wesberry*, 376 U.S. 1 (1964); *Reynolds*, 377 U.S. 533 (1964).

35. Oberst, "The Genesis of the Three States-Rights Amendments of 1963," 39 *Notre Dame Lawyer* 644, 650 (1964); McGovern, "Confederation vs. Union," 9 *South Dakota Law Review* 1 (1964); Morgan, "Seventeen States Vote to Destroy Democracy as We Know It," *Look*, Dec. 3, 1963, at 76; Swindler, "The Current Challenge to Federalism: The Confederating Proposals," 52 *Georgetown Law Journal* 1 (1963).

36. "Warren Cautions on Amendments," *New York Times*, May 23, 1963, at 1, 23. The appraisal of *Baker* is reported at id., July 6, 1968, at 42.

37. *Washington Post*, May 27, 1963, at 20. On Eisenhower's civil rights views see 2 S. Ambrose, *Eisenhower: The President* 190–91 (1984).

38. Stasny, "The Constitutional Convention Provision of Article V: Historical Perspective," 1 *Cooley Law Review* 73, 88 (1982); 112 *Cong. Rec.* 5153–58 (1966); 111 id. at 19373 (1965); 112 id. at 8583, 8580–81 (1966).

39. *New York Times*, Dec. 13, 1964, §1 at 54; id., March 18, 1967, at 12.

40. 113 *Cong. Rec.* 9342, 10110 (1967) (Sens. Javits and McIntyre); Graham, "Efforts to Amend the Constitution on Districts Gain," *New York Times*, March 18, 1967, at 1, 12.

41. *New York Times*, March 18, 1967, at 1; 113 *Cong. Rec.* 10102 (1967); R. Dixon, Jr., *Democratic Representation: Reapportionment in Law and Politics* 431 (1968); 113 *Cong. Rec.* 10105, 10106 (1967) (Sen. Robert Kennedy); id at 10103, 10108, 10112 (Sens. Proxmire, Javits, and Dirksen). See Tydings, "They Want to Tamper with the Constitution," *Saturday Evening Post*, June 17, 1967, at 10.

42. Large, "Dirksen's Crusade," *Wall Street Journal*, June 2, 1969, at 1; 113 *Cong. Rec.* 10107 (1967).

43. "Dirksen's Crusade," *Wall Street Journal*, June 2, 1969, at 1; Petuskey v. Rampton, 307 F. Supp. 235 (D. Utah 1969), *reversed on other grounds*, 431 F.2d 378 (10th Cir. 1970), *certiorari denied*, 401 U.S. 913 (1971).

44. C. Vose, *Constitutional Change: Amendment Politics and Supreme Court Litigation Since 1900*, at 354 (1972). On the Dirksen campaign: American Enterprise Institute, *Special Analysis: A Convention to Amend the Constitution?* 7–16 (1967); "Symposium on the Article V Convention Process," 66 *Michigan Law Review* 837 (1968), reprinted as L. Levy, ed., *The Article V Convention Process* (1971); "Symposium," 39 *Notre Dame Lawyer* 623 (1964).

45. *Federal Constitutional Convention: Hearings on S. 2307 Before the Subcommittee on Separation of Powers of the Senate Committee on the Judiciary*, 90th Congress, 1st Session (1967) (hereinafter *1967 Hearings*); S. 215, 92d Congress, 1st Session, 117 *Cong.*

Rec. 36804–6 (1971); S. 1272, 93d Congress, 1st Session, 119 *Cong. Rec.* 22731–32 (1973).

46. American Enterprise Institute, *Proposed Procedures for a Limited Constitutional Convention* 1 (1984); M. Kammen, *A Machine That Would Go of Itself* at 11.

47. E. Schapsmeier and F. Schapsmeier, *Dirksen of Illinois* 175 (1985).

48. A. Grimes, *Democracy and the Amendments to the Constitution* 162 (1978).

49. Roger Sherman to William Williams, May 4, 1784, in L. Boutell, *The Life of Roger Sherman* 122 (1896); Thomas Jefferson to John Taylor, Nov. 26, 1798, in 7 P. Ford, ed., *The Writings of Thomas Jefferson* 310 (1896); Council of State Governments, *The Book of the States 1986–87*, at 246 (1986). An amendment requiring "That no money be borrowed on the credit of the United States without the assent of two thirds of the senators and representatives present in each house" was proposed in the ratification acts sent by New York and Rhode Island. 1 *Elliot* at 330, 336.

50. M. Myers, *A Financial History of the United States* 62 (1970); Dreier and Stubblebine, "The Balanced Budget/Tax Limitation Amendment," 10 *Hastings Constitutional Law Quarterly* 809, 811–12 (1983); 102 *Cong. Rec.* 1217 (1956); 103 *Cong. Rec.* 6475 (1957). Indiana's application was superseded by a later submission, 125 id. at 9188 (1979).

51. Johnson, "How a Small Crusade Grew," *Washington Post*, Feb. 14, 1979, at A23. The NTU grew from 20,000 members in 1976 to 150,000 as of 1985. The convention campaign also has received assistance from the "New Christian Right," religious fundamentalist organizations allied to ultraconservative political lobbying groups, as well as from the American Farm Bureau Federation, a coalition of 49 state farm bureaus with an asserted membership of over three million. "Tax Union Playing Chief Role in Drive," *New York Times*, May 15, 1979, at D18; id., March 19, 1985, at B4; Stevens, "Tearing up the Constitution," 36 *Church & State* 10, 12 (March 1983); Comment, " 'The Monster Approaching the Capital:' The Effort to Write Economic Policy into the United States Constitution," 15 *Akron Law Review* 733, 735–36 (1982).

52. 124 *Cong. Rec.* 16472 (1978); Pritchett, "Why Risk a Constitutional Convention?," 13 *Center Magazine* 14, 17 (March 1980).

53. Davenport, "Amending the Constitution Is a Dubious Way to Curb Federal Spending," *Fortune*, March 12, 1979, at 114; G. Wills, *Reagan's America: Innocents at Home* 432 n.27 (1987); *Christian Science Monitor*, April 22, 1982, at 1, 6; M. Friedman and R. Friedman, *Free to Choose: A Personal Statement* 301–2, 313–14 (1980) (on adoption of NTLC anti-spending amendment by convention, with text of amendment); Bork, "Would a Budget Amendment Work?," *Wall Street Journal*, April 4, 1979, at 20. The NTLC amendment was originally to be proposed by Congress, but the half-million-member NTLC has since become active in the convention drive.

54. 125 *Cong. Rec.* 328 (1979); *Washington Post*, Jan. 16, 1979, at A17; California Assembly Committee on Ways and Means, *Transcript of Hearings on the Balanced Federal Budget Resolutions* (1979); Skelton, "Brown Loses Battle over Constitutional Convention," *Los Angeles Times*, Feb. 23, 1979, pt. I at 1.

55. *Washington Post*, May 29, 1979, at A2; "Group Wants to Balance Nation's Checkbook," 37 *Congressional Quarterly Weekly Report* 277, 279 (Feb. 17, 1979).

56. *Washington Post*, Feb. 14, 1979, at A4; 125 *Cong. Rec.* 3159 (1979). Former President Gerald Ford has written that a budget amendment is contrary to "abundant evidence that government cannot legislate fiscal responsibility any more than it can

morality." Ford, "On Flying High Today and Paying Tomorrow," *Life*, Oct. 1987, at 28, 29.

57. *Washington Post*, Jan. 19, 1979, at A9; id., March 28, 1979, at A10; id., April 27, 1979, at A5. See Shrum, ed., "The Con Con Papers: Memos to Jimmy Carter and Jerry Brown," *Politics Today*, May/June 1979, at 26 (excerpting memoranda from Prof. Tribe to Carter opposing budget convention and amendment, and from J. Anthony Kline to Brown justifying a limited convention).

58. *Washington Post*, May 29, 1979, at A2; Weaver, "2 Senators Dispute Tax-Parley Figures," *New York Times*, Feb. 7, 1979, at A16. See Cohen, "Working Against a Balanced Budget Convention," 11 *National Journal* 659 (April 21, 1979).

59. *Washington Post*, Feb. 25, 1979, at A13; Reid, "Balanced-Budget Amendment Campaign Falters," id., May 29, 1979, at A2.

60. Drew, "Phase: In Search of a Definition," *New Yorker*, Aug. 27, 1979, at 45, 54, 59.

61. Peterson, "The New Politics of Deficits," in J. Chubb and P. Peterson, eds., *The New Direction in American Politics* 365, 386–89 (1985); *New York Times*, Jan. 19, 1982, at A18; Malbin, "Huge Budget Deficit Projections Fuel Drive for Balanced Budget Amendment," 14 *National Journal* 757, 762 (May 1, 1982). See Green, "Showdown in 1984? Cries Grow for Balanced U.S. Budget," *Los Angeles Times*, Feb. 18, 1984, pt. I at 1, 22 (Davidson "would prefer to have a convention . . . . I think we can get a stronger amendment from a convention than from the Congress").

62. 129 *Cong. Rec.* H4942 (daily ed., July 11, 1983); *Christian Science Monitor*, June 23, 1983, at 3; Bell, "Constitutional Convention: Oh, Stop the Hand-Wringing," *Washington Post*, April 14, 1984, at A15; 42 *Congressional Quarterly Weekly Report* 1752 (July 21, 1984); id. at 2098 (Aug. 25, 1984); *New York Times*, Aug. 15, 1984, at B6.

63. *Washington Post*, Sept. 14, 1984, at A7; AFL-CIO v. Eu, 36 Cal.3d 687, *stay denied*, 468 U.S. 1310 (1984) (Rehnquist, as Circuit Justice); Montana *ex rel.* Harper v. Waltermire, 691 P.2d 826, *stay denied*, 469 U.S. 1301 (1984) (Rehnquist, Cir. J.).

64. 21 *Weekly Compilation of Presidential Documents* 68 (1985); *New York Times*, March 19, 1985, at B4; id., May 19, 1985, §23 (*Connecticut Weekly*) at 17. These legislative hearings now attracted numerous interest groups. At a Michigan senate hearing on March 13, 1985, speakers included representatives from the Chamber of Commerce, the National Tax Limitation Committee, Common Cause, the Michigan Manufacturing Association, the Coalition of Retiree Groups in Kalamazoo, the American Civil Liberties Union, B'nai B'rith, the Michigan Association of School Boards, the Jewish Community Council of Metro Detroit, and the Michigan Association of Realtors. At the Connecticut hearing a similar range of groups appeared, with the addition of the National Organization for Women, the AFL-CIO, and the National Association of Realtors. Weber, "The Constitutional Convention: A Safe Political Option," 3 *Journal of Law & Politics* 51, 62 n.27 (1986).

65. *New York Times*, March 26, 1986, at D20; *MacNeil/Lehrer NewsHour*, March 24, 1986, transcript #2736.

66. 22 *Weekly Compilation of Presidential Documents* 419–20 (1986); Brandt, "Balanced Budget Convention May Be Backed by President," *Washington Times*, March 28, 1986, at 3A; id., April 3, 1986, at 9A.

67. *Public Papers of the Presidents of the United States: Ronald Reagan, 1982* (pt. I), at 55 (interview with reporters from the *Los Angeles Times*, Jan. 20, 1982); Associated Press news release, Sept. 8, 1984.

68. Bowsher v. Synar, 478 U.S. 714 (1986), *affirming* 626 F. Supp. 1374 (D.D.C. 1986); *Washington Post*, Oct. 24, 1986, at A11; Note, "The Proposed Federal Balanced Budget Amendment: The Lesson from State Experience," 55 *University of Cincinnati Law Review* 563, 563 (1986). As this book went to press, Alabama in April 1988 became the first to rescind an application, its legislature overriding a gubernatorial veto imposed at White House urging. *Washington Post*, May 9, 1988, at A6. In May, Florida followed.

69. Brief for the Comptroller General at 14, Bowsher v. Synar, 478 U.S. 714 (1986); "Md. Urged to Cancel Call for Constitution Parley," *Washington Post*, April 8, 1987, at D1; *New York Times*, April 2, 1987, at A28.

70. "The State of Reagan," *Time*, Feb. 9, 1987, at 16, 17; Ronald Reagan to Gary Aklestead, March 16, 1987; "Schlafly Aims to Block Parley on Constitution," *Washington Times*, Feb. 23, 1987, at 1A; Bureau of National Affairs, Daily Report for Executives, Aug. 14, 1987, at LL-2.

71. Associated Press news release, May 23, 1987; Irwin, "Reagan Notes Support for Constitutional Convention," *Los Angeles Times*, May 24, 1987 (final ed.), pt. I at 4; United Press International news release, May 12, 1987.

72. Martin, "Views on Constitution: Promises Kept, Miles to Go," *New York Times*, May 26, 1987, at A20; *Washington Post*, Feb. 15, 1987, at A13; McGrath and McDaniel, "In Order to Form a More Perfect Union," *Newsweek*, May 25, 1987, at 50, 51.

73. *New York Times*, April 16, 1987, at C22; Rosen, "Is It Time to Make Some Changes in the Constitution?," *National Law Journal*, April 27, 1987, at S-2.

74. 23 *Weekly Compilation of Presidential Documents* 766 (1987); *New York Times*, Aug. 13, 1987, at A8; id., Aug. 18, 1987, at A24. The affair involved a controversial sale of weapons to Iran keyed to the release of American hostages in Lebanon, and the funneling of profits on the sale to rebels ("contras") in Nicaragua. For other Reagan statements on the convention option, see 23 *Weekly Compilation of Presidential Documents* 321, 463 (1987) (remarks at 1987 meeting of the Executive Forum, March 30, and at a White House briefing for the American Legislative Exchange Council, May 1, 1987).

75. Bureau of National Affairs, Daily Report for Executives, Aug. 14, 1987, at LL-1; *New York Times*, Sept. 27, 1987, §1 at 1; Osterlund, "Two-Year Federal Budget Compromise in Sight: Then What?," *Christian Science Monitor*, Oct. 30, 1987, at 1.

5. Judging Applications

1. 5 *Hamilton Papers* at 164. The Philadelphia delegates had, in fact, rejected Gouverneur Morris's suggestion that Congress be left to call a convention "whenever they please." 2 *Records* at 468.

2. Bureau of National Affairs, Daily Report for Executives, Nov. 8, 1985, at LL-2 (in releasing draft House Judiciary subcommittee report, members state that Congress "would be compelled to defend the position that [rejected] petitions are technically flawed and are inadequate to call a convention").

3. Rabushka, "Tax and Spending Limits," in P. Duignan and A. Rabushka, eds., *The United States in the 1980s*, at 103–4 (1980); Gunther, "Constitutional Brinksmanship: Stumbling Toward a Convention," 65 *American Bar Association Journal* 1046 (1979).

4. *House Journal*, 1st Congress, 1st Session 28, 29 (1789) (identical entries for Virginia and New York); 1 *Annals of Cong.* 260 (1789). See Owings v. Speed, 18 U.S. (5

Wheat.) 420, 422 (1820) (Marshall, C. J.) (the 1789 government "did not commence on the Constitution being ratified by the ninth State; for these ratifications were to be reported to Congress").

5. Mullins, "Amending the Federal Constitution," 13 *Law Notes* (New York) 146, 147 (1909) (Alabama resolution requesting Congress to submit amendment for direct vote of senators is a "memorial expressing the desire of the legislature," not "a legal application for a national convention"); 84 *Cong. Rec.* 3320 (1939); Fensterwald, "Constitutional Law: The States and the Amending Process—A Reply," 46 *American Bar Association Journal* 717, 718 (1960); D. Huckabee, "Constitutional Convention Applications: Addressing the Controversy of Counting State Applications Relating to a Deficit Spending Amendment," in 125 *Cong. Rec.* 4013, 4014, Table 2 nn. 1 and 3 (1979); 125 *Cong. Rec.* 4372, 9188 (1979).

6. Black, "Amending the Constitution: A Letter to a Congressman," 82 *Yale Law Journal* 189, 196, 198 (1972). Similarly, Ackerman, "Unconstitutional Convention," *New Republic*, March 3, 1979, at 8; Dellinger, "The Recurring Question of the 'Limited' Constitutional Convention," 88 *Yale Law Journal* 1623, 1636–38 (1979).

7. Lords of Trade to William Shirley, Sept. 18, 1753, in 2 C. H. Lincoln, ed., *Correspondence of William Shirley, Governor of Massachusetts* 14 (1912); 15 *Acts and Resolves, Public and Private, of the Province of the Massachusetts Bay* 157 (1908) (passed April 19, 1754).

8. E. de Vattel, *Le Droit des gens ou principes de la loi naturelle* (The Law of Nations or the Principles of Natural Law), bk. II, ch. 12, §156 at 161 (C. Fenwick, trans., 1916) (1st ed., London, 1758).

9. 9 I. Hammond, ed., *Collections of the New Hampshire Historical Society* 251–52 (1889); 3 C. Hoadly, ed., *The Public Records of the State of Connecticut* 566 (1922); *Journal of the House of Delegates of Virginia* 151 (Richmond, 1786) (proceedings of Jan. 21, 1786).

10. Richard Henry Lee to Samuel Adams, Oct. 5, 1787, in 13 *Ratification History* at 324 ("for the present" it is "sufficient so to alter the Confederation as to allow Congress full liberty to make Treaties . . . and the power of Regulating trade").

11. James Madison to Edmund Randolph, April 8, 1787, in 9 *Madison Papers* at 369; George Washington to James Madison, March 31, 1787, in id. at 342.

12. *The Federalist* No. 40 at 258; John Jay to George Washington, Jan. 7, 1787, in 3 H. Johnston, ed., *The Correspondence and Public Papers of John Jay* 228 (1891). Similarly, Letter No. 2 of "A Republican Federalist" (attributed to James Warren), *Massachusetts Centinel* (Boston), Jan. 2, 1788, in 4 H. Storing, ed., *The Complete Anti-Federalist* 168 (1981).

13. 3 *Elliot* at 101–2; see id. at 637 (James Innes at Virginia ratifying convention), 2 id. at 138 (Francis Dana at Massachusetts convention); 2 *Ratification History* at 709, 719–25, 717. To the same effect as Nicholas is an anonymous pamphlet by "A Native of Virginia" once ascribed to James Monroe, "Observations upon the Proposed Plan of Federal Government" (Petersburg, Va., 1788), in 1 S. Hamilton, ed., *The Writings of James Monroe* 347, 392 (1898).

14. James Madison to Thomas Jefferson, Dec. 8, 1788, in 11 *Madison Papers* at 382–83; Massachusetts Delegates to the Governor of Massachusetts (James Bowdoin), Nov. 2, 1785, in 8 E. Burnett, *Letters* at 246. See Ware v. Hylton, 3 U.S. (3 Dall.) 199, 223 (1796) (opinion of Chase, J.) (Virginia's 1776 convention framed constitution by virtue of

power delegated by the people, who as the source of all power had a "*right* to grant it to whom they pleased, and under what restrictions or limitations they thought proper"); 2 *Elliot* at 456 (James Wilson).

15. 3 *Records* at 367.

16. Letter No. 11 of "Cassius" (James Sullivan), *Massachusetts Gazette* (Boston), Dec. 25, 1787, in P. Ford, ed., *Essays on the Constitution of the United States* 43, 45 (1892); *The Federalist* No. 85 at 592, 592 n.*†. The founders' understanding may have survived in Dodge v. Woolsey, 59 U.S. (18 How.) 331, 348 (1856) (amendments are initiated either by Congress "or where the legislatures of two thirds of the several States shall call a convention for proposing amendments").

17. *In re* Opinion of the Justices, 373 Mass. 877, 881 (1977) (framers anticipated that the state legislatures would propose specific amendments); Rees, "Constitutional Conventions and Constitutional Arguments: Some Thoughts About Limits," 6 *Harvard Journal of Law and Public Policy* 79, 87 (1982); Van Alstyne, "The Limited Constitutional Convention—The Recurring Answer," 1979 *Duke Law Journal* 985 (specification allows Congress to judge when a consensus has been reached on a "felt need"); but see L. Orfield, *Amending the Federal Constitution* at 42 (ground of the applications immaterial because the mere fact of petitions from two thirds of the states conclusively shows "a widespread desire for constitutional changes").

18. 2 *Records* at 630; Black, "Amending the Constitution: A Letter to a Congressman," 82 *Yale Law Journal* 189, 196–97 (1972); similarly, Ackerman, "Unconstitutional Convention," *New Republic*, March 3, 1979, at 8.

19. *The Federalist* No. 85 at 592.

20. 1 H. Commager, *Documents of American History* at 66–67 (circular letter of Feb. 11, 1768, from Massachusetts House of Representatives to the other state legislatures, detailing the measures taken by Massachusetts in response to the Townshend Acts imposed by England); P. Maier, *From Resistance to Revolution: Colonial Radicals and the Development of American Opposition to Britain, 1765–1776*, at 77–112 (1974).

21. George Lee Turberville to James Madison, Dec. 11, 1787, in 10 *Madison Papers* at 318 (the bill referred to is the act passed Dec. 12, 1787); *Virginia Delegate Journal* at 43 (proceedings of Nov. 14, 1788).

22. Bailyn, General Introduction to 1 B. Bailyn, ed., *Pamphlets of the American Revolution 1750–1776*, at 91–92 (1965). Robert Luce traces the earliest American instructions to a Boston town meeting of March 14, 1652/53. R. Luce, *Legislative Principles* 448 (1930). Jack Pole considers the practice to have begun in earnest, at least in Massachusetts, around 1740. J. Pole, *Political Representation in England and the Origins of the American Republic* 72 (1966).

23. M. Zuckerman, *Peaceable Kingdoms: New England Towns in the Eighteenth Century* 21–22, 212–15 (1970); Franklin, "Some Aspects of Representation in the American Colonies," 6 *North Carolina Historical Review* 38, 46 (1929) (Rhode Island legislature in 17th century "simply promulgated the laws with which the towns had instructed them"); Morison, "The Struggle over the Adoption of the Constitution of Massachusetts, 1780," 50 *Proceedings of the Massachusetts Historical Society* 353, 383 (1917); 6 *Madison Papers* at 152 n.32 (editorial footnote).

24. George Washington to James Madison, March 31, 1787, in 9 *Madison Papers* at 344; 1 *Records* at 178.

25. O. Libby, *The Geographical Distribution of the Vote of the Thirteen States on the*

Federal Constitution, 1787–8, at 94 (1894); *New York Advertiser*, Feb. 8, 1788, in S. Harding, *The Contest over the Ratification of the Federal Constitution in the State of Massachusetts* 57 n.1 (1896); Edmund Randolph to James Madison, Aug. 13, 1788, in 11 *Madison Papers* at 232.

26. Hawke v. Smith (No. 1), 253 U.S. 221, 226–27 (1920); 1 *Annals of Cong.* 496 (1789) (Rep. Madison: as a general constitutional rule, "the power of removal result[s] by a natural implication from the power of appointing"); Rufus King to Elbridge Gerry, Jan. 7, 1787, in 8 E. Burnett, *Letters* at 527.

27. *In re* Opinion of the Justices, 132 Me. 491 (1933); *In re* Opinions of the Justices, 204 N.C. 806 (1933); State *ex rel.* Donnelly v. Myers, 127 Ohio 104 (1933); State *ex rel.* Tate v. Sevier, 333 Mo. 662, *cert. denied*, 290 U.S. 679 (1933). In the minority, holding the contrary: *In re* Opinions of the Justices, 226 Ala. 565 (1933).

28. 127 Ohio at 106; Robert Hale to Joseph H. Choate, Jr., April 3, 1933, in C. Vose, *Constitutional Change: Amendment Politics and Supreme Court Litigation Since 1900*, at 125 (1972).

29. W. Pullen, "The Application Clause of the Amending Provision" at 138–39; Hawke v. Smith (No. 1), 253 U.S. 221, 227 (1920); National Prohibition Cases, 253 U.S. 350 (1920); Kimble v. Swackhamer, 439 U.S. 1385, 1388 (Rehnquist, Cir. J.), *appeal dismissed*, 439 U.S. 1041 (1978) (upholding a nonbinding, advisory referendum on question of ratifying proposed equal rights amendment to federal Constitution).

30. Taft, "Can Ratification of an Amendment to the Constitution Be Made to Depend on a Referendum?," 29 *Yale Law Journal* 821, 824 (1920); *The Federalist* No. 69 at 464 (Hamilton). See Note, "The Unconstitutionality of Voter Initiative Applications for Federal Constitutional Conventions," 85 *Columbia Law Review* 1525 (1985).

31. *Virginia Delegate Journal* at 44 (proceedings of Nov. 14, 1788); *Virginia Senate Journal* at 31 (Nov. 19); *New York Assembly Journal* at 105 (proceedings of Feb. 5, 1789); *New York Senate Journal* at 56 (Feb. 7) (emphasis deleted). See 1 *Annals of Cong.* 787 (1789) (Rep. Tucker: amendments submitted for ratification by state legislatures "must meet the approbation of the majority" in each chamber).

32. Dyer v. Blair, 390 F. Supp. 1291, 1306 (N.D. Ill. 1975); see id. at 1305 n.34 (summarizing ratification majority requirements of the states), Coleman v. Miller, 307 U.S. 433 (1939) (simple majority in state legislature sufficient for ratification); 390 F. Supp. at 1303, quoting Leser v. Garnett, 258 U.S. 130, 137 (1922) (ratification is a federal function that "transcends" any limits a state might wish to impose).

33. W. Pullen, "The Application Clause of the Amending Provision" at 108; 125 *Cong. Rec.* 2928 (1979) (Rep. Volkmer); id. at 2112; *In re* Opinion of the Justices, 373 Mass. 877 (1977).

34. B. Bailyn, *The Origins of American Politics* 89 (1970); L. Friedman, *A History of American Law* 106–7 (1973). The standard treatments are E. Greene, *The Provincial Governor in the English Colonies of North America* (1898), and L. Labaree, *Royal Government in America* (1930).

35. 9 M. Jensen, ed., *English Historical Documents: American Colonial Documents to 1776*, at 248–52 (1955) (contemporary reports of maladministration and mistreatment by colonial governors); R. Simmons, *The American Colonies* at 43, 47, 74, 86, 135; Surrency, "The Courts in the American Colonies" (pts. 1 and 2), 11 *American Journal of Legal History* 253, 347 (1967); R. D. Brown, "The Massachusetts Convention of Towns, 1768," 26 *William and Mary Quarterly* 94, 99 n.14 (3d ser., 1969); G. Warden, *Boston 1689–1776*, at 274, 277–78 (1970).

36. Kamper v. Hawkins, 3 Va. (3 Wash.) 20, 69–70 (Gen. Ct. 1793), reprinted with alterations in 1 *Tucker's Blackstone*, Appendix at 86–88. Similarly, T. Jefferson, *Notes on Virginia* at 121.

37. J. Main, *The Sovereign States 1775–1783*, at 188–95 (1973); B. Bailyn, *Origins of American Politics* at 67–68; E. Greene, *The Provincial Governor* at 145–57, 162; L. Labaree, *Royal Government* at 190, 207–8. South Carolina's temporary constitution of 1776 gave the executive an absolute veto, a feature never copied by any other state. Two years later, South Carolina's revised charter omitted the veto altogether. In New York's 1777 constitution, any bill passed by the legislature could be returned by a council of revision, which consisted of the governor, the chancellor, and the judges of the supreme court; the bill became law if repassed by two thirds of each house. The Vermont territory's 1786 constitution empowered the governor and council of revision to suspend the passing of a bill until the next session of the legislature.

38. F. Ames, "Equality" (No. 2) (1801 or 1802), in 2 S. Ames, ed., *Works of Fisher Ames* 210, 212 (Boston, 1854); J. Daniell, *Experiment in Republicanism: New Hampshire Politics and the American Revolution, 1741–1794*, at 177 (1970); J. Pancake, *Thomas Jefferson and Alexander Hamilton* 118 (1974).

39. 2 *Records* at 159–60. See id. at 467 (John Dickinson); Martin v. Hunter's Lessee, 14 U.S. (1 Wheat.) 304, 333–34 (1816) (Story, J.) (in article III, omission of particular language in similar context implies different intent).

40. 3 *Elliot* at 425; 7 *JCC* at 124 (on Feb. 15, 1777, Congress recommends appointment of commissioners "to the legislatures, or, in their recess, to the executive powers" of the states); J. Locke, *The Second Treatise of Government*, in P. Laslett, ed., *Two Treatises of Government* §153 at 415 (1965) (1st ed., London, 1690).

41. 3 *Records* at 560–63, 569–72, 575, 577.

42. Hawke v. Smith (No. 1), 253 U.S. 221, 229–31 (1920); L. Orfield, *Amending the Federal Constitution* at 66; J. A. Jameson, *Treatise* §581 at 630; Dodd, "Amending the Federal Constitution," 30 *Yale Law Journal* 321, 345 (1921); Taft, "Can Ratification of an Amendment to the Constitution Be Made to Depend on a Referendum?," 29 *Yale Law Journal* 821, 824–25 (1920); "A Survey of Statutory Changes in North Carolina in 1933," 11 *North Carolina Law Review* 191, 241 (1933). Amendments proposed for the Articles of Confederation, however, were apparently ratified like statutes, with the governor's signature. 6 *Madison Papers* at 370, 372 n.8.

43. Dellinger, "Con Con Con," *New Republic*, April 7, 1986, at 10, 11.

44. 9 *New Hampshire Collections* at 251–52; W. Jenkins, ed., *Records of the States of the United States of America: A Microfilm Compilation*, Rhode Island journals, reel 2 (1949) (senate entry made on or after Nov. 24, 1776); *Journal of the House of Delegates* 86, 93 (Richmond, 1785) (proceedings of Dec. 28 and 31, 1784); 1 *Records* at 250.

45. 2 New York State, *Messages from the Governors* 293 (C. Z. Lincoln, ed., 1909).

46. 1 *Annals of Cong.* 259 (1789); 2 *Elliot* at 414.

47. 3 *Elliot* at 657–61, 1 id. at 327–31 (proposed amendments submitted by Virginia and New York with their ratification acts).

48. Bonfield, "The Dirksen Amendment and the Article V Convention Process," 66 *Michigan Law Review* 949, 954–55 (1968) (states may apply for a convention limited to certain subjects, but cannot restrict the convention to adopting specific amendments). The texts of submitted balanced-budget convention applications may be found in 125 *Cong. Rec.* 2108–16 (1979) (texts of 22 applications); Cogan, "Comments on Regulating a Constitutional Convention," 50 *Journal of Air Law and Commerce* 587, 623–83 (1985)

(all 32 applying states); Barker, "A Status Report on the 'Balanced Budget' Constitutional Convention," 20 *John Marshall Law Review* 29, 77–96 (1986); see Committee on Federal Legislation, Association of the Bar of the City of New York, "An Analysis of State Resolutions Calling for a Constitutional Convention to Propose a Balanced Budget Amendment," 40 *Record of the Association of the Bar of the City of New York* 710, 727–28 n.2 (1985) (citations to the applications and memorials of the 32 states).

49. "Schlafly Aims to Block Parley on Constitution," *Washington Times*, Feb. 23, 1987, at 1A (conservative argues against budget convention, fearing "internationalists" who want to "get rid of the separation of powers and give us a European parliamentary-style government"); Noonan, "The Convention Method of Constitutional Amendment—Its Meaning, Usefulness, and Wisdom," 10 *Pacific Law Journal* 641, 644 (1979).

50. 19 JCC at 112–13 (text of amendment); 23 id. at 788–89 (letter of Nov. 30, 1782, from Rhode Island legislature to the Continental Congress, explaining the rejection); 2 I. Brant, *James Madison: The Nationalist* 214 (1948).

51. 10 W. Hening, *Statutes at Large* at 409–10, 451, 11 id. at 171. The legislative records indicate that repeal was effected by the same procedure as that by which the original ratification was accomplished. *Virginia Delegate Journal* at 55, 58 (proceedings of Dec. 6 and 7, 1782).

52. *Laws of the State of New-York, Commencing with the First Session of the Senate and Assembly, After the Declaration of Independency, . . . Anno 1777*, at 279–80 (Poughkeepsie, 1782–1783) (New York's repeal act promised to grant the requested power to Congress as soon as every other state passed acts granting the power); *Acts and Ordinances of the General Assembly of the State of South Carolina, Passed in the Year 1783*, at 57 (n.p., n.d. [Charleston? 1784?]); James Madison to Edmund Randolph, April 1, 1783, in 6 *Madison Papers* at 429; James Madison to Edmund Randolph, Dec. 24, 1782, in 5 id. at 449.

53. Edmund Randolph to James Madison, Dec. 13, 1782, in id. at 401; James Madison to Edmund Randolph, Dec. 30, 1782, in id. at 473; Notes on Debates Jan. 29 and 28, 1783, 6 id. at 164, 147; 24 JCC at 257–61 (text of 1783 amendment). On accommodation, see Alexander Hamilton to George Clinton, May 14, 1783, in 3 *Hamilton Papers* at 354.

54. *The Federalist* No. 22 at 145–46 (Hamilton); 2 *Records* at 88 (Mason); id. at 90 (Gorham); *The Federalist* No. 43 at 296–97 (Madison); see 2 *Elliot* at 197 (Oliver Ellsworth at Connecticut ratifying convention).

55. 3 *Elliot* at 29. See id. at 113, 303, 630 (Francis Corbin, Edmund Pendleton, and Madison at Virginia ratifying convention). Rescinding an application or ratification for an amendment to an existing government (before the procedure is complete) differed from conditional entry into that government. To Hamilton's news that the New York convention was considering ratification while reserving the right to secede, Madison answered: "The Constitution requires an adoption *in toto*, and *for ever*. . . . An adoption for a limited time would be as defective as an adoption of some of the articles only. In short any *condition* whatever must viciate the ratification." James Madison to Alexander Hamilton, July 20, 1788, in 11 *Madison Papers* at 189.

56. James Madison to Edmund Randolph, April 10, 1788, in id. at 19; *Acts of the General Assembly of the Commonwealth of Pennsylvania* 114 (Philadelphia, 1791); S. Bloom, *Formation of the Union* at 318–19.

57. Coleman v. Miller, 307 U.S. 433, 449–50 (1939) (14th and 15th amendments are

precedents for regarding the efficacy of a withdrawal as a question left to the ultimate authority of Congress); *Cong. Globe*, 40th Congress, 2d Session 453, 475 (1868) (Senate and House resolutions); id. at 890, 2225–26.

58. 15 United States Statutes at Large 707 (1868); *Cong. Globe*, 40th Congress, 2d Session 4296 (1868); 15 Stat. 711 (1868).

59. *Cong. Globe*, 41st Congress, 2d Session 377 (1870); 16 Stat. 1131 (1870); Reichelderfer v. Quinn, 287 U.S. 315, 318 (1932).

60. For authorities finding a recission power (at either the application or ratification stage), see 113 *Cong. Rec.* 10106, 10109 (1967) (Sens. Tydings and Javits); 124 *Cong. Rec.* 33151, 34289 (1978) (Sens. Helms and Garn); L. Orfield, *Amending the Federal Constitution* at 72; 2 J. Story, *Commentaries on the Constitution of the United States* §1930 at 680–81 n.1 (5th ed., 1891) (1st ed., Boston, 1833) (note by Thomas Cooley); Bonfield, "Proposing Constitutional Amendments by Convention: Some Problems," 39 *Notre Dame Lawyer* 659, 671 (1964) (permitting withdrawal recognizes "the extent to which each application reflects the . . . required contemporaneous agreement that an Article V convention is desired"); Grinnell, "Finality of a State's Ratification of a Constitutional Amendment," 11 *American Bar Association Journal* 192 (1925); Comment, "The Equal Rights Amendment and Article V: A Framework for Analysis of the Extension and Rescission Issues," 127 *University of Pennsylvania Law Review* 494 (1978); Note, "Proposing Amendments to the United States Constitution by Convention," 70 *Harvard Law Review* 1067, 1074 (1957); *1979 Hearing* at 67, 308 (1979) (statements of John D. Feerick and Gerald Gunther); Idaho v. Freeman, 529 F. Supp. 1107, 1148–50 (D. Idaho 1981), *certiorari before judgment granted and judgment stayed*, 455 U.S. 918, *judgment vacated and remanded to district court with instructions to dismiss as moot*, 459 U.S. 809 (1982) (state can repeal its ratification at any time until three fourths have acted to ratify). Compare Fletcher v. Peck, 10 U.S. (6 Cranch) 87, 135 (1810) (Marshall, C. J.) ("one legislature is competent to repeal any act which a former legislature was competent to pass").

61. Authorities finding no power to repeal include: *In re* Opinion of the Justices, 118 Me. 544 (1919); C. Burdick, *The Law of the American Constitution* 43–44 (1922); S. Freedman and P. Naughton, *ERA: May a State Change Its Vote?* (1978); 113 *Cong. Rec.* 12271 (1967) (Sen. Hruska); 124 *Cong. Rec.* 33162 (1978) (Sen. Bayh); Kanowitz and Klinger, "Can a State Rescind Its Equal Rights Amendment Ratification: Who Decides and How?," 28 *Hastings Law Journal* 979 (1977); Note, "Rescinding Memorialization Resolutions," 30 *Chicago-Kent Law Review* 339 (1952); *1979 Hearing* at 296–97 (statement of William W. Van Alstyne).

62. 1 *Records* at 422; Benjamin Franklin to Jean Baptiste LeRoy, Nov. 13, 1789, in 10 A. Smyth, ed., *The Writings of Benjamin Franklin* 69 (1907).

63. Dillon v. Gloss, 256 U.S. 368, 372 (1921); 71 *Cong. Rec.* 3369 (1929).

64. 256 U.S. 368, 374–75 (1921), *affirming Ex parte* Dillon, 262 F. 563 (N.D. Cal. 1920).

65. 256 U.S. at 375. But see Trombetta v. Florida, 353 F. Supp. 575, 577 n.5 (M.D. Fla. 1973) (amendment proposed in 1924 "may yet be outstanding since Congress imposed no time limit upon ratification"); 56 *Cong. Rec.* 10098 (1918) (Sen. Overman: "when an amendment is submitted to the people it can be submitted for a thousand years and be in force whenever ratified").

66. 256 U.S. at 375; id., quoting J. A. Jameson, *Treatise* §585 at 634; 256 U.S. at

375–76. See Henry W. Taft, "How Long Is a State Petition for Constitutional Convention Good?," 17 *American Bar Association Journal* 143 (1931) (New York Bar Association committee report applying *Dillon* contemporaneity requirement to convention applications).

67. *Coleman*, 307 U.S. 433, 450–51, 454 (1939), *reversing* 146 Kan. 390 (1937). Similarly, Chandler v. Wise, 307 U.S. 474 (1939) (Kentucky's ratification of child labor amendment).

68. 125 *Cong. Rec.* 2110, 2111–12 (1979) (applications of Georgia and Mississippi); W. Pullen, "The Application Clause of the Amending Provision" at 151. Regarding the applicability of presidential vetoes to repeals of statutes, Madison considered it "probable that in doubtful cases the policy would soon take place of limiting the duration of laws so as to require renewal instead of repeal." 2 *Records* at 587.

69. Wheeler, "Is a Constitutional Convention Impending?," 21 *Illinois Law Review* 782, 794 (1927); Council of State Governments, *The Book of the States 1986–87*, at 76 (1986); Dyer v. Blair, 390 F. Supp. 1291, 1303 (N.D. Ill. 1975) (supremacy clause prohibits state legislature's abolition of ratification function); 113 *Cong. Rec.* 10102 (1967) (Sen. Tydings); *Senate Report No.* 594, 98th Congress, 2d Session 73 (1984) (additional views of Sen. Leahy). See *Coleman*, 307 U.S. at 473 (Butler, J., dissenting) (thirteen years "more than a reasonable time" to ratify child labor amendment).

70. Paul A. Freund to Sen. Philip A. Hart, June 3, 1971, in 117 *Cong. Rec.* 36763 (1971) (recommending a four-year effective period for applications). See Bonfield, "Proposing Constitutional Amendments by Convention: Some Problems," 39 *Notre Dame Lawyer* 659, 668–69 (1964) (effective period should be just long enough for every state legislature to meet for one complete session, and should not exceed two and a half years).

71. American Enterprise Institute, *A Constitutional Convention: How Well Would It Work?* 31 (1979); John Jay to George Washington, Jan. 7, 1787, in 3 H. Johnston, ed., *The Correspondence and Public Papers of John Jay* 228 (1891).

72. James Madison to Martin Luther Hurlbert, May 1830, in 9 G. Hunt, *Writings of Madison* at 375; *The Federalist* No. 43 at 296; 4 *Elliot* at 254, 298–99. See 13 *Annals of Cong.* 775 (1803) (Rep. Eustis: "the State Legislatures as well as Congress [have] a right to institute amendments").

73. *Senate Report No.* 336, 92d Congress, 1st Session 11, 19 (1971) (majority report; separate views of Sens. Bayh, Burdick, Philip Hart, Edward Kennedy, and Tunney).

6. Congress, the Courts, and the President

1. Martineau, "The Mandatory Referendum on Calling a State Constitutional Convention: Enforcing the People's Right to Reform Their Government," 31 *Ohio State Law Journal* 421, 424 (1970); Martineau, "Maryland's 1967–68 Constitutional Convention: Some Lessons for Reformers," 55 *Iowa Law Review* 1196, 1198 (1970).

2. *Reapportionment of State Legislatures: Hearings on S.J. Res. 2, S.J. Res. 37, S.J. Res. 38 and S.J. Res. 44 Before the Subcommittee on Constitutional Amendments of the Senate Committee on the Judiciary,* 89th Congress, 1st Session 40 (1965) (statement of Sen. Paul H. Douglas). Similarly, Black, "The Proposed Amendment of Article V: A Threatened Disaster," 72 *Yale Law Journal* 957, 966 (1963) (hereinafter Black, "Threatened Disaster"); Bonfield, "Proposing Constitutional Amendments by Convention: Some

Problems," 39 *Notre Dame Lawyer* 659, 676 (1964); Dodd, "Judicially Non-Enforcible Provisions of Constitutions," 80 *University of Pennsylvania Law Review* 54, 82 (1931).

3. Mathias, "What's the Constitution Among Friends?," 67 *American Bar Association Journal* 861, 863 (1981). Similarly, *1967 Hearings* at 67 (statement of Alexander Bickel); Gunther, "The Convention Method of Amending the United States Constitution," 14 *Georgia Law Review* 1, 5 (1979); Van Alstyne, "Does Article V Restrict the States to Calling Unlimited Conventions Only?—A Letter to a Colleague," 1978 *Duke Law Journal* 1295, 1305.

4. United States v. Sprague, 282 U.S. 716, 730 (1931) (emphasis supplied); "A Friend to the Union" (John Marshall), *The Union* (Philadelphia), April 24, 1819, in G. Gunther, ed., *John Marshall's Defense of McCulloch v. Maryland* 91 (1969). Similarly, 2 J. Story, *Commentaries on the Constitution of the United States* §1830 at 600 (5th ed., 1891).

5. *The Federalist* No. 85 at 593.

6. 3 *Elliot* at 636; 4 id. at 178; Letter No. 8 of "Fabius" (John Dickinson), in P. Ford, ed., *Pamphlets on the Constitution of the United States* 204, 210 (1888) (letters first published serially in the *Delaware Gazette* [Wilmington], 1788; first pamphlet ed., 1797).

7. James Madison to Thomas Mann Randolph, Jan. 13, 1789, in 11 *Madison Papers* at 417. The letter was published in the *Virginia Herald* on January 15, in the *Virginia Independent Chronicle* on January 28, and in other periodicals. R. Ketcham, *James Madison: A Biography* 276 (1971). Similarly, James Madison to George Eve, Jan. 2, 1789, in 11 *Madison Papers* at 405.

8. 1 *Annals of Cong.* 260 (1789). Similarly, id. at 260–61 (Reps. Boudinot, Bland, and Tucker); 5 id. at 498, 530 (1796) (Reps. Smith and Lyman).

9. 2 *Elliot* at 205–6 (resolution of New York legislature providing for ratification convention); 2 *Ratification History* at 101–2 (resolutions of Pennsylvania legislature).

10. 3 *Ratification History* at 90–91, 367–68 (Delaware and Connecticut); *New York Senate Journal* at 56 (Feb. 7, 1789) ("*Ordered*, That Mr. Tredwell and Mr. L'Hommedieu, deliver a copy of the preceding concurrent resolution to the Honorable the Assembly"); 4 *Elliot* at 3 (report of North Carolina ratifying convention's select committee: "the resolve of Congress of the 21st of February, 1787, recommending a Convention of Delegates to meet at Philadelphia"); Kamper v. Hawkins, 3 Va. (3 Wash.) 20, 70 (Gen. Ct. 1793) (state framing conventions assembled "in pursuance of recommendations from Congress"); J. Goebel, *Antecedents* at 201.

11. *Senate Report No.* 293, 93d Congress, 1st Session 7 (1973); similarly, Black, "Threatened Disaster" at 964; 2 *Elliot* at 151. See Gunther, "The Convention Method of Amending the United States Constitution," 14 *Georgia Law Review* 1, 23–24 (1979) (Congress lacks plenary legislative power over national convention, notwithstanding the necessary and proper clause); Tampa Water Works Co. v. Tampa, 199 U.S. 241 (1905) (Holmes, J.) (in state constitution, "a power of the legislature" signifies "the *possibility* of its exercise") (emphasis supplied).

12. 1 *Annals of Cong.* 744 (1789). During consideration of the 12th amendment, the Senate ruled that all questions preliminary to final proposal of an amendment may be decided by a simple majority. 13 id. at 81–84 (1803).

13. J. Greene, *The Quest for Power: The Lower Houses of Assembly in the Southern Royal Colonies 1689–1776* (1963); R. Simmons, *The American Colonies* at 247–53; J. Main, *The Upper House in Revolutionary America 1763–1788*, at 3–96 (1967); 129 *Cong. Rec.* S588, S587 (daily ed., Jan. 26, 1983) (Sen. Hatch).

14. Fortson v. Morris, 385 U.S. 231, 233–34 (1966) (in absence of overriding constitu-

tional directive, state may permit its legislature to choose the governor). See Eiselen, "Dare We Call a Federal Convention?," 244 *North American Review* 27, 34 (1937) (best results obtained from a national convention that is partly elected and partly appointed).

15. Roll, "We, Some of the People: Apportionment in the Thirteen State Conventions Ratifying the Constitution," 56 *Journal of American History* 21, 22 (1969); Hadley v. Junior College District, 397 U.S. 50, 58 (1970) ("the guarantee of equal voting strength for each voter applies in all elections of government officials"); Fortson v. Toombs, 379 U.S. 621 (1965) (upholding injunction mandating that if the Georgia legislature called a state constitutional convention, the representation of the convention must be based on population, as required by the state constitution); Note, "Constitutional Safeguards in the Selection of Delegates to Presidential Nominating Conventions," 78 *Yale Law Journal* 1228, 1247 (1969).

16. 1 *Records* at 8, 11 n.*. Maryland's 1776 constitutional convention, according to the journal, itself decided that all questions would be determined by a majority of the members. *Proceedings of the Convention of the Province of Maryland, Held at the City of Annapolis* 70 (Annapolis [1776?]) (proceedings of Nov. 5, 1776). The intent to allow future national conventions to make these determinations may be partly responsible for Madison's reservation about a convention clause, in that "difficulties might arise as to the form, the quorum &c. which in Constitutional regulations ought to be as much as possible avoided." 2 *Records* at 630.

17. 117 *Cong. Rec.* 36770 (1971); *ABA Study* at 19 ("unwise and of questionable validity" for Congress to impose a voting requirement on the convention); Note, "Proposed Legislation on the Convention Method of Amending the United States Constitution," 85 *Harvard Law Review* 1612, 1633 (1972) (two-thirds requirement imposed by Congress is unconstitutional, since convention may decide its own proposing vote).

18. 2 W. Holdsworth, *A History of English Law* 431 (1923); J. Locke, *Second Treatise* §§95–99 at 375–77; L. Cushing, *Elements of the Law and Practice of Legislative Assemblies in the United States of America* 47, 996 (1st ed., Boston, 1856); 1 *Records* at 198; 2 id. at 557; "A Citizen of New York" (John Jay), *An Address to the People of the State of New-York on the Subject of the Constitution* (New York, 1788), in P. Ford, ed., *Pamphlets on the Constitution of the United States* 67, 82 (1888).

19. Dyer v. Blair, 390 F. Supp. 1291, 1306 (N.D. Ill. 1975) (Stevens, J.); United States v. Ballin, 144 U.S. 1, 6 (1892); Penhallow v. Doane's Administrators, 3 U.S. (3 Dall.) 54, 93–94 (1795) (opinion of Iredell, J.); T. Jefferson, *A Manual of Parliamentary Practice for the Use of the Senate of the United States* (1st ed., Washington, D.C., 1801), reprinted in *House Document No.* 271, 97th Congress, 2d Session 240 (1983); J. Locke, *Second Treatise* §99 at 377. This majority is actually a majority of a quorum: 51 percent not of the total membership, but of the number required to transact business. A quorum generally is a simple majority of the total membership. FTC v. Flotill Products, Inc., 389 U.S. 179, 183 (1967).

20. *Dyer*, 390 F. Supp. at 1307 n.38 (Stevens, J.) ("such procedural matters were left to be determined by such a [national] convention itself"). A convention probably can determine the vote needed to expel a delegate. The members could theoretically decide that a simple majority would do, but might well settle on the two-thirds figure of article I, Madison having "observed that the right of expulsion was too important to be exercised by a bare majority of a quorum." 2 *Records* at 254.

21. 2 *Elliot* at 205.

22. 1 *Records* at 386–87, 392–93; 2 id. at 288, 490–91. See *The Federalist* No. 76 at 514 (Hamilton); 10 *Annals of Cong.* 131 (1800) (Sen. Charles Pinckney: "every officer of the United States is nominated by the President"); James Madison to James Monroe, Dec. 28, 1820, in 9 G. Hunt, *Writings of Madison* at 43 ("the tenure of the Office . . . is the pleasure of the P. alone"); United States v. Maurice, 26 F. Cas. 1211, 1214 (C.C.D.Va. 1823) (No. 15,747) (John Marshall, as Circuit Justice); James Monroe to the President of New Hampshire (John Sullivan), Aug. 16, 1786, in 8 E. Burnett, ed., *Letters* at 430 (1936).

23. 13 *Ratification History* at 235 (remarks of Madison, Sept. 27, 1787); "An American Citizen" (Tench Coxe), "Thoughts on the Subject of *Amendments* of the Federal Constitution" (No. 4), *The Federal Gazette and Philadelphia Evening Post*, Dec. 31, 1788, at 2. For the attribution of the "American Citizen" essays to Coxe, see J. Cooke, *Tench Coxe and the Early Republic* 128 n.57 (1978). Two Philadelphia appointees then in Congress declined their commission, but only because they perceived a conflict of interest sitting in both bodies rather than a constitutional infirmity in the appointment. Richard Henry Lee to John Adams, Sept. 5, 1787, in 2 J. Ballagh, ed., *The Letters of Richard Henry Lee* 434 (1914); Jonathan Dayton to David Brearley, June 7, 1787, in J. Hutson, ed., *Supplement to Max Farrand's The Records of the Federal Convention of 1787*, at 59 (1987) (on Abraham Clark's resignation).

24. R. Hoar, *Constitutional Conventions: Their Nature, Powers, and Limitations* 177–80 (1917); Platz, "Article Five of the Federal Constitution," 3 *George Washington Law Review* 17, 47 (1934); State *ex rel.* Constitutional Convention v. Evans, 80 N. Mex. 720 (1969) (rejecting argument that state constitutional convention has intrinsic power to draw funds from treasury).

25. 11 *Madison Papers* at 373 (Madison's statement of expenses for attendance at the Philadelphia Convention, tendered to Virginia legislature); 2 *Records* at 510; Pennhurst State School and Hospital v. Halderman, 451 U.S. 1, 17 (1981).

26. Eric Hanushek, Congressional Budget Office, to Sen. Strom Thurmond, Aug. 13, 1985, in *Senate Report No. 135*, 99th Congress, 1st Session 48 (1985).

27. 1 *Records* at 2; 2 *Ratification History* at 272 (Nov. 9, 1787).

28. 3 *American Archives* (5th ser.) at 87 (Maryland convention of 1776, proceedings of Aug. 15); 9 *Collections of the New Hampshire Historical Society* at 279 (New Haven convention of 1778, proceedings of Jan. 22); *Proceedings of the Convention of the Delaware State, held . . . August, 1776* (Wilmington, 1776) (proceedings of Aug. 30, 1776), in C. Bushman, H. Hancock, and E. Homsey, eds., *Proceedings of the Assembly of the Lower Counties on Delaware 1770–1776, of the Constitutional Convention of 1776, and of the House of Assembly of the Delaware State 1776–1781*, at 206 (1986).

29. 1 *Records* at 7–17.

30. On adopting rules, see 2 *Elliot* at 1, 207–8, 416–17 (Massachusetts, New York, Pennsylvania); 3 id. at 3 (Virginia). See also 3 id. at 5–6 (Virginia convention's committee of privileges and elections issues report on doubtful elections).

31. 4 *Elliot* at 3.

32. 1 W. Blackstone, *Commentaries* *164; 10 *Annals of Cong.* 72 (1800) (Sen. Charles Pinckney). Clauses similar to article I are in *Mass. Const.* of 1780, pt. 2, ch. 1, §3, art. 10; *Md. Const.* of 1776, art. 24. On parliamentary privilege, see M. Clarke, *Parliamentary Privilege in the American Colonies* (1943); C. Wittke, *The History of English Parliamentary Privilege* (1921).

33. H. McIlwaine, ed., *Journals of the House of Burgesses of Virginia* 241–42 (1910) (address of John Randolph, Speaker of the House, Aug. 6, 1736); M. Clarke, *Parliamentary Privilege in the American Colonies* at 202; J. Greene, *The Quest for Power: The Lower Houses of Assembly in the Southern Royal Colonies 1689–1776*, at 171, 185, 189, 198–99, 206–7, 216–19 (1963) (power of southern colonial legislatures to settle elections, determine qualifications, punish and expel members, appoint officers, and fix rules of procedure); S. George, B. Nead, and T. McCamant, eds., *Charter to William Penn, and Laws of the Province of Pennsylvania*, Appendix B at 473–76 (1879) (Pennsylvania legislature, on its first day of meeting, Dec. 4, 1682, chose its officers, appointed committees, settled a contested election, adopted rules of proceeding); Potts, "Power of Legislative Bodies to Punish for Contempt," 74 *University of Pennsylvania Law Review* 691, 704, 706–8 (1926) (early 18th-century examples of power to expel members, settle elections).

34. For early colonial examples of the privilege from arrest, see R. Luce, *Legislative Assemblies* 492–93 (1924); Potts, "Power of Legislative Bodies" at 700–701. Article V of the Confederation was taken from the 1689 English Bill of Rights, 1 W. & M. sess. 2, ch. 2, §19.

35. M. Clarke, *Parliamentary Privilege in the American Colonies* at 81–82, 84, 155; Potts, "Power of Legislative Bodies" at 692, 698–99, 715, 725.

36. 1 U.S. (1 Dall.) 296, 303 (1788) (Philadelphia Cty. Ct. C.P.).

37. *Journal of the Convention for Framing a Constitution of Government for the State of Massachusetts Bay* 45 (Boston 1832).

38. 5 *Annals of Cong.* 498 (1796); 2 *Ratification History* at 270 (Nov. 9, 1787); W. Staples, *Rhode Island in the Continental Congress* 659 (1870).

39. T. May, *A Treatise on the Law, Privileges, Proceedings and Usage of Parliament* 52, 226 (14th ed., 1946); M. Clarke, *Parliamentary Privilege in the American Colonies* at 227–33; 1 *Records* at 15.

40. George Mason to George Mason, Jr., May 27, 1787, in 3 R. Rutland, ed., *The Papers of George Mason* 884 (1970); Thomas Jefferson to John Adams, Aug. 30, 1787, in 12 *Jefferson Papers* at 69; 3 *Elliot* at 170; 3 *Records* at 479 (Journal of Jared Sparks, notes of a visit to James Madison, April 19, 1830); R. Luce, *Legislative Procedure* 337 (1922).

41. James McHenry to Peggy McHenry, Aug. 23, 1787, in J. Hutson, ed., *Supplement to Max Farrand's The Records of the Federal Convention of 1787*, at 236 (1987); George Washington to Henry Knox, Aug. 19, 1787, in 29 *Washington Writings* at 261; "A Citizen of New York" (John Jay), *An Address to the People of the State of New-York on the Subject of the Constitution* (New York, 1788), in P. Ford, ed., *Pamphlets on the Constitution of the United States* 67, 83 (1888).

42. Note, 18 *American Political Science Review* 329 (1924); *Acts and Resolves Passed at the General Assembly of the State of Rhode Island* 1533 (1969). The average length of the state constitutional conventions held from 1938 through 1968 is 4.4 months. This figure plummets to 2.6 months if the Rhode Island convention of 1964–1969 is excluded. Kofmehl, Memorandum to Sen. Birch Bayh on Constitutional Convention Procedures, July 4, 1980, in *1979 Hearing* at 445, 451.

43. E. Brown, ed., *Ratification of the Twenty-First Amendment to the Constitution of the United States* 516 (1938).

44. Id. at 525–26.

45. Id. at 278.

46. James Madison to Edmund Randolph, Dec. 30, 1782, in 5 *Madison Papers* at 473 (Virginia's repeal of its ratification of the 1781 impost amendment valid, since Rhode

Island's rejection meant that the full number had not ratified); *Idaho*, 529 F. Supp. at 1150 (state can rescind its ratification at any time up to the point at which three fourths of the states have assented).

47. Sprague, "Shall We Have a Federal Constitutional Convention, and What Shall It Do?," 3 *Maine Law Review* 115, 123 (1910); Wheeler, "Is a Constitutional Convention Impending?," 21 *Illinois Law Review* 782, 790 (1927). See 125 *Cong. Rec.* 2108–16 (1979) (texts of 22 applications for a balanced-budget convention, many giving Congress the option of proposing an amendment in lieu of calling a convention). There has been debate as to whether such conditional applications are valid, see California Assembly Committee on Ways and Means, *Transcript of Hearings on the Balanced Federal Budget Resolutions* (1979) (Feb. 1 session at 91, 97–98, Prof. Laurence Tribe: petitions allowing Congress to propose its own amendments instead of calling a convention are "of no effect at all"; Feb. 15 session at 125, Dean Gerhard Casper: if it becomes clear that Congress will not propose the amendment, Congress must call the convention). The evidence favors validity, as the purpose of a conditional application is to obtain the amendment from one or the other body, not permit indefinite delay by Congress. When in 1788 Francis Corbin moved his substitute petition giving Congress the option of proposal or calling, there was no indication that it was not consistent with article V.

48. Platz, "Article Five of the Federal Constitution," 3 *George Washington Law Review* 17, 45 (1934); Rowley, "The Constitutional Route to Effective Budgetary Reform," in J. Buchanan, C. Rowley, and R. Tollison, eds., *Deficits* 391, 404 n.11 (1987); Note, "Proposing Amendments to the United States Constitution by Convention," 70 *Harvard Law Review* 1067, 1074 (1957).

49. *House Journal*, 1st Congress, 1st Session 29 (1789) (emphasis supplied); 2 *Ratification History* at 271 (Nov. 9, 1787).

50. *Cong. Globe*, 38th Congress, 1st Session 522, 2218 (1864).

51. Judge Jameson was of the like view. J. A. Jameson, *Treatise* §585 at 634; also, C. Burdick, *The Law of the American Constitution: Its Origin and Development* 39 (1922). Orfield leaned toward allowing Congress to withdraw the amendment any time before three fourths ratify, because it still has no legal effect, but thought the question ultimately political. L. Orfield, *Amending the Federal Constitution* at 52.

52. Eber Bros. Wine & Liquor Corp. v. United States, 337 F.2d 624 (Ct. Cl. 1964), *cert. denied*, 380 U.S. 950 (1965).

53. James Madison to George Washington, Sept. 30, 1787, in 10 *Madison Papers* at 180; Hillman v. Stockett, 183 Md. 641 (Md. Ct. App. 1945) (state legislature has power to propose any number of constitutional amendments, even if mutually contradictory, and courts will construe them only when they are adopted into the constitution).

54. Turner v. Bank of North-America, 4 U.S. (4 Dall.) 8, 10 n.(1) (1799); Bowen v. Michigan Academy of Family Physicians, 476 U.S. 667, 681 n.12 (1986); *The Federalist* No. 43 at 291 (Madison: "a right implies a remedy"). Article III grants the Supreme Court original jurisdiction over suits "in which a State shall be a Party," but article V is clear that the convention route involves only "*the Legislatures* of two thirds of the several States," not the states as entire governing entities. Judicial review is available also to challenge actions taken by a convention, such as expulsion. United States v. Ballin, 144 U.S. 1, 5 (1892) (courts will not interfere when houses of Congress determine their rules of proceedings, but no house may "ignore constitutional restraints or violate fundamental rights").

55. 307 U.S. at 459. It has been plausibly suggested that the Court's lavish deference to

Congress in *Coleman* may be connected with the "Court-packing" plan of 1937. The plan was President Franklin Roosevelt's response to the Court's invalidating piece after piece of his New Deal legislation. Of the four concurring justices, three (Black, Frankfurter, and Douglas) were appointed by Roosevelt. Justice Roberts switched sides, becoming a swing vote in cases upholding important New Deal acts. L. Baker, *Back to Back: The Duel Between FDR and the Supreme Court* (1967); Henkin, "Is There a 'Political Question' Doctrine?," 85 *Yale Law Journal* 597, 625 (1976); Millet, "The Supreme Court, Political Questions, and Article V—A Case for Judicial Restraint," 23 *Santa Clara Law Review* 745, 756 (1983).

56. *Coleman*, 307 U.S. at 460 (opinion of Frankfurter, J.); Baker v. Carr, 369 U.S. 186, 217 (1962). See 13 C. Wright, A. Miller, and E. Cooper, *Federal Practice and Procedure* 296–323 (1975).

57. 2 *Records* at 92. From the context, it appears that "Legislative alterations" (perhaps Madison's shorthand for Morris's actual phrase) refers to amendments ratified by state legislatures.

58. *Hollingsworth*, 3 U.S. (3 Dall.) 378, 382, 379 (1798); National Archives Microfilm Publications, *Minutes of the Supreme Court of the United States February 1, 1790–August 4, 1828*, entry for Feb. 14, 1798 (Washington, D.C., 1954).

59. Letter No. 5 of "A Landholder" (Oliver Ellsworth), *Connecticut Courant*, Dec. 3, 1787, in 3 *Ratification History* at 484; H. Bourguignon, *The First Federal Court: The Federal Appellate Prize Court of the American Revolution 1775–1787* (1977); United States v. Peters, 9 U.S. (5 Cranch) 115, 119–20 (1809); Appendix, 131 U.S. i, xxix (1889) (historical overview of federal courts prior to adoption of Constitution).

60. L. Tribe, *Constitutional Choices* 284 n.15 (1985); *The Federalist* No. 1 at 3; Marbury v. Madison, 5 U.S. (1 Cranch) 137, 176 (1803).

61. L. Tribe, *Constitutional Choices* 22–23 (1985); Leser v. Garnett, 258 U.S. 130, 137 (1922); *Dyer*, 390 F. Supp. at 1301 n.24 (Stevens, J.). See 76 *Cong. Rec.* 4150 (1933) (Sen. Alben Barkley: Congress would be unjustified in recognizing ratification of an amendment if a state failed to act, and "a sort of rump convention . . . called by the people" purported to ratify).

62. *Marbury*, 5 U.S. (1 Cranch) at 177 (Marshall, C. J.); Dodge v. Woolsey, 59 U.S. (18 How.) 331, 348 (1856); White v. Hart, 80 U.S. (13 Wall.) 646, 649 (1872).

63. Leser v. Garnett, 258 U.S. 130, 136 (1922); United States v. Sprague, 282 U.S. 716, 734 (1931) (implying the valid adoption of 13th, 14th, 15th, 16th, and 19th amendments).

64. National Prohibition Cases, 253 U.S. 350, 386 (1920); United States v. Sprague, 282 U.S. 716 (1931).

65. Hawke v. Smith (No. 1), 253 U.S. 221 (1920).

66. *Leser*, 258 U.S. at 136. See United States v. Chambers, 291 U.S. 217, 222 (1934) (validity of 21st amendment). In Luther v. Borden, two rival governments contended for recognition in Rhode Island: one the result of an unofficial convention that produced a "People's Constitution," the other of a convention called by the legislature. The United States Supreme Court deferred to Congress as the final authority, under the guarantee clause, in determining the established government of a state. 48 U.S. (7 How.) 1, 42 (1849). Only federal-state relations were involved in *Luther*, not article V.

67. Maryland Petition Committee v. Johnson, 265 F. Supp. 823 (D. Md. 1967), *affirmed*, 391 F.2d 933 (4th Cir.), *certiorari denied*, 393 U.S. 835 (1968) (14th amendment); Peter Hand Co. v. United States, 2 F.2d 449 (7th Cir. 1924) (18th amendment).

68. Idaho v. Freeman, 529 F. Supp. 1107 (D. Idaho 1981) (whether states may rescind their ratifications of a constitutional amendment); Dyer v. Blair, 390 F. Supp. 1291 (N.D. Ill. 1975) (Stevens, J.) (whether states may specify legislative majority needed to ratify an amendment); Trombetta v. Florida, 353 F. Supp. 575 (M.D. Fla. 1973) (voiding state constitutional provision that prohibited state legislature from ratifying a federal amendment unless majority of the legislature was elected after amendment's proposal); Petuskey v. Rampton, 307 F. Supp. 235 (D. Utah 1969) (voiding state application for a national convention because it was adopted by a malapportioned legislature).

69. AFL-CIO v. Eu, 36 Cal.3d 687, *stay denied sub nom.* Uhler v. AFL-CIO, 468 U.S. 1310 (1984) (Rehnquist, Cir. J.) (initiative measure requiring state legislature to submit a convention application is unconstitutional under article V, since legislature must retain its independent judgment); Montana *ex rel.* Harper v. Waltermire, 691 P.2d 826, *stay denied sub nom.* Montanans for a Balanced Federal Budget Committee v. Harper, 469 U.S. 1301 (1984) (Rehnquist, Cir. J.) (same).

70. *In re* Opinion of the Justices, 60 Mass. (6 Cush.) 573 (1833); State v. McBride, 4 Mo. 303 (1836) (first court decision in the nation expressly holding justiciable the issue of an amendment's valid adoption); Collier v. Frierson, 24 Ala. 100 (1854) (first decision invalidating an improperly adopted amendment).

71. Huff v. Selber, 10 F.2d 236 (W.D. La. 1925).

72. Uhler v. AFL-CIO, 468 U.S. 1310, 1312 (1984). But see Goldwater v. Carter, 444 U.S. 996, 1001 n.2 (1979) (Powell, J., concurring) (when legitimacy of a state's ratification is challenged, "it may be entirely appropriate" for the judiciary to "step aside").

73. Weston, "Political Questions," 38 *Harvard Law Review* 296, 307 (1925). Similarly, L. Orfield, *Amending the Federal Constitution* at 13–14.

74. United States *ex rel.* McLennan v. Wilbur, 283 U.S. 414, 420 (1931) (mandamus order will issue where the duty is "ministerial" and "plainly defined"); see 5 *Annals of Cong.* 530 (1796) (Rep. Lyman: calling an article V convention is "ministerial").

75. *In re* Opinion of the Justices, 262 Mass. 603, 606 (1928) (article V excludes the voters from the amending process, vesting "all power over the subject . . . exclusively in the Legislatures of the several States"). The modern test for article III standing is set out in Valley Forge Christian College v. Americans United for Separation of Church and State, Inc., 454 U.S. 464, 472 (1982).

76. Riegle v. Federal Open Market Committee, 656 F.2d 873, 881 (D.C. Cir.), *certiorari denied*, 454 U.S. 1082 (1981) (when the dispute is among members of Congress, i.e., is really about the lawmaking process itself, equitable discretion counsels dismissal). On the ineligibility of the general public, see *Valley Forge*, 454 U.S. at 482–83; Fairchild v. Hughes, 258 U.S. 126 (1922) (private citizen lacked standing to have 19th amendment declared void).

77. Note, "Proposed Legislation on the Convention Method of Amending the United States Constitution," 85 *Harvard Law Review* 1612, 1643 (1972). The Kansas legislators in *Coleman* had standing because of their constitutionally "adequate interest in maintaining the effectiveness of their votes." 307 U.S. at 438.

78. United States *ex rel.* Widenmann v. Colby, 265 F. 998, 1000 (D.C. Cir. 1920) (action lies against official charged with proclaiming the adoption of amendments to federal Constitution).

79. Tenney v. Brandhove, 341 U.S. 367, 376 (1951); Powell v. McCormack, 395 U.S. 486, 505 (1969); Packard, "The States and the Amending Process," 45 *American Bar*

Association Journal 161, 196 (1959) (mandamus suit would lie against every member of Congress to call a convention).

80. See National Treasury Employees Union v. Nixon, 492 F.2d 587 (D.C. Cir. 1974) (suit will lie against the President to perform nondiscretionary statutory duties, when no subordinate official has authority to enforce the statute); Kendall v. United States, 37 U.S. (12 Pet.) 524 (1838) (against Postmaster General).

81. McPherson v. Blacker, 146 U.S. 1, 24 (1892); 113 *Cong. Rec.* 12272 (1967); 1 *Annals of Cong.* 787 (1789); Note, "Proposed Legislation on the Convention Method of Amending the United States Constitution," 85 *Harvard Law Review* 1612, 1644 (1972); Stasny, "Toward a Civically Militant Electorate: A National Constitutional Convention," in 122 *Cong. Rec.* 8985, 8988 (1976).

82. 30 *Washington Writings* at 295.

83. *Cong. Globe*, 38th Congress, 2d Session 630 (1865) (Sen. Howe); D. Currie, *The Constitution in the Supreme Court: The First Hundred Years 1789–1888*, at 21–22 (1985); Black, "Amending the Constitution: A Letter to a Congressman," 82 *Yale Law Journal* 189, 208 (1972).

84. "A Friend of Society and Liberty," *Maryland Journal and Baltimore Advertiser*, Aug. 12, 1788, at 3; 2 *Records* at 637–40. The federalist passage is here reprinted for the first time since its original publication.

85. 3 U.S. (3 Dall.) 378, 382, 381 (1798).

86. Id. at 381 n.*. Full, written opinions explaining the Court's reasoning were at this time the exception rather than the rule; not until 1834 were opinions required to be filed. D. Currie, *The Constitution in the Supreme Court* at 9.

87. 1 *Records* at 21; id. at 94; 2 id. at 298. See 4 *Elliot* at 27 (James Iredell: if the President vetoes a bill, "it depends on Congress afterwards to say whether it shall be a law or not").

88. 2 *Records* at 301, 304.

89. *The Federalist* No. 73 at 495; No. 85 at 592 n.*†.

90. James Madison to George Hay, Aug. 23, 1823, in 9 G. Hunt, *Writings of Madison* at 147.

91. 13 *Annals of Cong.* 215 (1803); W. Rawle, A *View of the Constitution of the United States of America* 291 (2d ed., Philadelphia, 1829) (1st ed., Philadelphia, 1825). Similarly, 1 *Tucker's Blackstone*, Appendix at 270.

92. Cohens v. Virginia, 19 U.S. (6 Wheat.) 264, 389 (1821).

7. The Convention's Proposing Agenda

1. *ABA Study* at 14; similarly, C. Brickfield, *Problems Relating to a Federal Constitutional Convention* 19–20 (85th Congress, 1st Session, Committee Print 1957); W. Dodd, *The Revision and Amendment of State Constitutions* 92–93 (1910) (state conventions are restricted by provisions of state and federal constitutions and popular referenda, though not by legislative enabling acts); W. Edel, A *Constitutional Convention: Threat or Challenge?* 124 (1981); R. Hoar, *Constitutional Conventions: Their Nature, Powers, and Limitations* 108, 120–24 (1917) (state convention may ignore acts of the legislature, but not the terms of referenda); J. A. Jameson, *Treatise* §389 at 383; Noonan, "The Conven-

tion Method of Constitutional Amendment—Its Meaning, Usefulness, and Wisdom," 10 *Pacific Law Journal* 641 (1979); Note, "Proposed Legislation on the Convention Method of Amending the United States Constitution," 85 *Harvard Law Review* 1612, 1628–30 (1972); Committee on Federal Legislation, Association of the Bar of the City of New York, "Legislation to Establish Procedures for a 'Limited Issues' Constitutional Convention," 39 *Record of the Association of the Bar of the City of New York* 593, 603 (1984); Van Alstyne, "The Limited Constitutional Convention—The Recurring Answer," 1979 *Duke Law Journal* 985.

2. *In re* Opinion of the Justices, 373 Mass. 877, 882 (1977); similarly, L. Orfield, *Amending the Federal Constitution* at 45; Ackerman, "Unconstitutional Convention," *New Republic*, March 3, 1979, at 8; P. Bator, "Thoughts on the Value of the Convention Alternative," in W. Moore and R. Penner, eds., *The Constitution and the Budget* 24 (1980); Black, "Amending the Constitution: A Letter to a Congressman," 82 *Yale Law Journal* 189, 196 (1972); Dellinger, "The Recurring Question of the 'Limited' Constitutional Convention," 88 *Yale Law Journal* 1623 (1979); E. D. Elliott, "Constitutional Conventions and the Deficit," 1985 *Duke Law Journal* 1077, 1109; Goldberg, "The Proposed Constitutional Convention," 11 *Hastings Constitutional Law Quarterly* 1, 2 (1983); Graham, "The Role of the States in Proposing Constitutional Amendments," 49 *American Bar Association Journal* 1175, 1178 (1963); Gunther, "The Convention Method of Amending the United States Constitution," 14 *Georgia Law Review* 1, 13 (1979); Mathias, "What's the Constitution Among Friends?," 67 *American Bar Association Journal* 861 (1981); Moynihan, "The Imprudence of Forcing a Balanced Budget," *Wall Street Journal*, March 18, 1981, at 28; Swisher, "In Convention Assembled," 13 *Villanova Law Review* 711, 731 (1968); Tribe, "Thinking About a New Constitutional Convention," in *1979 Hearing* at 502, 504 n.1; *1967 Hearings* at 61 (statement of Alexander Bickel).

3. American Enterprise Institute, *A Constitutional Convention: How Well Would It Work?* 22–23 (1979).

4. 3 *Elliot* at 102 (proceedings of June 6, 1788, erroneously printed as June 16).

5. Silas Lee to George Thatcher, Feb. 14, 1788, in Goodwin, ed., "The Thatcher Papers" (pt. 2), 6 *Historical Magazine* 337, 338–39 (2d ser., 1869).

6. "A Federalist," *The Maryland Gazette; or, the Baltimore Advertiser*, Sept. 30, 1788, at 2; "A.B.," *Maryland Journal and Baltimore Advertiser*, Oct. 3, 1788, at 3.

7. Thomas Jefferson to William Carmichael, Dec. 25, 1788, in 14 *Jefferson Papers* at 385. Similarly, Thomas Jefferson to James Madison, Nov. 18, 1788, in id. at 188; Thomas Jefferson to William Short, Dec. 8, 1788, in id. at 344.

8. 1 *Annals of Cong.* 688 (1789).

9. The credentials of the Philadelphia delegates are set out in 1 *Elliot* at 126–39; 1 *Ratification History* at 195–225; 3 *Records* at 559–86.

10. 13 *Ratification History* at 231; 33 JCC at 549; Edward Carrington to Thomas Jefferson, Oct. 23, 1787, in 12 *Jefferson Papers* at 253. For the proceedings of Congress during consideration of the draft Constitution, see 1 *Ratification History* at 325–42, 13 id. at 229–42; E. Burnett, *The Continental Congress* 694–97 (1941).

11. 3 *Elliot* at 23; "A Columbian Patriot" (Mercy Otis Warren), *Observations on the New Constitution, and on the Foederal and State Conventions* 13 (New York, 1788) (1st ed., Boston, 1788).

12. *The Federalist* No. 40 at 258, 259; 3 *Elliot* at 603.

13. *The Federalist* No. 40 at 265–66; 3 *Elliot* at 38.

14. James Madison to George Lee Turberville, Nov. 2, 1788, in 11 *Madison Papers* at 331; 4 *Elliot* at 203. See State *ex rel.* McCready v. Hunt, 20 S.C.L. (2 Hill) 1, 222 (Ct. App. 1834) (opinion of O'Neall, J.) (if a state convention exceeds its express purpose "their act is void, unless it is submitted to the people and affirmed by them"). Bruce Ackerman argues that since the Philadelphia Convention assumed "the constitutional right to revise the preexisting formal ratification procedures," future conventions may "assert a similar right to modify the formalities of Article V." Ackerman, "The Storrs Lectures: Discovering the Constitution," 93 *Yale Law Journal* 1013, 1059 (1984).

15. 2 *Records* at 476; *The Federalist* No. 39 at 254. Similarly, 1 *Records* at 283 (Hamilton), 2 id. at 92 (King); 2 *Elliot* at 433, 459 (James Wilson).

16. *The Federalist* No. 40 at 263, 267; No. 78 at 524.

17. C. Rossiter, *1787: The Grand Convention* 263 (1966); *The Federalist* No. 40 at 265. See also *Pennsylvania Herald* (Philadelphia), Nov. 28, 1787, in 2 *Ratification History* at 368 (James Wilson); 2 *Records* at 477 (Rufus King).

18. G. Wills, *Cincinnatus: George Washington and the Enlightenment* 158 (1984). Whether Madison's understanding of "natural law" was of that which is eternal, unchanging, and taking precedence over positive law, as contended in Grey, "Do We Have an Unwritten Constitution?," 27 *Stanford Law Review* 703, 715–16 (1975), or which simply represents the social conditions necessary for positive law to flourish, as argued in Berns, "Judicial Review and the Rights and Laws of Nature," 1982 *Supreme Court Review* 49, 58–66, Madison invoked a standard of legitimacy independent of the Articles of Confederation. Natural law figured throughout early Supreme Court decisions, from Calder v. Bull, 3 U.S. (3 Dall.) 386, 387–89, 399 (1798), through Loan Association v. Topeka, 87 U.S. (20 Wall.) 655, 662–63 (1874).

19. 2 *Records* at 91; T. Jefferson, *Notes on Virginia* at 118.

20. 9 *JCC* at 911; see 4 *Elliot* at 20 (William R. Davie at North Carolina ratifying convention).

21. Ware v. Hylton, 3 U.S. (3 Dall.) 199, 232 (1796) (opinion of Chase, J.) ("The powers of Congress originated from necessity, and arose out of, and were only limited by, events; or, in other words, they were *revolutionary* in their very nature"); Penhallow v. Doane's Administrators, 3 U.S. (3 Dall.) 54, 111 (1795) (opinion of Blair, J.) (approval subsequently given by the states to actions of the early Continental Congress were "as legitimate a source of authority, as if it had been given at first"); similarly, 2 *Records* at 92 (Rufus King).

22. *The Federalist* No. 40 at 265; E. Burnett, *The Continental Congress* 20–21, 61 (1941); A. McLaughlin, *Constitutional History* at 83–84 n.3; Morris, "The Forging of the Union Reconsidered: A Historical Refutation of State Sovereignty over Seabeds," 74 *Columbia Law Review* 1056, 1068–69, 1091–93 (1974); Henry Knox to Stephen Higginson, Jan. 28, 1787, in East, "The Massachusetts Conservatives in the Critical Period," in R. Morris, ed., *The Era of the American Revolution* 349, 387–88 (1939).

23. James Madison to George Washington, Sept. 30, 1787, in 10 *Madison Papers* at 179–80. Similarly, *The Federalist* No. 38 at 248 (Madison); 6 *Jefferson Papers* at 587–88 (editorial note).

24. 19 *JCC* at 124, 125; James Madison to James Monroe, Dec. 24, 1784, in 8 *Madison Papers* at 199–200; John Jay to George Washington, Jan. 7, 1787, in 3 *The Correspondence and Public Papers of John Jay* 229 (H. Johnston, ed., 1891).

25. Stephen Higginson to Henry Knox, Feb. 13, 1787, in J. Franklin Jameson, ed., "Letters of Stephen Higginson, 1783–1804," in 1 American Historical Association, *Annual Report, 1896*, at 704, 750 (1897).

26. J. O'Connor, *William Paterson: Lawyer and Statesman 1745–1806*, at 138, 140–42, 150 (1979).

27. Edmund Randolph to James Madison, Sept. 3, 1788, in 11 *Madison Papers* at 247; *Senate Report No. 594*, 98th Congress, 2d Session 72 (1984).

28. State *ex rel.* McCready v. Hunt, 20 S.C.L. (2 Hill) 1, 244 (Ct. App. 1834) (opinion of Johnson, J.); *1967 Hearings* at 34.

29. Adrian, "Trends in State Constitutions," 5 *Harvard Journal on Legislation* 311, 322–23 (1968).

30. *Idaho*, 529 F. Supp. at 1153.

31. See Bonfield, "Proposing Constitutional Amendments by Convention: Some Problems," 39 *Notre Dame Lawyer* 659, 677 (1964) (Congress should disregard proposed *ultra vires* amendments).

32. 2 *Records* at 478; James Madison to George Washington, Sept. 30, 1787, in 10 *Madison Papers* at 180; Hugh Williamson to James Iredell, July 22, 1787, in 3 *Records* at 61; 1 id. at 203 (Mason); 13 *Ratification History* at 238 (Madison in Confederation Congress, Sept. 27, 1787); Corwin and Ramsey, "The Constitutional Law of Constitutional Amendment," 26 *Notre Dame Lawyer* 185, 210–11 (1951).

33. 2 *Records* at 151, 152; Dellinger, "The Legitimacy of Constitutional Change: Rethinking the Amendment Process," 97 *Harvard Law Review* 386, 409 n.120 (1983) (power to choose mode of ratification is the power to decide *who* shall ratify; it does not necessarily include the power to tell states *when* ratification must occur); Forkosch, "The Alternative Amending Clause in Article V: Reflections and Suggestions," 51 *Minnesota Law Review* 1053, 1080 (1967) (convention probably can set time limits for its own amendments); *Popular Sources* at 432; 9 N. Bouton, ed., *Documents and Records Relating to Towns in New Hampshire* 842, 877, 895–96 (1875).

34. Carton v. Secretary of State, 151 Mich. 337, 346–47 (1908) (a state convention attempting to exercise powers not conferred upon it may be restrained in the same fashion as any other body acting beyond its powers); R. Cotner, ed., *Theodore Foster's Minutes of the Convention Held at South Kingstown, Rhode Island, in March 1790*, at 78 (1929).

35. *New York Times*, March 21, 1984, at 1; Gunther, "The Convention Method of Amending the United States Constitution," 14 *Georgia Law Review* 1, 9–10 (1979).

36. Mishkin, "A Question of Trust," *Newsweek*, March 5, 1979, at 17.

37. National Prohibition Cases, 253 U.S. 350, 386 (1920). See Platz, "Article Five of the Federal Constitution," 3 *George Washington Law Review* 17, 31 (1934) (if an amendment were proposed by less than two thirds of each house but validly ratified by the states, "the Supreme Court would be forced to declare it void"). Numerous cases exist in which the state courts have invalidated constitutional amendments because they were irregularly adopted, yet sometimes irregularly adopted amendments that were acquiesced in by the state governments over time were left undisturbed by the courts. Yawitz, "The Legal Effect Under American Decisions of an Alleged Irregularity in the Adoption of a Constitution or Constitutional Amendment," 10 *St. Louis Law Review* 279, 288–89 (1925).

38. W. Rawle, *A View of the Constitution of the United States of America* 291 (2d ed., Philadelphia, 1829) (President "cannot *recommend* to the people an amendment").

39. Ohio *ex rel.* Erkenbrecher v. Cox, 257 F. 334 (S.D. Ohio 1919) (plaintiff, a private

citizen, can have no cognizable injury under Prohibition amendment until it is ratified by the requisite number of states); *Brown*, 347 U.S. 483 (1954). The example is taken from Note, "Proposed Legislation on the Convention Method of Amending the United States Constitution," 85 *Harvard Law Review* 1612, 1641–43 (1972).

40. Allen v. Louisiana, 103 U.S. 80, 83–84 (1881); Livingston v. Ogilvie, 43 Ill.2d 9, 23 (1969).

41. Hammond v. Clark, 136 Ga. 313 (1911) (collecting authorities); Louisiana v. Pilsbury, 105 U.S. 278, 289 (1882); Posados v. Warner, Barnes & Co., 279 U.S. 340, 344 (1929).

42. State *ex rel.* Hudd v. Timme, 54 Wis. 318, 336 (1882).

43. State *ex rel.* McClurg v. Powell, 77 Miss. 543, 576–77 (1900); Carter v. Burson, 230 Ga. 511, 519 (1973).

44. See Committee on Federal Legislation, Association of the Bar of the City of New York, "Legislation to Establish Procedures for a 'Limited Issues' Constitutional Convention," 39 *Record of the Association of the Bar of the City of New York* 593, 609 (1984) (a proposed amendment must have a "bona fide, reasonable" relation to the subjects for which the convention was called); Note, "Proposed Legislation on the Convention Method of Amending the United States Constitution," 85 *Harvard Law Review* 1612, 1630–32 (1972) (determining the convention's compliance "should focus on the grievance which motivated state legislatures to apply for a convention rather than on the nature of the amendments to be proposed").

45. State *ex rel.* McCready v. Hunt, 20 S.C.L. (2 Hill) 1 (Ct. App. 1834) (three-judge panel agreed that state convention's power was limited to its express purpose, i.e., to consider the 1832 tariff; majority held that requiring militia officers to take an oath of allegiance to South Carolina was beyond the power of the convention to prescribe and of no legal effect; the dissenting judge maintained that the oath was comprehended within the convention's purpose).

46. Schlesinger v. Reservists Committee to Stop the War, 418 U.S. 208, 227 (1974); Note, "The Process of Constitutional Amendment," 79 *Columbia Law Review* 106, 140 n.140 (1979); *Ex parte* Lévitt, 302 U.S. 633 (1937) (interest of petitioner, as citizen and member of Supreme Court bar, insufficient to show direct injury from allegedly unconstitutional appointment of Hugo Black to the Supreme Court).

47. White, "Amendment and Revision of State Constitutions," 100 *University of Pennsylvania Law Review* 1132, 1152 (1952) (acquiescence in improperly adopted amendment treated by courts as political question); Note, "Will Acquiescence Validate an Irregularly Adopted State Constitutional Amendment?," 35 *Harvard Law Review* 593, 596 (1922) (cases espousing acquiescence are "exceptional and not to be followed as general authorities"); Kamper v. Hawkins, 3 Va. (3 Wash.) 20, 28 (Gen. Ct. 1793) (opinion of Nelson, J.); Leser v. Garnett, 258 U.S. 130, 136 (1922) (Brandeis, J.). See Pease v. Peck, 59 U.S. (18 How.) 595, 596–97 (1856) (upholding erroneously printed statute because "acknowledged by the people and the courts . . . for thirty years"), but see Smiley v. Holm, 285 U.S. 355, 369 (1932) (Hughes, C. J.) ("General acquiescence cannot justify departure from the law").

48. L. Tribe, *American Constitutional Law* 429–34, 567–69 (1978).

49. James Madison to George Lee Turberville, Nov. 2, 1788, in 11 *Madison Papers* at 331.

50. 5 *Annals of Cong.* 537 (1796).

51. 2 *Ratification History* at 269; see also id. at 267 (Thomas FitzSimons).

52. Gatewood v. Matthews, 403 S.W.2d 716, 721–22 (Ky. Ct. App. 1966); *New York Times*, Nov. 9, 1966, at 28. See Malinou v. Powers, 333 A.2d 420 (R.I. 1975) (two of seven amendments proposed by state convention went outside the subject matter restrictions of the call; one of the two was popularly ratified).

53. 1 *Annals of Cong.* 767 (1789); McCreary v. Speer, 156 Ky. 783, 791 (1914) (of Kentucky's constitution).

54. Woods's Appeal, 75 Pa. 59, 68–69 (1874).

55. Foley v. Democratic Parish Committee, 138 La. 220 (1915); Note, "The Powers of Constitutional Conventions," 29 *Harvard Law Review* 528, 531 (1916); J. A. Jameson, *Treatise* §578 at 627 n.1. See Brickhouse v. Brooks, 165 F. 534 (C.C.E.D. Va. 1908) (rejecting as political question a challenge to constitution said to be irregularly adopted by Virginia's 1901 convention, but when appropriate, court will invalidate any portion that conflicts with federal Constitution or statutes), but see Frantz v. Autry, 18 Okla. 561, 605 (1907) (after adoption, state constitution "becomes subject to judicial cognizance").

56. 5 *Annals of Cong.* 776 (1796).

57. 2 *Records* at 88; 1 *Annals of Cong.* 741, 742 (1789); similarly id. at 738 (Rep. Stone); 1 *Annals of Cong.* 739 (1789) (Rep. Gerry). Sherman implies that a new constitution ratified by state legislature, even if proposed by an authorized plenary convention, might still be invalid. But since Congress would claim the power to select the mode, and likely choose the invalid method, a convention bent on peaceful revolution would have to take it upon itself to stipulate ratification by state convention, perhaps by less than three fourths—a maneuver akin to that of the Philadelphia Convention.

58. E. Brown, ed., *William Plumer's Memorandum of Proceedings in the United States Senate 1803–1807*, at 518 (1923) (remarks of Sen. Baldwin, Nov. 30, 1806); 1 *Annals of Cong.* 451 (1789); see 2 *Elliot* at 432 (James Wilson).

59. T. Farrar, *Manual of the Constitution of the United States of America* 392 (Boston, 1867).

Conclusion: The Politics of Uncertainty

1. *The Federalist* No. 46 at 320.

2. 1 *Records* at 423, 422.

3. J. Goebel, *Antecedents* at 420 n.31 (citing examples). See also *The New-York Packet*, Dec. 12, 1788, at 2.

4. James Madison to Edmund Randolph, Jan. 10, 1788, in 10 *Madison Papers* at 355; George Washington to Bushrod Washington, Nov. 10, 1787, in 29 *Washington Writings* at 311.

5. Hucker, "Constitutional Convention Poses Questions," 37 *Congressional Quarterly Weekly Report* 273, 274, 275 (Feb. 17, 1979); Discussion of Sorauf, "The Political Potential of an Amending Convention," in K. Hall, H. Hyman, and L. Sigal, eds., *The Constitutional Convention as an Amending Device* 113, 131 (1981) (remarks of Frank J. Sorauf).

6. American Enterprise Institute, *A Constitutional Convention: How Well Would It Work?* 12 (1979).

7. Id. at 37; *The Federalist* No. 49 at 340; John Jay to Edward Rutledge, Oct. 15, 1788, in 3 H. Johnston, ed., *The Correspondence and Public Papers of John Jay* 362 (1891).

8. Slaughter-House Cases, 83 U.S. (16 Wall.) 36, 67 (1873).

9. 1 *Tucker's Blackstone*, Appendix at 371, 223.

Appendix

1. The text of the Virginia application is taken from 1 *Annals of Cong.* 258–60 (1789). Other printed sources: *Virginia Delegate Journal* at 42–43 (proceedings of Nov. 14, 1788); *House Journal*, 1st Congress, 1st Session 28–29 (1789); 14 *Jefferson Papers* plate facing page 329 (official, signed copy). The text of the New York application is taken from *House Journal*, 1st Congress, 1st Session 29–30 (1789). Other sources: *New York Assembly Journal* at 106 (proceedings of Feb. 5, 1789); R. Bernstein and K. Rice, *Are We to Be a Nation? The Making of the Constitution* 262 (1987) (first page of official copy).

Bibliography

Primary Sources

Adams, John. *Diary and Autobiography of John Adams*. Vol. 2, Lyman H. Butterfield, ed., Cambridge, Mass., 1961.

Annals of the Congress of the United States, 1789–1824. 42 vols., Washington, D.C., 1834–1856.

Bailyn, Bernard, ed. *Pamphlets of the American Revolution 1750–1776*. Vol. 1, Cambridge, Mass., 1965.

Ballagh, James Curtis, ed. *The Letters of Richard Henry Lee*. 2 vols., New York, 1911 and 1914.

Basler, Roy P., ed. *The Collected Works of Abraham Lincoln*. Vol. 4, New Brunswick, N.J., 1953.

Bouton, Nathaniel, ed. *Documents and Records Relating to Towns in New Hampshire*. Vol. 9, Concord, N.H., 1875.

Boyd, Julian P., et al., eds. *The Papers of Thomas Jefferson*. 22 vols. to date, Princeton, N.J., 1950– .

Brown, Everett Somerville, ed. *William Plumer's Memorandum of Proceedings in the United States Senate 1803–1807*. New York, 1923.

Burnett, Edmund C., ed. *Letters of Members of the Continental Congress*. 8 vols., Washington, D.C., 1921–1936.

Chittenden, Lucius E., ed. *A Report of the Debates and Proceedings in the Secret Sessions of the Conference Convention, for Proposing Amendments to the Constitution of the United States*. New York, 1864.

Congressional Globe. 46 vols., Washington, D.C., 1834–1873.

Congressional Record. Washington, D.C., 1873– .

Elliot, Jonathan, ed. *The Debates in the Several State Conventions on the Adoption of the Federal Constitution.* 2d ed., 4 vols., Philadelphia, 1836.

Farrand, Max, ed. *The Records of the Federal Convention of 1787.* 2d ed., 4 vols., New Haven, Conn., 1937.

Fitzpatrick, John C., ed. *The Writings of George Washington.* 39 vols., Washington, D.C., 1931–1944.

Ford, Paul L., ed. *Pamphlets on the Constitution of the United States, Published During Its Discussion by the People 1787–1788.* Brooklyn, N.Y., 1888.

———. *Essays on the Constitution of the United States, Published During Its Discussion by the People 1787–1788.* Brooklyn, N.Y., 1892.

Ford, Worthington Chauncey et al., eds. *Journals of the Continental Congress 1774–1789.* 34 vols., Washington, D.C., 1904–1937.

Gardiner, C. Harvey, ed. *A Study in Dissent: The Warren-Gerry Correspondence 1776–1792.* Carbondale, Ill., 1968.

Goebel, Julius, ed. "Melancton Smith's Minutes of Debates on the New Constitution," 64 *Columbia Law Review* 26 (1964).

Hammond, Isaac W., ed. *Collections of the New Hampshire Historical Society.* Vol. 9, Concord, N.H., 1889.

Handlin, Oscar, and Mary Handlin, eds. *The Popular Sources of Political Authority: Documents on the Massachusetts Constitution of 1780.* Cambridge, Mass., 1966.

Haw, James A. "Samuel Chase's 'Objections to the Federal Government,'" 76 *Maryland Historical Magazine* 272 (1981).

Hening, William Waller, ed. *The Statutes at Large; Being a Collection of All the Laws of Virginia, from the First Session of the Legislature, in the Year 1619.* 13 vols., New York, Philadelphia, and Richmond, 1819–1823.

Henry, William Wirt, ed. *Patrick Henry: Life, Correspondence and Speeches.* 3 vols., New York, 1891.

Hoadly, Charles J., ed. *The Public Records of the State of Connecticut.* Vols. 1–3, Hartford, 1894, 1895, and 1922.

Hunt, Gaillard, ed. *The Writings of James Madison.* 9 vols., New York, 1900–1910.

Hutchinson, William T., William M. E. Rachal, et al., eds. *The Papers of James Madison.* 15 vols. to date, Chicago and Charlottesville, Va., 1962– .

Hutson, James H., ed. *Supplement to Max Farrand's The Records of the Federal Convention of 1787.* New Haven, Conn., 1987.

Jefferson, Thomas. *Notes on the State of Virginia.* William Peden, ed., Chapel Hill, N.C., 1955.

Jensen, Merrill, ed. *English Historical Documents*. Vol. 9, *American Colonial Documents to 1776*, New York, 1955.

———— et al., eds. *The Documentary History of the Ratification of the Constitution*. 6 vols. to date, Madison, Wis., 1976–   .

Johnston, Henry P., ed. *The Correspondence and Public Papers of John Jay*. Vol. 3, New York, 1891.

Journal of the House of Delegates of the Commonwealth of Virginia. October 1787 session. Richmond, 1828.

Madison, James, Alexander Hamilton, and John Jay. *The Federalist*. Jacob E. Cooke, ed., Middletown, Conn., 1961.

Massachusetts General Court. *State Papers on Nullification*. Boston, 1834.

Peterson, Merrill D., ed. *Democracy, Liberty, and Property: The State Constitutional Conventions of the 1820's*. Indianapolis, 1966.

Rutland, Robert A., ed. *The Papers of George Mason 1725–1792*. 3 vols., Chapel Hill, N.C., 1970.

Smith, Paul H., et al., eds. *Letters of Delegates to Congress 1774–1789*. 13 vols. to date, Washington, D.C., 1976–   .

Smyth, Albert Henry, ed. *The Writings of Benjamin Franklin*. 10 vols., New York, 1907.

Sparks, Jared, ed. *The Life of Gouverneur Morris, with Selections from His Correspondence and Miscellaneous Papers*. 3 vols., Boston, 1832.

Storing, Herbert J., ed. *The Complete Anti-Federalist*. 7 vols., Chicago, 1981.

Syrett, Harold C., Jacob E. Cooke, et al., eds. *The Papers of Alexander Hamilton*. 26 vols., New York, 1961–1979.

Thorpe, Francis Newton, ed. *The Federal and State Constitutions, Colonial Charters, and Other Organic Laws of the States*. 7 vols., Washington, D.C., 1909.

Tucker, St. George, ed. *Blackstone's Commentaries: With Notes of Reference, to the Constitution and Laws, of the Federal Government of the United States; and of the Commonwealth of Virginia*. 5 vols., Philadelphia, 1803.

Secondary Sources

Books

Adams, Willi Paul. *The First American Constitutions: Republican Ideology and the Making of the State Constitutions in the Revolutionary Era*. Chapel Hill, N.C., 1980.

American Bar Association Special Constitutional Convention Study Committee. *Amendment of the Constitution by the Convention Method Under Article V*. Chicago, 1974.

American Enterprise Institute. *A Constitutional Convention: How Well Would It Work?* Washington, D.C., 1979.

Ames, Herman V. *The Proposed Amendments to the Constitution of the United States During the First Century of Its History.* Washington, D.C., 1897.

Andrews, Charles M. *The Colonial Period of American History.* 4 vols., New Haven, Conn., 1934–1938.

Auchampaugh, Philip G. *James Buchanan and His Cabinet on the Eve of Secession.* Lancaster, Pa., 1926.

Bailyn, Bernard. *The Ideological Origins of the American Revolution.* Cambridge, Mass., 1967.

————. *The Ordeal of Thomas Hutchinson.* Cambridge, Mass., 1974.

Bauer, Elizabeth K. *Commentaries on the Constitution, 1790–1860.* New York, 1952.

Beeman, Richard. *The Old Dominion and the New Nation, 1788–1801.* Lexington, Ky., 1972.

————, Stephen Botein, and Edward C. Carter II, eds. *Beyond Confederation: Origins of the Constitution and American National Identity.* Chapel Hill, N.C., 1987.

Billias, George A. *Elbridge Gerry: Founding Father and Republican Statesman.* New York, 1976.

Bloom, Sol, ed. *History of the Formation of the Union Under the Constitution.* Washington, D.C., 1941.

Borgeaud, Charles. *Adoption and Amendment of Constitutions in Europe and America.* New York, 1895.

Boyd, Steven R. *The Politics of Opposition: Antifederalists and the Acceptance of the Constitution.* Millwood, N.Y., 1979.

Brant, Irving. *James Madison.* 6 vols., Indianapolis, 1941–1961.

Brickfield, Cyril F. *Problems Relating to a Federal Constitutional Convention.* Dissertation, George Washington University School of Law, published as a committee print, Committee on the Judiciary, United States House of Representatives, 85th Congress, 1st Session, 1957.

Burdick, Charles K. *The Law of the American Constitution: Its Origin and Development.* New York, 1922.

Burnett, Edmund C. *The Continental Congress.* New York, 1941.

Clarke, Mary P. *Parliamentary Privilege in the American Colonies.* New Haven, Conn., 1943.

Cochran, Thomas C. *New York in the Confederation.* Philadelphia, 1932.

Collier, Christopher. *Roger Sherman's Connecticut.* Middletown, Conn., 1971.

Conway, Moncure D. *Omitted Chapters of History Disclosed in the Life and Papers of Edmund Randolph.* New York, 1888.

Currie, David P. *The Constitution in the Supreme Court: The First Hundred Years 1789–1888.* Chicago, 1985.

Dixon, Robert G. *Democratic Representation: Reapportionment in Law and Politics.* New York, 1968.

Dodd, Walter F. *The Revision and Amendment of State Constitutions.* Baltimore, 1910.

Dumond, Dwight Lowell. *The Secession Movement 1860–1861.* New York, 1931.

Edel, Wilbur. *A Constitutional Convention: Threat or Challenge?* New York, 1981.

Elliott, William Yandell. *The Need for Constitutional Reform.* New York, 1935.

Ellis, Richard E. *The Union at Risk: Jacksonian Democracy, States' Rights, and the Nullification Crisis.* New York, 1987.

Farrand, Max. *The Framing of the Constitution of the United States.* New Haven, Conn., 1913.

Freehling, William W. *Prelude to Civil War: The Nullification Controversy in South Carolina 1816–1836.* New York, 1966.

Freeman, Douglas Southall. *George Washington: A Biography.* 7 vols., New York, 1948–1957.

Goebel, Julius. *Antecedents and Beginnings to 1801.* Vol. 1 of the Oliver Wendell Holmes Devise History of the Supreme Court of the United States, New York, 1971.

Gunderson, Robert Gray. *Old Gentlemen's Convention: The Washington Peace Conference of 1861.* Madison, Wis., 1961.

Hall, Kermit L., Harold M. Hyman, and Leon V. Sigal, eds. *The Constitutional Convention as an Amending Device.* Washington, D.C., 1981.

Hall, Van Beck. *Politics Without Parties: Massachusetts, 1780–1791.* Pittsburgh, 1972.

Harding, Samuel B. *The Contest over the Ratification of the Federal Constitution in the State of Massachusetts.* New York, 1896.

Henderson, H. James. *Party Politics in the Continental Congress.* New York, 1974.

Hoar, Roger S. *Constitutional Conventions: Their Nature, Powers, and Limitations.* Boston, 1917.

Hyman, Harold M. *A More Perfect Union.* Boston, 1975.

Hyneman, Charles S., and Donald S. Lutz, eds. *American Political Writing During the Founding Era.* 2 vols., Indianapolis, 1983.

Jameson, John Alexander. *A Treatise on Constitutional Conventions: Their History, Powers, and Modes of Proceeding.* 4th ed., Chicago, 1887.

Jennings, Thelma. *The Nashville Convention: Southern Movement for Unity, 1848–1851.* Memphis, Tenn., 1980.

Jensen, Merrill. *The Articles of Confederation: An Interpretation of the Social-Constitutional History of the American Revolution 1774–1781.* Madison, Wis., 1940.

―――. *The New Nation: A History of the United States During the Confederation 1781–1789.* New York, 1965.

Kammen, Michael. *A Machine That Would Go of Itself: The Constitution in American Culture.* New York, 1986.

Ketcham, Ralph. *James Madison: A Biography.* New York, 1971.

Kimmel, Lewis H. *Federal Budget and Fiscal Policy 1789–1958.* Washington, D.C., 1959.

Kirwan, Albert D. *John J. Crittenden: The Struggle for the Union.* Lexington, Ky., 1962.

Klein, Philip Shriver. *President James Buchanan.* University Park, Pa., 1962.

Lee, Charles R. *The Confederate Constitutions.* Chapel Hill, N.C., 1963.

Lutz, Donald S. *Popular Consent and Popular Control: Whig Political Theory in the Early State Constitutions.* Baton Rouge, La., 1980.

MacDonald, William. *A New Constitution for a New America.* New York, 1921.

McDonald, Forrest. *Novus Ordo Seclorum: The Intellectual Origins of the Constitution.* Lawrence, Kans., 1985.

McLaughlin, Andrew C. *A Constitutional History of the United States.* New York, 1936.

Main, Jackson Turner. *The Antifederalists: Critics of the Constitution 1781–1788.* New York, 1974.

Moore, W. S., and Rudolph G. Penner, eds. *The Constitution and the Budget.* Washington, D.C., 1980.

Morris, Richard B. *Government and Labor in Early America.* 2d ed., Boston, 1981.

―――. *The Forging of the Union 1781–1789.* New York, 1987.

Myers, Denys P. *The Process of Constitutional Amendment.* Senate Document No. 314, 76th Congress, 3d Session, 1940.

Nevins, Allan. *The American States During and After the Revolution 1775–1789.* New York, 1924.

Oates, Stephen B. *With Malice Toward None.* New York, 1977.

O'Connor, John E. *William Paterson: Lawyer and Statesman 1745–1806.* New Brunswick, N.J., 1979.

Orfield, Lester Bernhardt. *The Amending of the Federal Constitution.* Ann Arbor, Mich., 1942.

Osgood, Herbert L. *The American Colonies in the Seventeenth Century.* 4 vols., New York, 1904–1907.

Penello, Penny, ed. *Electing Delegates to a Constitutional Convention.* Proceedings of an Annual Meeting Presidential Showcase Program, held

July 1985, under the auspices of the American Bar Association, Washington, D.C., 1986.

Peterson, Merrill D. *Thomas Jefferson and the New Nation*. New York, 1970.

Polishook, Irwin. *Rhode Island and the Union, 1774–1795*. Evanston, Ill., 1969.

Pullen, William Russell. "The Application Clause of the Amending Provision of the Constitution." Dissertation, University of North Carolina, Chapel Hill, 1951.

Rakove, Jack N. *The Beginnings of National Politics: An Interpretive History of the Continental Congress*. New York, 1979.

Reardon, John J. *Edmund Randolph: A Biography*. New York, 1974.

Risjord, Norman K. *Chesapeake Politics 1781–1800*. New York, 1978.

Rollins, Richard M. *The Long Journey of Noah Webster*. Philadelphia, 1980.

Rossiter, Clinton. *1787: The Grand Convention*. New York, 1966.

Rutland, Robert Allen. *The Ordeal of the Constitution*. Norman, Okla., 1966.

Savage, James D. *Balanced Budgets and American Politics*. Ithaca, N.Y., 1988.

Saye, Albert B. *A Constitutional History of Georgia*. Athens, Ga., 1970.

Schechter, Stephen L., ed. *The Reluctant Pillar: New York and the Adoption of the Federal Constitution*. Troy, N.Y., 1985.

Simmons, R. C. *The American Colonies*. New York, 1981.

Smith, James Morton. *Freedom's Fetters: The Alien and Sedition Laws and American Civil Liberties*. Ithaca, N.Y., 1956.

Smith, Page. *John Adams*. 2 vols., Garden City, N.Y., 1962.

Szatmary, David P. *Shays' Rebellion: The Making of an Agrarian Insurrection*. Amherst, Mass., 1980.

Varg, Paul A. *Foreign Policies of the Founding Fathers*. East Lansing, Mich., 1963.

Vose, Clement E. *Constitutional Change: Amendment Politics and Supreme Court Litigation Since 1900*. Lexington, Mass., 1972.

Wagner, Richard E., and Robert D. Tollison. *Balanced Budgets, Fiscal Responsibility, and the Constitution*. San Francisco, 1980.

Ward, Harry M. *"Unite or Die:" Intercolony Relations 1690–1763*. Port Washington, N.Y., 1971.

Wills, Garry. *Inventing America: Jefferson's Declaration of Independence*. Garden City, N.Y., 1978.

Wood, Gordon S. *The Creation of the American Republic 1776–1787*. Chapel Hill, N.C., 1969.

Wooster, Ralph A. *The Secession Conventions of the South*. Princeton, N.J., 1962.

Zuckerman, Michael. *Peaceable Kingdoms: New England Towns in the Eighteenth Century*. New York, 1970.

Articles

Ackerman, Bruce A. "The Storrs Lectures: Discovering the Constitution," 93
    Yale Law Journal 1013 (1984).
Adrian, Charles R. "Trends in State Constitutions," 5 *Harvard Journal on
    Legislation* 311 (1968).
Bagehot, Walter. "The American Constitution at the Present Crisis," 13 *Na-
    tional Review* (London) 465 (1861).
Baldwin, Simeon E. "The New Haven Convention of 1778," 3 *Papers of the
    New Haven Colony Historical Society* 33 (1882).
Bancroft, George. "A Hartford Convention in 1780," 8 *Magazine of American
    History* 688 (1882).
Barker, William T. "A Status Report on the 'Balanced Budget' Constitutional
    Convention," 20 *John Marshall Law Review* 29 (1986).
Bishop, Hillman M. "Why Rhode Island Opposed the Federal Constitution,"
    pts. 1–4, 8 *Rhode Island History* 1, 33, 85, 115 (1949).
Black, Charles L. "The Proposed Amendment of Article V: A Threatened
    Disaster," 72 *Yale Law Journal* 957 (1963).
———. "Amending the Constitution: A Letter to a Congressman," 82 *Yale
    Law Journal* 189 (1972).
———. "Amendment by National Constitutional Convention: A Letter to a
    Senator," 32 *Oklahoma Law Review* 626 (1979).
Bonfield, Arthur. "Proposing Constitutional Amendments by Convention:
    Some Problems," 39 *Notre Dame Lawyer* 659 (1964).
Boyd, Julian P. "Attempts to Form New States in New York and Pennsylvania
    1786–1796," 12 *Quarterly Journal of the New York State Historical
    Association* 257 (1931).
Braxton, A. Caperton. "Powers of Conventions," 7 *Virginia Law Register* 79
    (1901).
Brown, Richard D. "The Massachusetts Convention of Towns, 1768," 26
    William and Mary Quarterly 94 (3d ser., 1969).
Buckwalter, Doyle W. "Constitutional Conventions and State Legislators," 20
    Journal of Public Law 543 (1971).
Castello, James E. "The Limits of Popular Sovereignty: Using the Initiative
    Power to Control Legislative Procedure," 74 *California Law Review*
    491 (1986).
Clark, Homer. "The Supreme Court and the Amending Process," 39 *Virginia
    Law Review* 621 (1953).
Committee on the Federal Constitution, New York State Bar Association.
    "Article V and the Proposed Federal Constitutional Convention Pro-
    cedures Bills," 3 *Cardozo Law Review* 529 (1982).
Committee on Federal Legislation, Association of the Bar of the City of New

York. "Legislation to Establish Procedures for a 'Limited Issues' Constitutional Convention," 39 *Record of the Association of the Bar of the City of New York* 593 (1984).

Connely, Dwight W. "Amending the Constitution: Is This Any Way to Call for a Constitutional Convention?," 22 *Arizona Law Review* 1011 (1980).

Cover, Robert M. Book review of 1969 reprint of St. George Tucker's edition of *Blackstone's Commentaries*, 70 *Columbia Law Review* 1475 (1970).

Corwin, Edward S. "The Progress of Constitutional Theory Between the Declaration of Independence and the Meeting of the Philadelphia Convention," 30 *American Historical Review* 511 (1925).

———, and Mary Louise Ramsey. "The Constitutional Law of Constitutional Amendment," 26 *Notre Dame Lawyer* 185 (1951).

Crowl, Philip A. "Anti-Federalism in Maryland, 1787–1788," 4 *William and Mary Quarterly* 446 (3d ser., 1947).

Dellinger, Walter. "The Recurring Question of the 'Limited' Constitutional Convention," 88 *Yale Law Journal* 1623 (1979).

———. "The Legitimacy of Constitutional Change: Rethinking the Amendment Process," 97 *Harvard Law Review* 386 (1983).

Dodd, Walter F. "Amending the Federal Constitution," 30 *Yale Law Journal* 321 (1921).

———. "State Constitutional Conventions and State Legislative Power," 2 *Vanderbilt Law Review* 27 (1948).

Douglas, William O. "Interposition and the *Peters* Case, 1778–1809," 9 *Stanford Law Review* 3 (1956).

Dreier, David, and William Stubblebine. "The Balanced Budget/Tax Limitation Amendment," 10 *Hastings Constitutional Law Quarterly* 809 (1983).

Eaton, Amasa M. "Recent State Constitutions," 6 *Harvard Law Review* 53 (1892).

Elder, Judith L. "Article V, Justiciability, and the Equal Rights Amendment," 31 *Oklahoma Law Review* 63 (1978).

Elliott, E. Donald. "Constitutional Conventions and the Deficit," 1985 *Duke Law Journal* 1077.

Feerick, John D. "Amending the Constitution Through a Convention," 60 *American Bar Association Journal* 285 (1974).

Fordham, Jefferson B. "Some Observations upon Uneasy American Federalism," 58 *North Carolina Law Review* 289 (1980).

Foster, Edward. "The Balanced Budget Amendment and Economic Thought," 2 *Constitutional Commentary* 353 (1985).

Goldberg, Arthur J. "The Proposed Constitutional Convention," 11 *Hastings Constitutional Law Quarterly* 1 (1983).

Gooch, Robert K. "The Recent Limited Constitutional Convention in Virginia," 31 *Virginia Law Review* 708 (1945).

Graham, Fred P. "The Role of the States in Proposing Constitutional Amendments," 49 *American Bar Association Journal* 1175 (1963).

Gunther, Gerald. "The Convention Method of Amending the United States Constitution," 14 *Georgia Law Review* 1 (1979).

Heller, Francis H. "Article V: Changing Dimensions in Constitutional Change," 7 *University of Michigan Journal of Law Reform* 71 (1973).

————. "Limiting a Constitutional Convention: The State Precedents," 3 *Cardozo Law Review* 563 (1982).

Henkin, Louis. "Is There a 'Political Question' Doctrine?," 85 *Yale Law Journal* 597 (1976).

Hoober, John A. "Popular Prejudice and Constitutional Amendatory Conventions," 1 *Yale Law Journal* 207 (1892).

Howard, A. E. Dick. "Constitutional Revision: Virginia and the Nation," 9 *University of Richmond Law Review* 1 (1974).

Hutson, James H. "Country, Court, and Constitution: Antifederalism and the Historians," 38 *William and Mary Quarterly* 337 (3d ser., 1981).

————. "The Creation of the Constitution: The Integrity of the Documentary Record," 65 *Texas Law Review* 1 (1986).

Jameson, John Franklin. "The Early Political Uses of the Word Convention," 3 *American Historical Review* 477 (1898).

Kay, Richard S. "The Illegality of the Constitution," 4 *Constitutional Commentary* 57 (1987).

Kenyon, Cecelia M. "Men of Little Faith: The Anti-Federalists on the Nature of Representative Government," 12 *William and Mary Quarterly* 3 (3d ser., 1955).

Linder, Douglas. "What in the Constitution Cannot Be Amended?," 23 *Arizona Law Review* 717 (1981).

Martig, Ralph R. "Amending the Constitution Article Five: The Keystone of the Arch," 35 *Michigan Law Review* 1253 (1937).

Martin, William Logan. "The Amending Power: The Background of the Income Tax Amendment," 39 *American Bar Association Journal* 21 (1953).

Miller, Maxwell A., and Lincoln C. Oliphant. "Evenly Dividing a Nine-Member Court: The Political Question Doctrine in *Coleman v. Miller, Goldwater v. Carter,* and *Idaho v. Freeman,*" 1980 *Detroit College of Law Review* 789.

Morris, Richard B. "John Jay and the Adoption of the Federal Constitution in New York," 63 *New York History* 133 (1982).

Morton, Stephen C. "Amending the Tennessee Constitution by Limited Convention: Judicial Invalidation of Unauthorized Proposals After Voter Approval," 9 *Memphis State University Law Review* 533 (1979).

Noonan, John T. "The Convention Method of Constitutional Amendment—Its Meaning, Usefulness, and Wisdom," 10 *Pacific Law Journal* 641 (1979).

Packard, Frank E. "The Inherent Safety in Calling a Convention for the Purpose of Proposing Amendments to the Constitution of the United States," 56 *Dickinson Law Review* 373 (1952).

———. "Problems Arising from an Attempt to Amend the Constitution by Convention Concerning the Limiting of Income Tax Rates to 25 Percent," 31 *Nebraska Law Review* 407 (1952).

Parker, Robert M., and Price Ainsworth. "A 1986 Constitutional Convention?," 48 *Texas Bar Journal* 896 (1985).

Platz, William A. "Article Five of the Federal Constitution," 3 *George Washington Law Review* 17 (1934).

Potts, C. S. "Power of Legislative Bodies to Punish for Contempt," 74 *University of Pennsylvania Law Review* 691 (1926).

Rhodes, Robert M. "A Limited Federal Constitutional Convention," 26 *University of Florida Law Review* 1 (1973).

Rodino, Peter W. "The Proposed Balanced Budget/Tax Limitation Constitutional Amendment: No Balance, No Limits," 10 *Hastings Constitutional Law Quarterly* 785 (1983).

Roll, Charles W. "We, Some of the People: Apportionment in the Thirteen State Conventions Ratifying the Constitution," 56 *Journal of American History* 21 (1969).

Sears, Kenneth C. "Voting on Constitutional Conventions and Amendments," 2 *University of Chicago Law Review* 612 (1935).

Smith, Edward P. "The Movement Towards a Second Constitutional Convention in 1788," in John Franklin Jameson, ed., *Essays in the Constitutional History of the United States in the Formative Period 1775–1789*, at 46 (Boston, 1889).

Sprague, Robert J. "Shall We Have a Federal Constitutional Convention, and What Shall It Do?," 3 *Maine Law Review* 115 (1910).

Stasny, James N. "The Constitutional Convention Provision of Article V: Historical Perspective," 1 *Cooley Law Review* 73 (1982).

———. "A National Constitutional Convention: Bibliography Updated February 1984," in *Constitutional Convention Procedures: Hearing Before the Subcommittee on the Constitution of the Senate Committee on the Judiciary*, 98th Congress, 2d Session, 63–89 (1985).

Stern, Robert L. "Separability and Separability Clauses in the Supreme Court," 51 *Harvard Law Review* 76 (1937).

Swindler, William F. "Seedtime of an American Judiciary: From Independence to the Constitution," 17 *William and Mary Law Review* 503 (1976).

Synar, Mike, Vincent LoVoi, and Donald Pongrace. "Congressional Perspective on the Balanced Budget and Emergency Deficit Control Act of 1985," 7 *Pace Law Review* 675 (1987).

Tribe, Laurence H. "Issues Raised by Requesting Congress to Call a Constitutional Convention to Propose a Balanced Budget Amendment," 10 *Pacific Law Journal* 627 (1979).

Tuller, Walter K. "A Convention to Amend the Constitution—Why Needed—How It May Be Obtained," 193 *North American Review* 369 (1911).

Turner, Frederick Jackson. "Western State-Making in the Revolutionary Era," pts. 1 and 2, 1 *American Historical Review* 70, 251 (1895–1896).

Van Alstyne, William W. "Does Article V Restrict the States to Calling Unlimited Conventions Only?—A Letter to a Colleague," 1978 *Duke Law Journal* 1295.

———. "The Limited Constitutional Convention—The Recurring Answer," 1979 *Duke Law Journal* 985.

Voegler, Douglas G. "Amending the Constitution by the Article V Convention Method," 55 *North Dakota Law Review* 355 (1979).

Weber, Paul J. "The Constitutional Convention: A Safe Political Option," 3 *Journal of Law & Politics* 51 (1986).

Webster, William C. "Comparative Study of the State Constitutions of the American Revolution," 9 *Annals of the American Academy of Political and Social Science* 380 (1897).

Wheeler, Wayne B. "Is a Constitutional Convention Impending?," 21 *Illinois Law Review* 782 (1927).

White, Thomas R. "Amendment and Revision of State Constitutions," 100 *University of Pennsylvania Law Review* 1132 (1952).

Yawitz, Milton. "The Legal Effect Under American Decisions of an Alleged Irregularity in the Adoption of a Constitution or Constitutional Amendment," 10 *St. Louis Law Review* 279 (1925).

Symposium, "The Article V Convention Process," 66 *Michigan Law Review* 837 (1968). Articles by Everett McKinley Dirksen, Sam J. Ervin, Paul G. Kauper, Ralph M. Carson, Robert G. Dixon, Arthur Bonfield, and Clifton McCleskey, reprinted as Leonard Levy, ed., *The Article V Convention Process: A Symposium*. New York, 1971.

Symposium, "Massachusetts Constitution of 1780," 14 *Suffolk University Law Review* 841 (1980).

Comment, "Amendment by Convention: Our Next Constitutional Crisis?," 53 *North Carolina Law Review* 491 (1975).

Comment, "A Constitutional Convention: Scouting Article Five's Undiscovered Country," 134 *University of Pennsylvania Law Review* 939 (1986).

Comment, "Enabling and Implementing Legislation and State Constitutional Convention Committee Reports," 6 *University of Hawaii Law Review* 523 (1984).

Comment, "The Equal Rights Amendment and Article V: A Framework for Analysis of the Extension and Rescission Issues," 127 *University of Pennsylvania Law Review* 494 (1978).

Comment, " 'The Monster Approaching the Capital:' The Effort to Write Economic Policy into the United States Constitution," 15 *Akron Law Review* 733 (1982).

Note, "Article V: Political Questions and Sensible Answers," 57 *Texas Law Review* 1259 (1979).

Note, "Article III Problems in Enforcing the Balanced Budget Amendment," 83 *Columbia Law Review* 1065 (1983).

Note, "The Balanced Budget Amendment: An Inquiry into Appropriateness," 96 *Harvard Law Review* 1600 (1983).

Note, "By Whom Shall a State Constitution Be Adopted?," 9 *Harvard Law Review* 471 (1896).

Note, "The Constitutional Convention, Its Nature and Powers—and the Amending Procedure," 1966 *Utah Law Review* 390.

Note, "Constitutional Revision by a Restricted Convention," 35 *Minnesota Law Review* 283 (1951).

Note, "Critical Details: Amending the United States Constitution," 16 *Harvard Journal on Legislation* 763 (1979).

Note, "Enforcing the One-Subject Rule: The Case for a Subject Veto," 38 *Hastings Law Journal* 563 (1987).

Note, "The Judiciary and Popular Democracy: Should Courts Review Ballot Measures Prior to Elections?," 53 *Fordham Law Review* 919 (1985).

Note, "The Legislature's Power to Judge the Qualifications of Its Members," 19 *Vanderbilt Law Review* 1410 (1966).

Note, "The Powers of Constitutional Conventions," 29 *Harvard Law Review* 528 (1916).

Note, "The Process of Constitutional Amendment," 79 *Columbia Law Review* 106 (1979).

Note, "Proposed Legislation on the Convention Method of Amending the United States Constitution," 85 *Harvard Law Review* 1612 (1972).

Note, "The Proposed National Initiative Amendment: A Participatory Perspective on Substantive Restrictions and Procedural Requirements," 18 *Harvard Journal on Legislation* 429 (1981).

Note, "Proposing Amendments to the United States Constitution by Convention," 70 *Harvard Law Review* 1067 (1957).

Note, "Reversals in the Federal Constitutional Amendment Process: Efficacy of State Ratifications of the Equal Rights Amendment," 49 *Indiana Law Journal* 147 (1973).

Note, "State Constitutional Conventions: Limitations on Their Powers," 55 *Iowa Law Review* 244 (1969).

Note, "The Unconstitutionality of Voter Initiative Applications for Federal Constitutional Conventions," 85 *Columbia Law Review* 1525 (1985).

Note, "The United States and the Articles of Confederation: Drifting Toward Anarchy or Inching Toward Commonwealth?," 88 *Yale Law Journal* 142 (1978).

Popular Publications

Ackerman, Bruce A. "Unconstitutional Convention," *New Republic*, March 3, 1979, at 8.

Anderson, Martin. "A Safe and Effective Constitutional Convention," *Wall Street Journal*, March 11, 1987, at 36.

Armstrong, William L. "George Mason, Article V and the Deficit," *Human Events*, March 30, 1985, at 20.

Bell, Griffin B. "Constitutional Convention: Oh, Stop the Hand-Wringing," *Washington Post*, April 14, 1984, at A15.

Berry, Mary Frances. "How Hard It Is to Change," *New York Times*, September 13, 1987, §6 (*Magazine*) at 93.

Bork, Robert H. "Would a Budget Amendment Work?," *Wall Street Journal*, April 4, 1979, at 20.

Davenport, John A. "Amending the Constitution Is a Dubious Way to Curb Federal Spending," *Fortune*, March 12, 1979, at 114.

Du Pont, Pierre S. "The Constitutional Way Out," *Washington Post*, May 2, 1982, at C8.

Eisenhower, Milton S. "Balancing the Budget in a Conventional Way," *Wall Street Journal*, January 17, 1985, at 26.

Friedman, Milton. "Washington: Less Red Ink," *The Atlantic*, February 1983, at 18.

Garrett, Wilbur E. "Waterway That Led to the Constitution: George Washington's Patowmack Canal," 171 *National Geographic* 716 (June 1987).

"Give Us a Balanced Budget—But Not Yet," *The Economist* (U.S. edition), July 31, 1982, at 23.

Glen, Maxwell. "Balance-the-Budget Juggernaut Heads for Capitol Hill," 11 *National Journal* 306 (February 24, 1979).

Grant, James. "Pass the 27th Amendment and Make a Balanced Budget the Law of the Land," *Barron's*, February 22, 1982, at 11.

Green, Larry. "Showdown in 1984? Cries Grow for Balanced U.S. Budget," *Los Angeles Times*, February 18, 1984, pt. I at 1.

Halbrook, David. "States Have Legitimate Role in Balanced Budget Debate,"
     Governing, January 1988, at 66.
Hatch, Orrin G. "It's a Constitutional Right," *Washington Post*, February 18,
     1984, at A17.
Lacayo, Richard. "Is It Broke? Should We Fix It?," *Time*, July 6, 1987, at 54.
Laird, Melvin R. "James Madison Wouldn't Approve," *Washington Post*, Feb-
     ruary 13, 1984, at A13.
Lamm, Richard D., and Scott M. Matheson. "Deficits: A Noose," *New York
     Times*, November 10, 1983, at A27.
Malbin, Michael J. "Huge Budget Deficit Projections Fuel Drive for Balanced
     Budget Amendment," 14 *National Journal* 757 (May 1, 1982).
Mishkin, Paul J. "A Question of Trust," *Newsweek*, March 5, 1979, at 17.
Morgan, Thomas B. "Seventeen States Vote to Destroy Democracy as We
     Know It," *Look*, December 3, 1963, at 76.
Pei, Mario. "The Case for a Constitutional Convention," 12 *Modern Age* 8
     (Winter 1967–1968).
Pritchett, C. Herman. "Why Risk a Constitutional Convention?," *Center Mag-
     azine*, March 1980, at 14.
Rosen, Ellen L. "Is It Time to Make Some Changes in the Constitution?,"
     National Law Journal, April 27, 1987, at S-2.
Safire, William. "Doing the Con Con," *New York Times*, September 3, 1984,
     at 25.
Sorensen, Theodore. "The Quiet Campaign to Rewrite the Constitution,"
     Saturday Review, July 15, 1967, at 17.
Stanfield, Rochelle. "The Taxpayers' Revolt is Alive or Dead in the Water—
     Take Your Pick," 15 *National Journal* 2568 (December 10, 1983).
Stevens, John V. "Tearing up the Constitution," *Church & State*, March 1983,
     at 10.
Stevens, William K. "Outlook Doubtful on Charter Shift," *New York Times*,
     August 16, 1987, §1 at 28.
Thompson, Frank, and Daniel H. Pollitt. "A New Constitutional Convention?
     Harnessing the Tiger," 39 *Christianity and Crisis* 82 (April 16, 1979).
Will, George F. "The Folly of a Constitutional Convention," *Washington
     Post*, May 21, 1981, at A27.

Cases

AFL-CIO v. Eu, 36 Cal.3d 687, *stay denied*, 468 U.S. 1310 (1984) (Rehn-
     quist, Cir. J.).
Baker v. Carr, 369 U.S. 186 (1962).

Bolton v. Martin, 1 U.S. (1 Dall.) 296 (1788) (Philadelphia Cty. Ct. C.P.).

Bowsher v. Synar, 478 U.S. 714 (1986).

Bragg v. Tuffts, 49 Ark. 554 (1887).

Brickhouse v. Brooks, 165 F. 534 (C.C.E.D. Va. 1908).

Brown v. Board of Education, 347 U.S. 483 (1954).

Carton v. Secretary of State, 151 Mich. 337 (1908).

Coleman v. Miller, 307 U.S. 433 (1939).

Dillon v. Gloss, 256 U.S. 368 (1921).

Dodge v. Woolsey, 59 U.S. (18 How.) 331 (1856).

Dyer v. Blair, 390 F. Supp. 1291 (N.D. Ill. 1975).

Eber Bros. Wine & Liquor Corp. v. United States, 337 F.2d 624 (Ct. Cl. 1964), *cert. denied*, 380 U.S. 950 (1965).

Fortson v. Morris, 385 U.S. 231 (1966).

Fortson v. Toombs, 379 U.S. 621 (1965).

Hawke v. Smith (No. 1), 253 U.S. 221 (1920).

Hillman v. Stockett, 183 Md. 641 (Md. Ct. App. 1945).

Hollingsworth v. Virginia, 3 U.S. (3 Dall.) 378 (1798).

Idaho v. Freeman, 529 F. Supp. 1107 (D. Idaho 1981), *certiorari before judgment granted and judgment stayed*, 455 U.S. 918, *judgment vacated and remanded to district court with instructions to dismiss as moot*, 459 U.S. 809 (1982).

Kamper v. Hawkins, 3 Va. (3 Wash.) 20 (Gen. Ct. 1793).

Leser v. Garnett, 258 U.S. 130 (1922).

Montana *ex rel.* Harper v. Waltermire, 691 P.2d 826, *stay denied*, 469 U.S. 1301 (1984) (Rehnquist, Cir. J.).

National Prohibition Cases, 253 U.S. 350 (1920).

Ohio *ex rel.* Erkenbrecher v. Cox, 257 F. 334 (S.D. Ohio 1919).

Petuskey v. Rampton, 307 F. Supp. 235 (D. Utah 1969), *reversed*, 431 F.2d 378 (10th Cir. 1970), *certiorari denied*, 401 U.S. 913 (1971).

Powell v. McCormack, 395 U.S. 486 (1969).

Reynolds v. Sims, 377 U.S. 533 (1964).

Schechter Poultry Corp. v. United States, 295 U.S. 495 (1935).

Schlesinger v. Reservists Committee to Stop the War, 418 U.S. 208 (1974).

Scott v. Sandford, 60 U.S. (19 How.) 393 (1857).

Smith v. Union Bank of Georgetown, 30 U.S. (5 Pet.) 518 (1831).

State *ex rel.* McCready v. Hunt, 20 S.C.L. (2 Hill) 1 (Ct. App. 1834).

Trombetta v. Florida, 353 F. Supp. 575 (M.D. Fla. 1973).

Turner v. Bank of North-America, 4 U.S. (4 Dall.) 8 (1799).

United States v. Sprague, 282 U.S. 716 (1931).

Ware v. Hylton, 3 U.S. (3 Dall.) 199 (1796).

Wesberry v. Sanders, 376 U.S. 1 (1964).

Index